"Richly layered with meaning, refined as velvet, writing is thinking, here..."

NUALA O'FAOLAIN, author of *My Dream of You*

"When you sit down to read Treasa O'Driscoll's *Celtic Woman*, settle in as it is a thought train you'll not want to alight from. It is filled with play words, word play, poetry, history, romance, leaving no sense untouched. Off you go; it's a fulfilling journey."

MALACHY McCOURT, author of *A Monk Swimming*

"*Celtic Woman* is like a long walk with a dear friend deep into the landscape of the Irish heart, a place that offers glimpses of magic and food for the soul."

ORIAH MOUNTAIN DREAMER, author of *The Invitation*

"*Celtic Woman* is a magnificent chronicle of an individual's journey toward the process not only of self-healing, but of understanding and growing with the world around her. Had St. Augustine continued *The Confessions* into a record of his more mature years, assisted by science and modern spirituality, he would surely have found a fulfilling companion voice in Treasa O'Driscoll. There is a spirit of inquiry in this book that moves throughout these pages, animating every word and infusing the text with an energy that guides the will to love above the trials and tribulations of the world, and there it illumines as a beacon. On this truly remarkable journey, the stars not only shine above the road, but reach down and touch the soul."

BRUCE MEYER, author of *The Golden Thread*

"Treasa O'Driscoll's book is an enlightened journey back to the spiritual heart of Ireland."

JAMES REDFIELD, author of *The Celestine Prophecy*

"In speaking what most of the rest of us cannot speak, Treasa O'Driscoll has made an advance for humanity... Here, in this writing, we find a true language of the heart; it is strong, it is robust, it is full of will and action..."

ROBERT SARDELLO, author of *Freeing the Soul from Fear*

"*Celtic Woman*, is a rich feast of a book, part travelogue, part romance, part meditation—and all of it poetry! Like the best of memoir, it manages to touch on the most personal, intimate themes of a human life and at the same time to render them universal. Readers will want to shout both *Bravo!* and *Encore!*"

MICHAEL LIPSON, author of *Stairway of Surprise*

"Treasa is the fairy godmother of poetry—she has recited, to stunning effect and near supersensible memory, since childhood. Her book, like an intertwined laurel wreath takes her simultaneously from poem to poem like her own life."

RUFUS GOODWIN, author of *Give Us this Day*

"It's not only Ireland's enchanting landscape and the Irish spirit that Treasa's book welcomes the reader to experience, but through her life, we have a better appreciation for how that land and spirit enriches the world around us."

JOHN FOX, author of *Finding What You Didn't Lose*

"Treasa has taken the oral, literary and spiritual traditions of her Irish heritage and woven them into a living fabric that is uniquely feminine, transformative and contemporary."

THERESE SCHROEDER-SHEKER, author of *Transitus*

A reader's comment:

"By the way, I'm really enjoying your book. I'm still on the early chapters (time!!!!) but I find it fascinating—I keep flipping forward and getting engaged with new sections and then I have to go back and pick up the chapter flow where I left off. Your prose is lovely: full of life, energy and directness; your words are imbued with wisdom and perception. It's wonderful how you manage to pull so many things together in the flow of your narrative—there's not a page that doesn't have something that resonates deep inside me. The authority and purpose (but also the light, dancing movement) of your voice takes me back to a time in the early 1980s when I immersed myself in the writings of AE when I was at Carleton University. I look forward to continuing my reading..."

PETER SHEPPARD, Teacher-Librarian, Archbishop Denis O'Connor Catholic High School

celtic
woman

A Memoir of Life's
Poetic Journey

Treasa O'Driscoll

Blue Butterfly Books
THINK FREE, BE FREE

Blue Butterfly Book Publishing Inc.
2583 Lakeshore Boulevard West, Toronto, Ontario, Canada M8V 1G3
Tel 416-255-3930   Fax 416-252-8291   www.bluebutterflybooks.ca

Complete ordering information for Blue Butterfly titles is available at:
www.bluebutterflybooks.ca

First edition, paperback: 2008

LIBRARY AND ARCHIVES CANADA CATALOGUING IN PUBLICATION

O'Driscoll, Treasa, 1944–
Celtic woman : a memoir of life's poetic journey / Treasa O'Driscoll.

Includes bibliographical references and index.
ISBN 978-0-9781600-2-9

1. O'Driscoll, Treasa, 1944–. 2. Singers—Canada—Biography.
3. Performance artists—Canada—Biography.
4. Irish Canadian women—Ontario—Biography. I. Title.

ML420.O275A3 2008   782.42162'91620092   C2008-903975-0

Design and typesetting by Fox Meadow Creations
Set in Goudy Oldstyle
Printed and bound in Canada by Transcontinental-Métrolitho
Permanent paper ∞

No government grants were sought nor any public subsidies received for publication of this book. Blue Butterfly Books thanks book buyers for their support in the marketplace.

In memory of Celtic visionary,
writer, teacher, and scholar,
Robert O'Driscoll,
who once spread his dreams
under my feet…

Contents

Cover Picture

This portrait adorned the cover of my album Farewell But Whenever: Love Songs of Ireland from the 15th Century, a release of the Irish record company Gael-Linn. Colm Henry was the assigned photographer and I believe this was his first album credit in a distinguished career that links his name with U2, Riverdance, and other leading lights in the Irish musical and literary pantheon of the past three decades.

He decided to do the shoot on Killiney Hill on the south side of Dublin. Mary O'Donnell, a well-known Irish fashion designer, lived at the foot of the hill and I had recently modelled some costumes she had designed for a film about Tristan and Isolde in which Richard Burton played King Mark and which featured the music of The Chieftains.

The costumes were labours of love made from the finest woven tweeds from Mary's native Donegal. Mary was fortunately at home when Colm and I paid her a surprise visit and she graciously urged me to take my pick from Isolde's lavish wardrobe. Thus I came to be wearing her beautifully designed traditional Irish cloak in a fine weave of brilliant green.

I had attended a party in Mary's house a few months before and had responded to her request for a song in the Irish language in which she was fluent. As soon as I finished, she disappeared into her workroom and emerged with an antique hand-made lace garment. Thrusting it into my hands, she said: "You can always boast that you got this for a song!"

"My glory was I had such friends," I said, quoting from Mr. Yeats.

Arriving Where I Started

> *"Would you tell me please which way I ought to go from here?"*
> *"That depends a good deal on where you want to get to,"*
> *said the cat.*
>
> LEWIS CARROLL

Edging onto the tree-lined bank, I lowered the car window.
"Would you please tell me the way to Killaloe?" A burly
farmer, enthroned on his tractor, commanded the width
of that narrow country road. I had been confounded by
the choice of winding side-roads on the map, all purport-
ing to lead to the ancient capital of Ireland, now an unpre-
tentious town in County Clare that sits contentedly on
the shores of Lough Derg.

"I would indeed," said he, as he eyed the potholes in
the road. "But I wouldn't be setting out from here at all,
if I were you."

He then proceeded to put me "on the right road,"
where presumably I could make a better start.

"You will find your way from there," was what he said
in the distinctive accent of the place. I thanked him and

made my way to the crossroads, where a surer, somewhat wider, more evenly paved roadway stretched before me. The farmer's emphatic words echoed in my mind and gave me food for thought for the remainder of my journey. I recalled a few lines from a poem I'd learned as a child.

The little roads of Ireland
Go wandering up and down
O'er hill and moor and valley
By rath and tower and town.

The roads of Ireland, I mused, could be a metaphor for modern lives, caught in the swing of extremes and seeking an uncertain way forward. Interweaving and underpinning the sleek expressways that conduct the flow of Ireland's celebrated Celtic Tiger economy, is a network of straggling *boreens* or "little roads," replete with potholes. Because every highway inexorably gives way to a byway, drivers are required to adapt to the slower pace of crowded towns and narrow village streets. I remembered a familiar saying—without opposites there is no progress—being ever sensitive to the pull of opposites in myself, the swing from enthusiasm to apathy, generosity to meanness. I often reminded myself that the opposite is also true, when I tended towards one extreme or another. I believed that a continual awareness of the conflict of opposites in every area of our personal lives and an acceptance of this dynamic, could help us to generally withstand and resolve dramatic extremes of opposition now vying for supremacy on the world stage.

I was far removed from the world stage now, having travelled back to my native land from Canada, where I had lived for some thirty years, with the intention of writing this book. I wanted the rich tapestry of my life to unfold its gathered wisdom because I believed that in contemplating my own biography I would become more conscious of the ideals, inner forces, choices and challenges that have tried and tempered my soul. In writing this book, I would be able to reflect on the meetings that had so serendipitously touched my life to random or far-reaching effect. The quest for meaning would be my guiding force, whether found in the whys and wherefores of every encounter, or distilled in the wisdom of the writers I chose to celebrate, my kinsmen of the shelf. To unite with my star of meaning—that familiar guiding other or higher self—would be to muster my powers of attention in the service of memory, insight and understanding.

I had reached a metaphorical crossroads in 1998. I was then in my early fifties and had been pursuing a conscious path of self development since my marriage had ended ten years earlier. I had moved from Ontario to British Columbia and back again and had crossed the Atlantic several times in a peripatetic attempt to find a place where I might truly feel I belonged. I was trying to decide what I should do: Should I revert to the comfort of my Irish family ethos, now that my children all had lives of their own, or should I remain in North America where I have lived for most of my adult life?

I decided to consult my friend Alexander, whose astrological savvy was legendary. A quick survey of my planetary aspects elicited the following response in him: "I see you are writing a book … All the elements point towards your success—and 1999 is the ideal time to begin!" This suggestion struck me as preposterous at first but Alex was adamant. "Ask yourself what purpose writing would fulfill for you." "It would justify my 'bookworming' ways and allow me to share the riches I have gleaned from a life time of reading!" was my first response. "It would also give you a clear focus and allow for some soul searching and the possibility of settling in one spot for a while." I con-

fessed to him that the idea was not entirely new—a clair-
voyant had predicted to my husband, many years before,
that I would write a book. Bob had frequently encouraged
me to "Start now!" while placing pen and paper, with his
list of chapter titles, on the table before me when he came
upon me in an idle moment. I lacked the inner motivation
required for writing at the time but the more I contem-
plated this course of action now, the more exciting the
prospect appeared. I definitely had a story to tell.

Deepening self-awareness over the years had provided
a means of coping with difficult circumstances while at
the same time urging me on to greater involvement in the
world. I had honed my skills as a performer of poetry,
song and story and perhaps this was a form of prepara-
tion for writing. A live presentation has a fleeting exist-
ence, whereas the written word remains to be revisited
and revised. However, these modalities are mutually
supportive. Reaching for the meaning of a good poem
stimulates thinking which leads to writing. Engaging an
audience or a readership implies striking a fine balance
between the universal and the personal. I had often sensed
that an inner connection with members of a prospective
audience sometimes influenced my choice of programme.
Perhaps the process of writing would also yield me the
necessary inspiration and inner connection with prospec-
tive readers.

I regarded myself as a participant in an emerging spir-
ituality that did not stem from old forms but arose from
the daily struggle for balance and sanity in every indi-
vidual who adopts a meditative and intuitive approach
to life. I hoped that in charting the joys and sorrows of
my life I might contribute to that burgeoning conscious-
ness. My sense of urgency in the task reflects a passage
in the Gospel of St. Matthew that always gives me pause:
"And because deeds of violence against the heavenly law

multiply, the love of the many will grow cold." I wanted
my writing to warm the hearts of readers and provide a
means of expressing the deeper concerns of life. When I
attend to the media accounts of atrocities being perpetu-
ated around the globe, it engenders a feeling of power-
lessness in me because the gap between my concern and
sphere of influence is so great. Yet I know that it better to
feel pain than not to feel at all—my every intimate rela-
tionship has taught me that. I often meditated on the fol-
lowing verse by Rudolf Steiner:

> As long as you feel pain
> which I am spared
> So is Christ's deed
> unrecognized in the world.
> For weak is still the spirit
> who can only suffer
> in his own body.

A radical philosopher and cultural critic, the Austrian-born
Steiner lived from 1861 to 1925 and founded a movement
called anthroposophy, pronounced like anthropology,
and meaning a "wisdom of man." He dedicated his life to
developing a new framework for thinking that would, he
believed, lead to a healthy evolution of our culture and
of our world. I encountered the work of Steiner while
searching for meaning in my life and a new framework
for thinking. The study of his writings brought me into
contact with inspired initiatives in the fields of education,
agriculture, medicine, art and curative education for peo-
ple with special needs. Spiritual knowledge is valued for
its practical application in these endeavours which engage
a spirit of cooperation in the people involved that is remi-
niscent for me of the early Irish monastic movement and
the deeds of love that it inspired. Every task, no matter

how menial, was regarded as valuable to the whole and no work was considered too low or inconsequential. My Irish predecessors demonstrated what Rudolf Steiner's teachings later confirmed, that the whole aim of earth evolution is to permeate the world with human love through devoted attention to everyday needs. A conscious path of inner development, as I would gradually come to discover, enables the student of anthroposophy to find a middle way in soul-life between extremes of "too much" and "too little," making him or her more ready to serve with equanimity.

The poet John Keats, another of my soul-guides and a precursor of Steiner, lived fully from the heart, embracing a path of transformation that juxtaposed necessary suffering with a cultivated capacity to abide in uncertainties, mysteries, doubts, without any irritable reaching after fact and reason. An equally radical way of trial and error was recommended in earlier times by another great thinker, Meister Eckhart. He named it the way of paradox. Rainer Maria Rilke, a contemporary of Steiner's, understood how the exercise of creative imagination resolved the tension of opposites in the soul. In this way what Rilke termed "the god" could come to know himself in human hearts.

So as I navigated my own way forward on the twisting network of Irish roads, both metaphorically and practically that day, I had the benefit of guides—Steiner, Keats, Eckhart, Rilke, and the farmer. Part of my journey was outward, from the persuasive embrace of Irish Catholicism in which I'd been raised, even though those now stimulating and inspiring me in new directions shared a Christian consciousness.

To be sure, I was somewhat wary of adding to the ranks of would-be authors who dazzled captive audiences in pubs around the country with outlines of plots that would drown in pints of Guinness. I knew that certain preconditions attend creative endeavour. These preconditions were clearly outlined for me by Robert Fritz, whom I had encountered in Toronto many years before. A successful American composer, Fritz desired to probe the mysteries of creativity and so made a keen study of the process through which his completed works emerged. He discovered that inspiration was merely a starting point.

All visionary flights, he cautioned, must be tempered with a cold, clear look at one's current reality. Too often we take refuge in daydreams or wishful thinking that can never be realized, or, conversely, we are plunged into despair by adverse circumstances. When both vision and current reality are held together in consciousness, a structural tension is then created between these polarities, invariably resolving itself in favour of the vision. In always referring to current reality I could be honest about the circumstances of my life however disturbing they might be, and earn my right to whatever rewards the vision might bring. I had put this balancing technique into practice a few months before arriving in Ireland, envisioning my book as a *fait accompli* while conversely noting my inability to type and my lack of stable living conditions and funds. Current reality presented a very dismal picture indeed...

Holding focus on both vision and reality simultaneously, I referred to them from time to time and entered into the spirit of the following lines from T.S. Eliot's *Four Quartets*:

> ...*I said to my soul, be still and wait without hope*
> *For hope would be hope for the wrong thing; wait without love*
> *For love would be love for the wrong thing; there is yet faith*
> *But the faith and the love and the hope are all in the waiting...*

Right action in its rightful time arises out of the inner, plentiful
void of expectant waiting. Soon life began to arrange a
chain of events through which an ever-changing current
reality and stable vision edged closer to one another in
time. An American friend, Joy Redfield Kwapien, whose
brother is the author of *The Celestine Prophecy*, unexpect-
edly commissioned me to write a book. We first met
when I presented an evening of poetry, song and story at
a School of Spiritual Psychology conference in Hartford,
Connecticut, in August 1996. She and her husband, Bob,
subsequently accompanied me on an extensive tour of
Ireland and we became fast friends. Driving the winding
roads, I shared anecdotes and autobiographical footnotes
to prepare them for encounters with remarkable friends
who would host us on our travels.

Meeting artists in their natural habitats made a strong
impression on Joy and Bob. Attentive always to nuance,
they could sense in these encounters the immanence of
the "hidden Ireland," which is ever sustained through love
of place, history, legend, oral and written tradition, and
in vibrant community life. They wanted to know more
about the influences that shaped the consciousness they
were meeting. Like me, they were lovers of poetry and
avid readers of books by Rudolf Steiner, Robert Sardello,
and Georg Kühlewind, who traced an evolutionary path
of consciousness in the human story that includes what is
past, passing, and to come. This book is punctuated with
references to these three writers whose works often pro-
vided context for our conversations on the road.

This subsequent journey across Ireland to make sense
of my life and clarify its larger purpose had, in reality,
started several years earlier. Those same "waiting" words
of the poet Eliot, had also helped to give my life new direc-
tion in 1990 when, after considerable inner struggle, I had
managed to break loose from an intolerable domestic situ-

Joy Kwapien and her brother James Redfield bear a striking resemblance to one another and share a devotion to the written word. Born into a family of aspiring writers, the success of James's first book, the bestselling The Celestine Prophecy, *vindicated family tradition and gave the Redfield name well-deserved literary prominence. I spent several months at the Kwapiens' Alabama home in 2000 and often joined next-door neighbours James and his wife Salle for memorable Sunday outings like the one recorded in this snapshot.* PHOTO BY SALLE REDFIELD

ation. A firmly held conviction of the indissolubility of the marriage bond, however, died hard. The doctrines and teachings of Roman Catholicism were as deep as the marrow in my bones. Although friends and family encouraged the move, I only crossed the threshold of realization one day when I finally admitted to a trusted counsellor in a very small voice, "I do not want to be married any more." Like many other women in later life who have once been timid, I felt a gathering of forces that enabled me to say no to a way of life that I could no longer sustain but which was a source of material security to me.

To find myself at odds with many of the events of a household that was once my pride and joy caused great upheaval in the life of my family. All order was displaced for a time as though we were living in the wake of an earthquake. The illusions with which I had begun an earlier, more naive phase of my life all surfaced for review and redemption. Inner growth entails coming to terms with unexamined assumptions. I took refuge in the Toronto Institute of Self Healing to embark on a painful but necessary process of change, intent on releasing co-dependent patterns of behaviour while learning to accept the uncertainty of life with equilibrium.

Change intensified during the ensuing years. A new order of life was breaking through from within. This power is termed menopause. It was to be celebrated rather than deplored, I discovered, for a natural shift of focus occurred as my bodily reality altered to accommo-date awakening spiritual faculties. When the regenerative capacity of the body slows down, life forces that were pre-viously engaged for reproductive and nurturing purposes are liberated, and can be channelled into spiritual study, social activism and creativity.

Commercial ways and means have become more and more available in the so-called "fight" against the natu-ral aging process, presupposing a reductionist view of the body as having a purely external, objective reality. Because I believe the physical body reflects the larger real-ity of soul and spirit that encompasses and permeates it, it seemed appropriate to now direct my attention to the hoarded treasures of heart and mind that had nourished my soul. Released from my earlier emotional need to be special, I was more ready to acknowledge my autonomy and responsibility to the world at large.

With this new phase came an appetite for adventure, which I was amused to think was rather in the spirit of the three Irish monks who set out from the south of Ireland sometime during the sixth century. They pushed out in their little *currach*, or small boat, without benefit of oar or sail. After some time at sea they drifted ashore somewhere on the English coastline. Emerging from their frail vessel, they were questioned by an inhabitant.

"Why have you come here?"

"We do not know," they replied. "But we must be always on pilgrimage, we know not where."

So much were they imbued with an awareness of the love indwelling every human heart that they were impelled to go forth to meet as many people as possible in order to more fully live this mystery. Divine presence was known and not simply inferred. This is how I began to know divine presence at this time of my life. Encounters with other people seemed more than ever enchanted and sacred. I sense this realization in many women my age in the prevailing climate of freedom and changing values that is charged with the potential of future possibilities and no longer reliant on the conventions of the past.

Some fifty million women worldwide are just now moving through menopause, imbued with conscious spiritual intent, peaceful and loving, holding the focus of a more harmonious and unified whole and, disconcerting hot flashes notwithstanding, helping to bring mankind through the proverbial eye of the needle.

Ralph Waldo Emerson expressed the essence of what many of my contemporaries realize:

The secret of culture is to learn that a few great points steadily reappear ... and, that these few are alone to be graded: the escape from all false ties; courage to be what we are, and love of what is simple and beautiful; independence and cheerful relation; these are the essentials, these, and the wish to serve, to add something to the well-being of men and women.

The new feminine ideal advocates trust in the face of adversity, unconditional living on the edge of uncertainty, a freeing and schooling of our attention to help us meet the world with undivided interest, and a renewal of the imagination. The mother or "wise woman" principle was an essential element of ancient mystery rites that brought humanity into harmony with the divine and natural worlds. Whether recognized by the name of Natura, Sophia, Isis, Kwan Yin, Divine Mother or Mary, the invocation of an eternal feminine presence of mercy and forgiveness becomes a source of empowerment in human souls that supersedes religious conventions. I regard it as the common denominator of all spiritual paths and an essentially unifying force for all who would embrace it.

As I drove the winding country road to Killaloe, my attention was drawn to a large statue of Our Blessed Virgin, as she is fondly called there, her arms outstretched to gather in her children. Her figure commanded a stretch of road as I rounded another bend. A source of bemused speculation for scientist, sceptic and believer was a phenomenon that occurred in 1986, when no less than fifteen of these wayside statues of Mary began to perceptibly sway backwards and forwards and from side to side. I was living in County Cork at the time, my place of residence only six miles from the village of Ballinaspittle, where the most remarkable of these phenomena could be witnessed. Kathleen Raine, the English poet, wrote admonishing me to "go and see if the statue is really moving. Perhaps you can determine what it is the Virgin is trying to tell us."

Each time I cycled to the spot and knelt before the roadside shrine, I could distinctly observe the movement

in the statue. No communication of the Virgin's intent
entered my mind until, leafing through a newly acquired
book entitled *Ariadne's Awakening*, a poem called "The
New Mary" caught my eye. It is poet Paula Brown's testi-
mony of the compassionate feminine presence immanent
for her in the company of women keeping a vigil of peace
at Greenham Common in England:

> ... *there came upon the Earth a new Mary*
> *She sung songs*
> *She built a web*
> *She grew like a great flower in the light of her own truth and*
>   *sisterhood* ...

The new Mary fully and sadly acknowledges the painful
reality that men, women, children, and the old are living in
abject conditions of disease, war and poverty, that forests
and seas are dying, that many are condemned to home-
lessness and hopelessness. I knew the Virgin was drawing
the attention of women everywhere to the wellspring of
renewal that lies within our collective consciousness. The
New Mary addresses every woman in the final lines of
Brown's poem:

> *"We are the purpose," she said.*
> *"The vision is us."*

The task of transformation requires precision in think-
ing and expression, and a keen attention to the usage and
meaning of words as exemplified in a true poem. Just as
the biblical Mary pondered the words of her son, Jesus, I
made a practice of learning poems by heart to retain their
inspiration as a source of contemplation. As soon as the
words are imprinted on the mind, conventional thinking
about the content gives way to a more intuitive grasp of

the meaning that interlaces a fabric of vowels and conso-
nants. Poetry provides ground on which the spirit can rest.
W.B. Yeats went so far as to say: "Only in what poets have
affirmed in their finest moments have we come anywhere
close to an authentic religion."

The tenet most central to my Christian life was articu-
lated by St. Paul: "Not I but Christ in me." The words
gained more immediacy for me when I pondered and
memorized an inspired poem by D.H. Lawrence, entitled
"Song of a Man Who has Come Through." It conveys
the attitude of humility and readiness exemplified in Paul.
Here are the opening lines:

Not I, not I but the wind that blows through me!
A fine wind is blowing the new direction of Time.
If only I let it bear me, carry me, if only it carry me! ...

In response to his passionate declaration of poetic intent,
angels draw near to Lawrence in the last lines of the
poem.

A shift in the new direction of Time is occurring today with the
phenomena of healing circles where people gather together
for artistic and therapeutic purposes and to develop a
speech of the heart. Paul Matthews is a leader in the field,
actively involved in restoring the connection between the
spoken and written word. He establishes circles of poetry,
love and truth wherever he travels. When I met him at
Emerson College in Sussex where my son Declan was
studying, we acknowledged common sources of inspira-
tion. By coincidence, Paula Brown had also been a student
of his and he was glad to hear me recite "The New Mary"
in my evening presentation at the college.

Next day, Paul presented me with a copy of his book

Sing Me the Creation, in which he points out that the com-
mission to praise the work of the creator and to uphold
the sources of imagination and creativity is central to the
work of a poet. The title alludes to Caedmon, a stutter-
ing, unlettered stable hand who lived in the seventh cen-
tury, and who is the first English poet we can name. He
took flight from the campfire when he noticed the harp
was being passed to him, a sign that it was his turn to sing.
Making some excuse about having to feed the animals, he
repaired to the barn. Falling into a deep sleep, he dreamed
an angel stood before him.

"Caedmon, sing me something," the angel said.
"I cannot sing. I left the feasting and came here because I
    could not."
"Nevertheless, you can sing to me," responded the angel.
"What shall I sing?" questioned Caedmon.
"Sing me the creation!" ordered the angel.

With the help of his angelic muse, Caedmon composed
a hymn to the creator in his sleep. Next morning he
knocked on the door of the nearby monastery of Whitby,
where the Celtic Rule was observed by the Abbess Hilda.
The monks recorded his words in careful calligraphy.
His act of breaking the tribal circle epitomized a funda-
mental shift from oral to printed word. He later joined
the monastic community and produced many verses on
Christian themes when, like a clean animal he ruminated
and converted all into the sweetest music. Inspired by this
story, I resolved to uphold the sources of imagination and
creativity in my own humble paean of praise.

A repertoire of memorized poems and songs was a
legacy of my Irish schooling, and the foundation for a
lifelong practice of learning by heart—my guarantee of
mental wellbeing, and the basis of a performance career

that would blossom many years later. What began as enforced learning by rote with more care for sound than sense developed into as genuine a love for the words, ideas, imagination and rhythms as my youthful capacity could summon. My mother's beautiful singing voice and her gift of rhymes and stories had taught me to listen from infancy as though the whole skin surface of my body was an attenuated ear. A mother who sings prepares the soul of a child for poetry and forms the actual larynx of the child for musical speech and song.

When I was thirteen or so I had a conscious awakening to the mystery of speech when I encountered a remarkable teacher, Mairéad Nic Dhonncha, who had grown up with Irish as her first language in a remote area of Connemara. A person of great intellect, she had absorbed the riches of oral and written literature in the Irish language. When I heard her recite "Dónal Óg," the bitter remonstration of a jilted lover, its many verses describing in imaginative picture the pain of unrequited love, I was touched in a part of the soul which has ever since remained open.

> ... For you took what's before me and what's behind me,
> You took east and west when you wouldn't mind me,
> Sun and moon from my sky you've taken,
> And God as well, or I'm much mistaken.

This teacher commanded great respect in the classroom because her presence was imbued with the authority of her speech. Through her I first understood how soul-enhancing the sense of language is and how it carries through in the voice. Her way of speaking was characteristic of her place of birth: a total unity of sound and sense was natural to her, mellifluous intonation, a savouring of vowels, an appreciation of consonants, musicality of phrasing, an ability to convey deep feeling without reverting to sentimentality or excess. Her words carried weight and met with rapt attention tinged with awe in me.

Mairéad Nic Dhonncha coached me in the interpretation of *sean nós*, or old style songs, that are still a standard part of my repertoire. I have also dipped into the poetic continuum of East and West, choosing poems that reveal the subtle movement of the soul between self and surroundings. Poetry is my means of keeping faith with a stream of wordless thinking that hovers over everyday life as meaning but which requires a slowing down of tempo and mental alertness to capture in words. The act of memorizing a poem has often given rise to an unexpected context for its recitation. I was once called upon to stand on a dolmen in a field near Chartres in France before dawn, to recite appropriate words as a large assembly of people waited for the morning sun to rise. Only a few weeks beforehand I had been seized by the fever of memorization, fortuitously stumbling on a new poem, which now happily saved the day in a moment of unprecedented necessity.

As a young child it was already apparent to me that people had trouble articulating what was closest to their hearts. My own inability to communicate my real feelings had often made me miserable. I sought refuge in poems that could reveal to me what I already knew and would like to say, if I had the words. Making these words my own by memorizing them always brought relief and gradually helped me to express my thoughts more freely.

Good poetry is born out of a reverence for life. Arising out of our powerful instinct for self-preservation, the poetic tradition is a genuine source of joy and strength flowing from our human story, transcending historical fact by virtue of its enduring qualities of beauty and truth. As soon as I am drawn into the mystique of a poem, the import of the words sink in, often appearing to express my own hidden thoughts. I will repeat the words over and over until I have made them my own, deriving great pleasure from this exercise as my appreciation for the content grows like a source of inner light and strength.

The famous Irish four-seasons-in-one-day variable was evident as I sped along the road to Killaloe, noting the extensive flooding that was such a source of distress for small farmers that year. Cows, wading through mucky and waterlogged fields, looked disoriented and forlorn. Due to a lack of fodder they were brought to a state of famine in some areas. Gradually the rain ceased, and the sun slanted out and soon flooding light illumined a desolate landscape. Approaching a lay-by that overlooked the beautiful Shannon River, I stopped the car to admire the play of light on calm waters.

Retrieving a notebook from my handbag, I jotted down some of the thoughts the journey had afforded me. I had a definite sense that I was coming home—I was now only a few miles from Ogonolloe, which I knew to be the territory of my ancestors, Gradys and Costelloes, McNamaras, Armstrongs and Grealishs. I recalled the litany of names on my mother's lips when she spoke nostalgically of her youth in Clare. When I told my Aunt Lil that I would be living at Tinarana House, her face lit up. "Your great-grandmother provided fabrics for the quilt-making that went on there years ago ..."

To think that I would weave my tapestry of words under that same roof! I had so often thought about the continuity of tradition and how one skill metamorphosed into another between generations. Seamus Heaney's poem "Digging" expresses it best. In this poem he recalls his father's and grandfather's engagement in the farming activities that characterized his rural upbringing:

...But I've no spade to follow men like them

Between my finger and my thumb
The squat pen rests.
I'll dig with it.

In Ireland, past, present, and future seem woven in a time-less mantle over the events of everyday life. I enjoyed such moments of backward-forward-inward intensity as I drove through the open gateway and meandered up a driveway, past enchanting woodland populated by red and fallow deer. Tinarana House, the imposing nineteenth-century mansion that loomed behind the trees, was to be my home for the months ahead. The twenty-odd years spent in one house during my marriage seemed to have satisfied my need for a permanent dwelling. When that period of my life ended, a need arose like a hunger or thirst, which was only satisfied by new places, books and conversation.

I learned the importance of having long periods of solitude. I could enter more fully because of that into interaction with others. I knew that I could only be content with a lifestyle that allowed me this rhythm. A meditative approach to life, far from isolating me, actually led to more intense involvement with the world. I recognized outside what I was inwardly aware of in my soul. A gem of wisdom from a sixth-century Irish monk, written at a time when Rome represented the pinnacle of sanctity, confirms this truth.

Who to Rome goes
Little comfort knows
For God on earth
Though long you've sought Him
You'll miss in Rome
Unless you've brought Him!

And this, I believe, is the secret of happiness—that elusive state of being that we relentlessly seek. We can become erroneously convinced that the experience of happiness is dependent on external circumstance or causal relationship when in fact it is self-determined. It stems I feel from a sense of one's own inner worth, independent of external conditions. We all have flashes throughout our lives of what we term happiness and some salient memories of contrasting periods of unhappiness. W.B. Yeats describes an experience of sudden happiness welling up in his soul, in the following lines from "Vacillation":

> *My fiftieth year had come and gone,*
> *I sat, a solitary man*
> *In a crowded London shop,*
> *An open book and empty cup*
> *On the marble table top.*
>
> *While on the shop and street I gazed*
> *My body of a sudden blazed;*
> *And twenty minutes more or less*
> *It seemed, so great my happiness,*
> *That I was blessed and could bless.*

These are the words of a man who understands what it means to come home to his own spiritual nature. I could recall these words at will from the hundreds of lines from this poet's work I had memorized. Yeats had taken a radical path of poetry which enlivened and deepened his soul-life. It was also the path of friendship. The pattern of destiny that moved through Yeats's life included collaboration with many other gifted and famous men and women of his day. I had driven past Coole Park, in County Galway, on my way to Killaloe. Once the home of Lady Gregory, it had been the location for significant meetings between

her and Yeats and other writers and visionaries, a power-
ful stimulus for the artistic life of their time. Lady Gre-
gory, George Hyde-Lees, Maud Gonne, James Stephens,
John Millington Synge, Ezra Pound and John Quinn, had
helped shape the creative genius and public interests of
Yeats.

His life demonstrates that fulfilment is never self-cre-
ated. It must always be given by the world, by other peo-
ple, by the environment, by the attuning of one's own
destiny with the world, with the time and with the people
with whom one lives. We all have our own litany of names
of those people who have contributed to the totality of
who we are in thought and action and belonging. They
have shown us how wholeness results from the ability to
balance our own needs with the needs of others. We are
each other's teachers in this experiment in the art of living
and social renewal. I have learned most from those who
are the most conscious of what they do and say. I write in
praise of friends whose example of living has influenced
mine. I wish to also demonstrate the central tenet of the
life I lead; that it is the recognition of the presence of
love in each individual that transforms experience into
the stuff that dreams are made on. This demands adap-
tation to nuances of tradition and behaviour and chang-
ing mores. I knew that the content of my book would
emerge from the ethos of this particular place and time
as it impinged on my heart and mind. In this enterprise
I would be led backwards, forwards and inwards like the
movement of the threefold Celtic spiral, a metaphor for
life itself.

I knocked on the door of Tinarana House.

Tinarana House is situated four miles from Killaloe, the ancient capital of Ireland, in a beautiful valley along the shores of Lough Derg. This aerial view reveals its splendid setting. It was a favourite place of retreat for many of the visitors I encountered and a quiet haven for any aspiring writer.

A Sense of Place

*Tory Island, Knocknarea, Slieve Patrick, all of them steeped
in associations from the older culture, will not stir us beyond
a usual pleasure unless that culture means something to us,
unless the features of the landscape are a mode of commun-
ion with a something other than themselves, a something to
which we ourselves still feel we might belong.*

SEAMUS HEANEY
Preoccupations: Selected Prose 1968–1978

"Hello, I'm Treasa—I've come to stay." I stood hesitant on the
doorstep, surrounded by baggage and the chill of a Janu-
ary afternoon.

"Welcome. We have been expecting you," said the cheer-
ful woman who opened the heavy yellow door. All appre-
hension vanished and my sense was that of homecoming.
The hospitality of Clare people is legendary. My moth-
er's family was native to this county. My late grandmother
Bridget told me that there was a living memory amongst
her people of abject conditions that were the legacy of
famine and evictions. My forebears found ways to make

a stranger feel welcome, their own poverty notwithstanding. The greeting, "We'll spread green rushes under your feet!" conveyed the respect that was natural for them at the appearance of a visitor. Green rushes grew abundantly on the river banks. I can remember my mother and her friends laying them out on the kitchen floor when I was a child, before plaiting them into crosses for St. Bridget's Day, February 1. This tradition continues.

A Clare custom that also survived in our family was the inclusion of music and dance in every gathering. Anybody who could play a few tunes on the fiddle or piano, or dance a set, was called into action as soon as refreshments were served to the guests. My grandfather, a violinist, taught Irish dancing and was a fine flute player. He died before I was born—like many other Irishmen of the time, he was carried off by tuberculosis. It was from my mother that I inherited the gift of singing and imitated from an early age her spontaneous response to any request for a song. "Since the gift is God-given it must be shared with all," was what I was told. I imbibed the spirit of the following anonymous old rune with my mother's milk:

> *I saw a stranger yesterday*
> *I put food for him in the eating place*
> *Drink for him in the drinking place*
> *And in the Holy name of the Trinity*
> *He blessed myself and my house*
> *My possessions and my family.*
> *And the lark said as she sang:*
> *It is often, often, often,*
> *Christ comes disguised*
> *As a stranger.*

There were no rushes in sight as I crossed the threshold of the stately mansion that was far removed from the dirt

My maternal grandfather in his dancing regalia. Although he died before I was born he set a standard of excellence held aloft for me when I proved an enduring competitor myself.

floor hovels of famine time, but an equally inviting abun-
dance of greenery and long, white lilies met my eye as I
entered the reception area. A red carpet of welcome led
the way along an old pitch-pine stairway. The smell of
burning cedar mingled with the aroma of the perfumed
candles that flickered in every corner. Soft lights cast a
glow on polished wood and reflected in the elegantly
furnished adjoining rooms. Shadows of lives long gone
seemed to hover in the twilight. In such an atmosphere
as this, one might draw nearer to the old poets W.B. Yeats
so often talked about, the ones who had a seat at every
hearth, if one could only enter a condition of timeless-
ness and allow one's own longings and aspirations to min-
gle with theirs.

My reverie was broken as staff members rushed for-
ward to introduce themselves. They were few in number
compared with the swell of vassals and serfs of one hun-
dred years before—some of whom were likely ancestors
of mine—who had scurried and scrubbed and hauled to
meet the demands of a prestigious household. Soon swept
up in a whirl of welcome and relieved of the burden of
luggage by strong and eager hands, I was encouraged to
choose my own room from amongst the vacant ones.

It was off season and other paying guests were few.
After some careful deliberation I opted for a lovely "en
suite" in the attic that held the promise of solitude. It
would be beyond earshot of engaging conversations and
the rest of the household buzz. There were a few book-
shelves in the corner and at my request a desk was placed
in front of the window that afforded me a lovely view of
Lough Derg that was only slightly obscured by a lattice of
saplings, stark against a winter sky.

I heard once that angels assume as their form bodies
of water, and this imagination invariably causes me to
look with awe at all bodies of water, such as the one that

was now spread out before me. The shimmering pearl-grey surface of the lake betrayed a tremor of movement and perfectly mirrored the shade of the afternoon sky. I knew from the experience of growing up in Ireland and my frequent sojourns in stormy Connaught that before the month was out I would witness many variations on this now tranquil scene. Sudden weather changes would call wind and rain into capricious service amidst shifting cloud formations and the play of light and shadow. Slanting rays would shyly appear from behind a brightening curtain of sky to briefly highlight some new detail of the landscape. I knew that waters could stir at the blink of an eyelid from tranquil to storm-shrouded turbulence. Distant hills that were at one moment cast into a reflective tableau on a polished mirror of lake could, would, in the next moment, present a verticality of blue and purple hue interwoven with luminous patches of mossy green or peat brown. Sometimes dense clusters of woodland would come to light against the skyline or seem to plunge down into hidden depths and form fringes of inky black around the inlets.

One could not remain indifferent to natural forces in this setting. I began to hope that in living so close to volatile elements, I might become more sensitive to the invisible presences active in them. Becoming more observant of the subtle changes in the natural world around me would increase my sense of belonging here as I began to establish a daily rhythm of walking and working.

Living abroad for most of my adult life, the poetry of W.B. Yeats had provided imaginative continuity with the country of my birth. Through memorizing and pondering upon the content of his poems, I was often reminded that I too was one of a race that recognized its origins in an imaginative mythology that related us to rock and hill. Sligo, where Yeats spent his childhood summers, was further north on the Connaught coastline. Seamus Heaney recognized how Yeats and his friends, at the turn of the twentieth century, had restored fairies to the landscape and presented readers and play-goers with a literature rooted in a legendary vision of history to counter the increasing materialism of the time. Here was a country of the mind in which I could orient myself and here I was at the source of it once more!

Yeats's poetry conveys the urgency of nature spirits, their endless activity bred of the reciprocal relationship that operates between their realm and ours. W.B. and other Celtic Renaissance poets understood that it is through devotion to the Folk Spirit of Ireland, a nature goddess, that our heart-forces are united with the selfless activity of the spirits of air, water, fire, and earth. That these spirits lie enchanted in mineral, plant and animal life and that human beings could be perpetually engaged in releasing them though their loving attention was implicit in the Irish folk wisdom of previous centuries, a wisdom that I was now seeking to incorporate into my own life. In earlier times, country people experienced the cycle of the seasons, as some poets still do, and as urgently as we experience the life inside our own skin today. The transformative processes of dying and becoming were directly experienced in the unfolding destiny of their lives and in the changing seasons of the year. These realizations fostered an aesthetic feeling of nationhood, as opposed to a nationalism that was more politically based. The author AE (the pen name of George William Russell) remarked that a peculiar element of beauty exists in every nation and is the root cause of the love felt for it by its citizens. This beauty arises from the endearing features of the landscape evident in mountain, lake and sky; from the passionate commitment of countless individuals to ideals of freedom and justice, to the inspiration of poets and artists and to early Christian monks who, in the words of poet John Montague, to this day continue to "kneel among dark rocks, in incessant, contemplative prayer."

A devotion to the feminine deity of the land through which hope, protection, strength and harmony would issue had characterized poetry in the Irish language in the eighteenth and nineteenth centuries. Yeats was writing out of this tradition when he gave us his splendid, prayerful tribute to the one he named Cathleen, the daughter of Houlihan. Every cultural aspiration of the Irish nation seemed vested in her radiant presence. Often appearing as a woman in distress, bound by the shackles of English conquerors, she inspired visions of freedom and purpose in Irish writers that would spur her people to rebellion. Yeats wondered once if certain verses of this order, written by him, had sent young men out to die. It is interesting to note that the eternal feminine, by whatever name, makes her presence felt when people find common cause with those who suffer from injustice, war and poverty. Dark Rosaleen was another name by which poets could address the spirit of Ireland as she cast her mantle of protection over all her folk. The image of the spirit of Ireland was often mingled with the character traits of wives and mistresses beloved of Irish writers, in the shaping of some significant fictional characters. My late ex-husband, Robert, like many another scholar of Irish literature, was enamoured of the Yeatsian image of Cathleen and imagined he saw its reflection in me! He often recited "Red Hanrahan's Song about Ireland" to me in his wonderfully resonant voice and my heart still lifts with the musical cadence of the words that I recommend you read aloud:

The old brown thorn-trees break in two high over Cummen
  Strand,
Under a bitter, black wind that blows from the left hand;
Our courage breaks like an old tree in a black wind and
  dies,
But we have hidden in our hearts a flame out of the eyes
Of Cathleen, the daughter of Houlihan.

The wind has bundled up the clouds high over Knocknarea,
And thrown the thunder on the stones for all that Maeve
  can say.
Angers that are like noisy clouds have set our hearts abeat;
But we have all bent low and low and kissed the quiet feet
Of Cathleen, the daughter of Houlihan.

The yellow pool has overflowed high up on Clooth-na-
  Bare,
For the wet winds are blowing out of the clinging air;
Like heavy flooded water our bodies and our blood;
But purer than a tall candle before the Holy Rood
Is Cathleen, the daughter of Houlihan.

A flame of the new feminine stirred in my heart when
I made the words of this poem my own. It became my
inspiration for a one-woman show entitled *I Am of Ireland*,
which I performed throughout the seventies in North
America, Ireland, England, and Scotland. It took another
shape in the 1980s, when I teamed up with the American
composer Steven Scotti, who had set several of Yeats's
poems to music and who had a very popular following in
Massachusetts, where he lived. We met through a mutual
friend, Herb Kenny, who was for many years literary edi-
tor of the *Boston Globe*. Steven first introduced himself to
me over the telephone, within listening range of a grand
piano on which he accompanied himself while he sang

American composer Stephen Scotti as I remember him — even before meeting him in the flesh! He gave forth lusty renditions of the poems he had set to music wherever there was a piano in sight. Collaborating with him was a highlight of my performing career. PHOTO BY PAUL FOLEY, 1985

his catchy arrangements of poems by Yeats, in full voice over the wire. I soon learned his haunting air for the poem I quoted above, and many other original settings that proved to me that poetry was essentially song. The joint engagements he promised to arrange in the U.S. for us became a *fait accompli* as our friendship developed.

The late actor/singer Robert Heinlein and I in a Scotti production at Hammond Castle in Massachussets. We are performing a scene from Maureen Charlton's musical adaptation of J.M. Synge's Playboy of the Western World, in which Christy Mahon bids a fond farewell to Pegeen Mike. PHOTO BY PAUL FOLEY, 1985

I was called away from the window by a light knock on my bed-room door. Frieda, the owner of the estate, had come to welcome me. I had been delighted by the warmth of Frieda's response when I had telephoned some weeks earlier to inquire about accommodation. The mellifluous tones of her voice were now matched by her gentle presence and striking, black-Irish beauty. I had a sense of being restored to the company of a long-lost sister and sensed a similar recognition in her.

After we had discussed the practical details of my stay, I asked her to tell me the history of the house.

"The estate was owned since the seventeenth century by a family called Purdon, who distinguished themselves during the famine by their concern for the well-being of their tenants, making every effort to feed and clothe them. Those who survived the horrors of the time erected a plaque as an expression of gratitude to their landlord. This was most unusual. The title for the 300-acre property passed out of that family in 1901 and my husband and I acquired it in 1989, after it had fallen into a very dilapidated condition. We gradually managed to restore the property, preserving the original structure and character."

She continued animatedly, "We are, after all, at the heart of Ireland here. This area was the focus of national attention at the close of the first millennium when Brian Boru (whose seat of power, Kincora, was down the road) succeeded in vanquishing the Viking invaders. Ronald Reagan and others claim ancestry with the warrior king Brian.

"The Irish name *Tí na Ranna*, means 'house of the point.' I would like to establish a peaceful haven here for people seeking respite from the stress of modern life and provide a wide range of therapies for them.

"In the natural beauty of these surroundings, people can experience the benefit of a healing current which is available twenty-four hours a day," I replied. "I have lived for the past year in another such centre, called Kingview, close to the city of Toronto. In that community, I noticed that each member consciously served the good of the whole, which in turn reflected the talents and efforts of each individual. The spirit of cooperation generated by the permanent residents there, their responsibility in caring for the property and meticulous attention to the comfort of their guests, was conducive to the healing atmosphere that visitors were seeking. I saw there that when we pay attention to the needs of others our own needs are automatically served."

I could speak my mind freely to Frieda and was learning to know her by what I myself could say in her company.

In orienting myself to any new situation, I hold the question: "What is seeking to come forth and how can I serve?" I knew that some task would emerge for me in this location in due course. In adopting this approach, I have been able to establish homes for myself in several places to which I have no material claim, but where the rightness of my intention towards people and place assures me a constant welcome.

"It is as though I have known you for a long time..." Frieda spoke after a long pause.

"I hope we will be good friends," I said sincerely.

A male friend of mine once wisely observed that when two women meet for the first time they exchange chapter and verse of interests and attitudes and cover more ground than the opposite gender would in years of acquaintance! Thus it was with us. As soon as my new friend became aware of my familiarity with the types of therapy offered at Tinarana House, and the fact that I was a certified Attunement practitioner, she encouraged me to begin giving sessions on the morrow. In this way I could join with the other therapists in serving a common purpose in an entirely practical way. It would also afford me the opportunity of meeting Irish people, house guests drawn from every walk of life.

"You will still have lots of time to write! I will also show you some walking trails. Let us meet at eight a.m., one or two mornings a week," she called over her shoulder as she left.

I cast a rueful glance at the pile of blank pages on the table before me. The three essentials of the writing life—the coveted "room of one's own," the promise of solitude, and the prospect of hours to spare of unstructured time—had been serendipitously provided. Hundreds, even thousands of miles now lay between me and a variety of loved ones to whom I might have deferred. There was no telephone, fax machine, or computer in sight, no meals to cook, grocery lists or house cleaning to fret about in this tranquil setting. Free of the need to make extra money for several months to come, I had struck a low-season, all-in deal with Frieda that included the services of her reigning gourmet chef. In short, I had nothing to do but write, a terrifying prospect for one who had little notion of what writing a book entailed.

Producing that first draft over many months only served to prepare me for the more exacting and rewarding task of working with an experienced editor later on. I knew I was capable of churning out short prose pieces, having contributed to a variety of newspapers in the past, never however exceeding my limit of twelve hundred words on any topic. I had also written a series of radio scripts. In recent years, I had learned to perfect the shaping of themes around memorized poems and songs, the success of which depended on an art of selection and the resonance my interpretations would strike in the souls of listeners. Apart from these creative outlets, a habit of copious letter-writing had bolstered my writing skills over the years.

I began my book out of a genuine desire to communicate with my two friends, Bob and Joy, to inform and entertain them, while acknowledging our common debt to the poets they never tired of hearing me recite. I would layer ideas gleaned from writers we admired, from personal experience and memory on the palimpsest of my Irish heritage, a source of great fascination to my two non-Irish readers. I had discovered the Lewis Carroll quotation which inspired my opening chapter in a promotion catalogue for Tinarana House lying on my bedside table, my library consisting of only a handful of books to begin with. Getting directions from a farmer was a good anecdote to start me off since my travels around Ireland with the Kwapiens yielded many such yarns. We laughed heartily when Joy on one occasion, rolled down her window to enquire from a local person, "Can you tell us where we are going?"

Writing long-hand was a meditative process and slowed me down considerably, since a better formulation for every sentence occurred to me in mid stream. I carried on regardless, stitching and unstitching, like my great-grandmother before me and her quilt-making companions, until a pleasing pattern presented itself. I enjoyed rising early, bringing order and form to the muddle of a previous day with increasingly painstaking penmanship. An urgent mingling and sifting of ideas took shape in sleep, forming itself into a compelling stream of consciousness with the light of day. I noticed that questions consciously taken into sleep were invariably answered in these waking moments. My self-imposed rhythm of writing, walking and reading had a stabilizing effect on my days, carrying the emerging content of the book forward in surprising directions, the ideas for a subsequent chapter suggesting themselves as the one I was working on neared completion. I was driven by themes integral to my thinking life more than by the chronology of biographical details. The solitary exercise of writing and the eremitic lifestyle suited me well and was curiously invigorating since my attention was fully engaged and time seemed to fly as the day progressed until sleep overtook me again.

I woke up early on the morning of my first walk with Frieda and recited Rudolf Steiner's morning offering as I always do. The sun had not yet arisen but I felt the inner glow, the joy in living that these words convey:

> *In purest outpoured light*
> *Shines the Godhead of the world;*
> *In purest love for all that lives*
> *The divinity of my soul radiates;*
> *I rest in the divinity of the world;*
> *I shall find myself*
> *In the divinity of the world.*

This prayer articulates the essence of a sense of place. I only experience myself as truly at home anywhere when I have established my purpose in being there, when I have attuned myself to the landscape, inhabitants and history of the area and when my individual aspirations can contribute to the collective well-being.

As we walked the rugged country road, I told Frieda about an essay my friend of many years, Christopher Bamford, had written on the subject of walking and friendship. He suggests that friends walk together united in contemplation of the reality they aspire to, noting that the wish for friendship develops rapidly but friendship does not. According to Christopher, Aristotle maintained that friendships were based either in pleasure, utility or goodness. The latter was the most lasting because to wish for a friend's good for its own sake was the truest mark of friendship. I rely on the goodwill of friends when the chips are down. It is easy for the mind to identify with the depressing scenarios that can accompany blows of fate or even temporary setbacks. Even though to fail at something does not make one an ultimate failure, it can often make one doubt one's own abilities. At such times it does not serve to hear one's own negative inner dialogue repeated by anyone else. Blessed is the friend in that moment that can articulate the words that give comfort and hope for the future.

My most enduring friendships have survived misunderstandings, incompatibility of viewpoint, geographical distance, romantic attachment, and disappointment, as though to convince me of the unassailable unity of our bond. According to Ralph Waldo Emerson, friendship implies an alliance of formidable natures, joined by mutual respect and fear, in the recognition of an underlying bond that unites them even in the face of obvious disparity. It is not unusual to fear the people we love since they have the power to hurt us.

In his introduction to a favourite book, *James, Sēamus and Jacques*, which I had carried with me to County Clare, Irish writer James Stephens mentions a conversation he had with AE:

> *"If, when you come to my age,"* said AE, *"you can claim that you have had six friends in your life, you will be a luckier man than any man has a right to be."*
>
> *"I am one of your six,"* James boasted.
>
> *"You are one of my four,"* he replied severely; and something like desolation fell on him for half a minute.

AE was easily the most popular man in Ireland at the time and it seems odd that he would think his friends only numbered four when almost everyone whose life he had touched regarded him as a real friend. He had the ability to address and call forth the highest strivings of the person who stood before him. A conversation with him often represented a point of no return in the life of that person, since AE had the gift of clairvoyance, a clear seeing of the task that was foremost in the life of the person concerned.

I too have had the benefit of special friends who could see more clearly than I could myself the necessity of a certain course of action for me. I have, although sometimes reluctantly, usually followed their well-intended guidance to good effect. Such people never act out of self-interest and can place every event in the context of a greater whole. Jesus, a friend supreme, upon meeting Simon for the first time, is said to have gazed into him and, although acknowledging that he was Simon, son of John, said that he should from then on be called Kephas, which means "bedrock," or "Peter" in translation. He could fathom Peter's purpose in life in a pure moment of encounter.

I believe that friendship arises out of a predisposition towards another person that can often be intuited at first meeting. A memory has been imprinted on the heart further back than we can remember. There is a recognition that cannot consciously be accounted for, and sometimes even a feeling of awe that causes a shyness to descend. It's as though a mystery lies ready to unfold in subsequent interaction. Friendship is a means of balancing the intimacy and right relation that love demands of me.

When Jesus, at the end of his ministry, referred to his disciples as friends, a sacramental dimension was introduced to the ideal of friendship. All friendships will be tested by human shortcomings, but I believe that if we make brotherhood and sisterhood a constant recurring motif in our lives, we will come close to leading a heavenly life on earth. While fondness for my blood relations is always a given, I have noticed that the friends I carry in my heart as treasures constitute an extended family to which I am as equally bound in love and loyalty. I experience the vastness of my spiritual kin as I move from place to place. My son Declan, whose friends are legion, reached a similar realization when he took to the road with his extended family of Grateful Dead followers in the early nineties, excitedly exclaiming to me over the phone a few months later. "Mom there isn't a town in the United States where I'm not welcome!"

Rudolf Steiner recommended that we awaken spirit in each other by acknowledging and encouraging each other's unique creativity and calling, an outlook shared by his contemporaries W.B. Yeats and AE. The latter regarded the artist as spirit awakener supreme, believing that the artists are the true architects of a nation, shaping the collective consciousness out of their own imaginations. Native Americans proclaim the most eloquent amongst them, who can rouse the rest of their tribe from any lethargy, waker uppers. James Joyce chose to fulfill a similar purpose when he wrote *Finnegans Wake*, admonishing all readers to abandon cliché and be more creative in their use of language. He wanted to demonstrate, in his novel coining of words and phrases that we cannot do justice to the lives we lead with hackneyed expressions, plots that are too straightforward or grammar that is cut and dried.

Inspired literature can serve to prepare our minds for the awakening that can most effectively come about through spontaneous interaction with one another. The concepts I acquire in the turning of pages always seem to be tested in the exacting demands of relationship. I value the life-giving and soul-strengthening nature of human relations more than ever today, in the face of growing alienation, virtual reality, distrust, confusion and fear. Self-absorption is a phase that most people, on a path of self-development, pass through. In reality, I find my deepest self reflected back in the people and events I encounter. The poet Novalis spoke from personal experience when he said, "The heart is the key to life and to the world. If our life is as precarious as it is, it is so in order that we should love and support one another."

I believe that we need one another in order to know ourselves. We say "show me your friends and I will show you who you are." From early childhood, we have been registering the judgments and internal images that at first our families, and later our peers, have held of us and we have tended to form an identity around these thought forms. The trouble is that, later in life, we may need to take a new direction which might not be compatible with who we think we are. If we are fortunate, we will have acquired some new role models in the meantime, people who have learned how to be gloriously themselves in the way that Walt Whitman did when he declared "...there is no sweeter flesh than sticks to my very own bones." The best compliment I have received came after a poetry recital when someone in the audience said, "You do you so well, it helps me to do me!"

Whenever I am at a crossroads, not knowing what to do next, a friend (and not only a farmer), will come along and set me straight, sensing a capacity in me that I am not aware of in myself until actually engaged in the recommended task. Joy Kwapien, in calling upon me to write this book, proved herself a "friend indeed." Deepening friendships are truly the greatest gift of the ageing process, since it often takes almost a lifetime to truly be oneself and to value the companionship of kindred others who lead the life they choose in the face of all odds. Unconditional acceptance of one another is a given in these relationships as we discover together that it is mutual acceptance that unites us and helps us to create unprejudiced images of one another by which we may be recognized and cherished in this life and beyond.

Frieda and I talked of many things as the morning spread its light around us;: motherhood she had five school age children and I have four who are now grown up; and her life as a doctor—besides prescribing medicine, she could prescribe the life changes needed in local people, and most of her employees at Tinarana were former patients of hers. We talked about my life in Canada and the challenges I had faced when my husband had become mentally ill several years before. Our voices mingled with the twitter of bird song, the scampering, darting movements of small animals in hedges along the road, the more distant bellow of cows and morning echoes of rooster and sheep, and the random neighing of horses in fields. All these natural sounds seemed to bolster our flow of thoughts and underscore the animation of our exchange.

Conversation is the lifeblood of communication, an art form that has fascinated me since childhood. As a little girl I developed very long ears, straining to catch the content of muffled adult talk behind closed doors. "What are they talking about?" my sisters and I wondered. A protective silence hung around the affairs of the grown-up world, considered too profane for innocent ears. "Curiosity killed the cat!" was the invariable response, no matter how much the air was charged with the dynamic of some current happening.

Instinctively I turned to books for the answers to questions I was not yet capable of formulating. Television had not been introduced in Ireland, and I remained immersed in the kingdom of childhood while the soap operas of adult life unfolded around me and without my participation. I unconsciously adopted Rilke's approach to questions and answers and the importance of personal experience. "Live the questions now," he counselled. "Perhaps you will gradually, without noticing, live along some distant day into the answers." Nobody can have ready answers for the unprecedented challenges and cruelty of our time, and difficult as it may be for those who regard answers as being more important than questions, more and more people are learning to accustom themselves to not knowing. I find that when I entertain a question I soon begin to feel the steady beat of an answering response implicit in my environment, in the pages of a book, in conversation, on billboards or on the radio, in overheard exchanges between strangers. This in itself awakens gratitude in me for my own time and place and makes any difficulties I may be experiencing more tolerable.

Many clues to the mystery and meaning of life have fallen from the lips of good talkers. I was eighteen when I met my first inspired talker. He was courting a younger sister, Frances, the beauty of our family. They married in due course, although he was considerably older than she. His name was Tom Naughton and he had appeared in our small town in County Galway to salvage a business that was on the verge of ruin. He resembled the late John F. Kennedy, who was then a great hero of the Irish people. My sister was pregnant with their third child when Tom lost his life in a car accident.

His death left a void in the lives of hundreds of people—his absence is acutely felt even to this day, but he left us with an enhanced understanding of the meaning of friendship. His enduring support of friends in need, his gestures of practical assistance, depleted his own financial resources. People were the central focus of his life.

He could divine and appreciate the unique individuality of the people who would gather around him, as round a hearth, often in the small hours of the morning. He was at his most insightful late at night, intent on bringing out the best in everyone, chiding and praising, holding up mirrors in the hilarious vignettes he performed extemporaneously.

Years later, I spent many happy hours in the company of the Irish actress Siobhán McKenna, who spread a similar mantle of enchantment over any gathering, so that everyone could say afterwards, "Now I am more myself!" Time was away and somewhere else in the company of Tom or Siobhán who both taught me to be a good listener.

"What is a good listener?" James Stephens once asked on the radio, and he gave the answer himself, remarking that a good listener is one who likes the person who is talking. I could certainly agree with that. He said that "listening with affection is creative listening. No person, however gifted, is talking at his best unless he likes the people he is talking to and knows that they like him, he is then inspired almost as a poet is." Stephens, who lived into the 1950s, could boast some of the greatest talkers Ireland has ever known as his contemporaries. They cultivated their art in the salons of the day, which, in the sixties, were superseded by such pubs in Dublin as The Bailey and McDaids.

The tradition of home salon was still upheld by a few in the Ireland of my time. I was invited to author Arland Usher's Friday nights whenever I was in Dublin and thereby acquired a sense of the character of such gatherings. Arland, in earlier years, had himself enjoyed the soirees of AE and Yeats. He opted to telephone a number of people on his extensive list of acquaintances every week and I eagerly responded whenever I was one of the chosen. Struggling still with shyness at the time, I contributed little to the topics aired, basking in the reflected glory of my eloquent elders instead. However, I readily sang or recited on request. Arland, a prolific writer, rarely held forth at his own gatherings but sat chain-smoking unfiltered cigarettes in a corner, with a look of glee on his face. He was known in Dublinese to be a great man for the women, but he was seen to be resting from his escapades on these occasions. His silent focus seemed to fuel discussion in the assembled company of the voluble writers, academics and actors he attracted.

I cannot, however, remember encountering any talker there with the remarkable qualities of Stephen McKenna, to whom famous authors such as Yeats, AE and James Joyce had to accede when conversing in the salons of bygone years. James Stephens, who had been his friend, described McKenna thus: "His remarkable and never-absent great quality was that he not only made his listeners listen, he made his listeners talk. When you were with McKenna you discovered that you were talking just as much as he was. For the first time in your life, perhaps, you found that you were also a philosopher, a wit, a lover of the moon, and an intimate of Eve and of the dragon, the donkey and the duck."

Ireland has often been characterized as a nation of talkers and all the best talk can be traced in its origins to the Irish language, which playwright John Millington Synge termed "the language of a race that has tired the sun with talking." The English of Synge's plays carries the character of the Irish tongue, so full of hyperbole, cajolery, lamentations, euphemism, allusion, endearment, blessing and tirade. The people who shaped the language owed nothing to book learning but regarded an original turn of phrase as an expression of individuality to be cultivated and respected. Language to them was the fruit of the deeds and sufferings of life, which rendered one person distinct from another. How you spoke, the quality of your voice and intonation, and your novel turn of phrase were more important than how you looked or what you owned. Healthy speech was seen as a basis for physical health and for the spiritual well-being of the speaker. Synge's characters were closely modelled on people who surrounded him on the Aran Islands and on those he met walking the roads of County Wicklow. He described their talk as follows: "A fashion of speech which was not conned from books, the wild exuberant speech of isolated people. People who are as timid in action as they are bold in talk; being bold indeed in the only thing they have practice of."

Robin Flower was a scholar who immortalized the Gaelic speech and ways of the Blasket Islands, off the southwest coast of Ireland. Peig Sayers was one of its most famous inhabitants, living there in rhythmic harmony with the elements. Although illiterate, she had a great gift of articulation. He came upon her cursing one day.

"The people of the island have a fine gift of cursing," Flower said.

"We have," Sayers answered, "but there is no sin in it. If the curse came from the heart, it would be a sin. But it is from the lips they come, and we use them only to give force to our speech, and they are a great relief to the heart."

"Well," he said, "I make little of them, for if the blessings come from the heart I don't care where the curses come from."

More tragic than the disruption caused in the history of the Irish people by famine is the social disintegration that arose and that continues to prevail since the native language was virtually eliminated as a mother tongue. A concerted campaign was successfully conducted in the eighteenth and nineteenth centuries to cause people to

Peig Sayers sitting in the smoky confines of her humble cottage. The "wild exuberant speech of isolated people" found a good example in her. She lived on a Blasket Island, off the Kerry coastline, at the turn of the twentieth century. Robin Flower, scholar, linguist and folklorist, keeper of manuscripts in the British Museum, discovered her there and recorded and immortalized her legacy of tall tales and lively anecdotes delivered in a mellifluous flow of Irish language that sounded like music to his ears.

abandon Irish in all but the few peripheral pockets where it is still spoken today. Complex and cruel in its implementation, this campaign demanded that parents punish their children as a means of censor. The parents themselves were already enslaved and weakened in spirit by poverty and hunger. Its repercussions on the national psyche can still be felt.

The shift from Irish to English and the cultural fragmentation it entailed is one of the hidden causes of mass emigration from the country. Economic deprivation can be overcome by one generation but the loss of the natural expression of a collective psyche can never be overcome. I see the backlash in evidence in Ireland's metamorphosis into a consumer society. Greed and self-interest predominate in the absence of a common cultural ideal. When people lose spiritual identity they seek its substitute in material things. Seán de Fréine states in his seminal book *The Great Silence* that Irish life is like a plant that has been cut back to the roots, whose growth is stunted because it is being trampled on continuously.

AE, among others, sowed seeds of Ireland's spiritual renewal that remain yet to be harvested. The following lines are from his "Defence of some Irishmen not Followers of Tradition":

> *...We are less children of this clime*
> *Than of some nation yet unborn*
> *Or empire in the womb of time*
> *We hold the Ireland in the heart*
> *More than the land our eyes have seen*
> *And love the goal for which we start*
> *More than the thought of what has been...*

Frieda and I talked of these and other matters as we took our first walk through the unspoiled landscape of

County Clare, conversing in the Irish language so dear to our hearts. I struggled to keep pace with her, being unused to such early morning exertion. I had an occasion of *déjà vu* as we climbed uphill, talking excitedly. I could vividly recall similar walks and animated exchanges in Irish during my teenage years as a boarder in a convent in County Mayo, set like Tinarana on the shores of a lake, Lough Mask. Half of my classmates were from Connemara, and Irish was their first language. Some of them were descendants of the Aran Islanders who had inspired the plays of John Millington Synge. They spoke in musical tones, with the clear intonation, the attention to vowels and the richness of expression that I have ever since associated with the Irish language. As we rounded the hill, we both fell silent; a stillness hung in the air as the light became golden in a turquoise haze. Trees and landscape appeared embossed in a moment of unearthly radiance. We looked at one another, transfigured in a tableau that is etched in my memory. I felt touched by grace and I felt a cheerful confidence in all that lay ahead. Frieda's artist's eye was alert to the awesome beauty of the scene.

"I wish I had paint and canvas with me now," she murmured.

We began to talk about the connection between memory and feeling. "We have as it were, two memories. One recalls facts, details, dates, chapter and verse, and which can also go blank—a memory that can be stored in a computer. We need this memory to function effectively in the world. The other memory, the hidden aspect of remembrance, arises when feeling and intuition are at work," I ventured.

Looking at her watch Frieda remarked: "I am remembering that it is time for me to go to work!"

When I returned to my room, I looked up some notes I had written about Martin Heidegger's approach to memory. For him, memory did not initially refer to our power of recall, but signified devotion and the constant, concentrated abiding with something. He called it the power of unrelenting and unrelinquishing retention. He highlighted the fact that "thinking" and "thanking" were expressed at one time by the same word in the German language. He regarded "thankfulness for being" as the natural expression of the human heart. This gives rise to the impulse of poetry, which in turn gives birth to philosophy.

I resolved to recall the key relationships of my life in the spirit of thankfulness and devotion implicit in the following lines by Christian Morgenstern:

...With thankfulness resounds all life divine
Resounds from beings one and manifold
In giving thanks all beings intertwine.

Heresies of Truth

…One charge alone we give to youth
Against the sceptred myth to hold
The golden heresy of truth.
AE
"In Defence of Some Irishmen not Followers of Tradition"

Spring was at hand. Country roads became more enticing, sap was rising and circulating in every living thing. Hedges and trees were coming back to themselves, awakening from the anonymity of winter sleep. Skies appeared more clement, roadside streams and trickling waterfalls more musical, the swell of bird song more assured. Change was in the air, sweeping me up in its current…

Trunks bearing the totality of my earthly possessions arrived from Canada. I was eager to surround myself with cherished books and paintings once again. By fortunate synchronicity, the Tinarana gate lodge became available to rent and, comfortable as the attic of the main house had been, within days I was ensconced in the modest but modernized two-roomed dwelling. Built-in bookshelves were soon swelling, a sturdy desk and chair rested between heater and fireplace and the freshly painted walls afforded ample gallery space. I hung the prized works of Canadian painter friends between the windows so I could watch slanting sunlight enhance both the subtle and vibrant colours.

Never in all my wanderings had I found a more perfect setting for these paintings, nor felt so well surrounded by them. Cottage windows presented seasonal splendours of budding foliage, gnarled tree trunks, a blaze of yellow furze that would last several months, and the highs and lows of bushes. There was pleasure without end in the drama of skies, against which distant blue and purple hills presided majestically over acres of woodland and lake. The enchantment deepened when I stepped outside. Imposing oaks, beeches and sycamores, and a Spanish chestnut shading my doorway, were protective and reassuring in their sheltering presence.

> *A wall of forest looms above*
> *And sweetly the blackbird sings;*
> *All the birds make melody*
> *Over me and my books and things.*
>
> *There sings to me the cuckoo*
> *From bush citadels in grey hood,*
> *God's doom! May the Lord protect me*
> *Writing well, under the great wood.*

Curiously fitting for me now, this rhapsodic gloss was inscribed by a monk on the margin of a ninth-century manuscript. My fondness for the old mysteries could, I thought, be fruitfully sustained in the proximity of a grove of oak trees, named in Irish *doire*, root word for druid, he who plied his priestly craft underneath their shade.

I had been loathe to abandon the luxury of the big house and the illusions of grandeur I could indulge in there, but I was, I reminded myself, still within a pleasant, tree-lined walk of it. More peripheral to me now would be the comings and goings of guests and the idle chat I so enjoyed. The time had come for me to forego all distraction if I was to meet my deadline; in my new home, I could feel the earth beneath my feet, and face for the first time in my life the challenge of living alone.

As if to affirm the rightness of the move, a letter arrived from Jay Ramsay, a favourite contemporary poet, within hours of my settling in. Included was a poem entitled "For Treasa." It recalled the occasion, a few months before, when he and I, both impecunious artists, helped a group of wealthy people raise money for a worthy cause by giving a reading. We stayed at the time at an establishment known as An Cultúrlann, in rooms high up on the fourth floor, where we had ranged in rambling talk late into the night.

Jay's compassionate interest in my circumstances brought me close to tears and I could confess to him how difficult it was for me to adapt to a nomadic way of life. He urged me to embrace whatever reality I was faced with, explaining that acceptance would lead me into authenticity. My transference now from mansion to mews was a symptom of that newfound practicality. It was encouraging for me therefore to note the uncanny accuracy and timeliness of the lines Jay addressed to me:

… How are you going to descend?
And the temptation is to ignore it
When the sun comes out again
To let the universe bail us out
But isn't that the beginning of sadness?
Not to stand in our own two feet and in what we speak

But to embody it and bear the world
As the time demands, if we are to be what we dream.
Because as far as we reach upwards we have to come down
To grasp the nettle of matter beneath,
Powerless as we are beside the rain and falling leaves
And when we can let go to them; peace,
In the deep solace of quiet they seek.

In fact, the universe had bailed us out on that occasion and our good deed was rewarded a hundred-fold. We were both offered book contracts the morning after the reading, one of the most remarkable examples of divine providence I have ever witnessed! Jay, whom I had first met when he attended a poetry recital I gave in England earlier that year, had contacted me the day before to say he was in Dublin for a few days. I told him about the performance and spontaneously invited him to share the stage with me. There was a surprise in store for him since I intended to recite the seven-page poem of his I had just memorized, entitled "Rosa Mundi," during the first hour of the programme. This proved to be a very moving experience for him. Bob and Joy Kwapien had come over from London for the night and could revel in a quintessentially Irish turn of events. Wine had been flowing in the course of the readings and several members of the audience were itching to take the floor when Jay and I took our bow. An impromptu concert erupted, each performer outdoing the other in bursts of song that continued into the small

Celebrated English poet Jay Ramsey paid me a visit me at the gate lodge before we toured Connemara together. Charlie McGeever took this photo on a fine October evening I can vividly recall. We were only a stone's throw from the window of my writing room at the time.

hours. Jay and I were still high-flown from having been on both sides of the footlights when we joined Joy and Bob for a late breakfast at their hotel. Joy told us that she was willing to offer her financial support to both of us in the coming year if we agreed to write two books that she planned to eventually publish.

Later that month, she and I discovered Tinarana House on a drive through County Clare. Our curiosity aroused by the large roadside sign, we had entered through open gates and followed the tree-lined avenue that led to the house. The door was ajar but there was nobody in sight as we wandered around the lobby. Reluctantly returning to the car when our friendly calls fell on deaf ears, Joy started up the engine with a knowing look in my direction. "This would be the perfect place for you to write your book!" And so it came to pass.

When I had first surveyed the mere five hundred square feet of gate lodge floor, I remarked to the young man who had unlocked the door for me: "You couldn't swing a cat in here!"

"Well," he said somewhat scornfully, "it ought to be big enough for you. My relations managed to raise a family of ten here years ago."

No more complaints from me!

Stepping inside, I imagined how it might once have been—a one-roomed cottage, family all huddled around an open hearth, a hanging black kettle boiling over a turf fire, the smoky atmosphere permeated by the smell of burning peat, the glow of an oil lamp penetrating the darkness, bedding made of straw and horsehair dimly perceptible in a corner. Perhaps this cottage stood on the foundations of a cabin that might have fallen into ruin during the famine?

In Diarmaid Ó Muirithe's *A Seat Behind the Coachman*, I had recently come across accounts written in trembling hand by concerned visitors to Ireland in the early 1800s. Words often failed them in the depiction of the abject poverty of families living in hovels containing no furniture at all. One million people had perished from 1845 to 1850, their emaciated bodies withered or swollen with disease. In the towns, the straggling columns of haunted wretches, trooping to already overcrowded poorhouses, were a heart-wrenching sight. Lying on the streets were dying children, orphaned and alone, their empty expressions giving hunger and despair a face. The breathtaking beauty of the Clare landscape held a memory of suffering; the clay of skeletal corpses had mingled with the brown earth and nourished its verdure. The untimely surrender of bodies to mass graves on sloping hillsides released curses and blessings that still affect the living.

Some time after I had settled in, I resumed my reading of these moving accounts of famine in Ireland only to be interrupted by a knock on the door. Standing on the doorstep was an elderly friend, one of my first visitors at the gate lodge, whose grandparents had lived through the famine. We talked over a cup of tea about the hunger that had been artificially induced by landlords whose unfortunate tenants were condemned to subsist on potatoes and buttermilk.

"When the potato crop failed in the 1840s, they did not know how to grow anything else. Meanwhile," I protested, "grain was being steadily exported to England by the same heartless landlords!"

My friend remarked with characteristic insight, "Suffering has different meanings for people. Christianity has rooted itself deeply in the Irish psyche. The deed of Christ, his prolonged passion, inspired an art of suffering in those who would follow him. Perhaps it is not so prevalent in the Ireland of today, but it certainly was, up to thirty or forty years ago."

"What you say reminds me of something Simone Weil wrote," I countered, reaching for a book by Weil from one of the bookshelves. "She makes a distinction between suffering and affliction. Suffering, she argues, has a psychological connotation, which can sometimes be perversely indulged in—people have a tendency to view themselves as victims because of the attention it attracts. However, she describes affliction as a mechanical brutality of circumstances. And although affliction is something imposed, often to the horror and revulsion of the victim, Weil states that this is the very thing one must consent to for the sake of divine love. Leafing through the book, I found her unusual definition of love, which I had underlined: "...the necessary force of nature in its brute ongoing impulse of destruction leading to growth, leading to death," I read, closing the book.

My friend sat for a moment in silence, then he quietly responded, "I always sense that our famine ancestors were predisposed to make that consent and that our task is to live our lives all the more fully and freely because of their misfortune."

A report by an English traveller in Ireland in 1834 supported his viewpoint: "The lower orders of the Irish have much feeling for each other. It is a rare thing to hear an angry or contemptuous expression addressed to anyone who is poor; commiseration of the destitute condition of others is largely mingled in their complaints of their own poverty, and it is a fact that they are most exemplary in the care which they take of their destitute relatives and in the sacrifices which they willingly make for them."

Although this was written more than one hundred years before I was born, this mood of soul was prevalent in the people who surrounded me in childhood. Generosity was valued as the virtue that covered a multitude of sins. There was ample opportunity for giving to the poor. Tinkers, the descendants of tenants evicted during the famine who never again succeeded in settling, still, to this day, live in caravans along Irish roads. In my childhood, they were ever at our door and we knew them each by name. In my town they were all called Ward, the English version of bard, the bards being the first Irish itinerants who sang for their suppers. Instead of songs, the tinkers of my day offered prayers. They would need to be permanently on their knees to offer up all the supplications they rashly promised on the receipt of pennies or scraps of food!

Habits of prayer were also inculcated in me from an early age, the legacy of generations for whom every act was accompanied by the remembrance of God: getting up, kindling the fire, sitting down to eat, working, going to bed. There were of course prayers for special occasions and always aspirations—the constant remembrance of the souls in purgatory. One of my favourite translations from the Irish covers all eventualities: "May neither the grass that grows, nor the sand on the shore, nor the dew on the pasture be more plentiful than the blessings of the King of Grace on every soul that was, that is and that will be."

For many years of my life, I lost this mindfulness of Divine presence, but increased understanding led me back to its simple effectiveness again. Mother Meera, an Indian avatar who makes her home in Frankfurt, demonstrates through word and deed how simplicity can restore us to wholeness. Her description of her way is consistent with traditional Irish practice: "Offering everything, pure and impure, is the best and quickest way to develop spiritually.

If you offer everything to the divine, the divine will accept and change it, even the worst things. What is important is not what you offer but that you offer."

As a child I was always being admonished to "offer everything up to Our Lady!" I deplored public displays of piety, although shamelessly bargaining with God on the eve of exams went with the territory of convent schooling. I frequently stormed the doors of heaven for results that would be, in reality, more reflective of my hours of study than the hoped for miracle. I became infected with distrust in my own abilities, and suffered, as well, a subtle transference of fear, doubt and guilt from the automatic reactions of adults around me. I imagined myself the butt of a watchful "God" whose chief occupation from morning until night was in documenting my misdemeanours. "God's will be done" was a mantra to be trotted out in all seasons, as if abnegation of individual impulse was a virtue in itself and the will of a child a potentially subversive force to be moulded in accordance with more predictable conventions from the past.

According to the poet Robert Frost, "something there is that does not love a wall." I suffered as a child the discomfort of interminable church ceremonies, the rigmarole of sermons and the moribund adherence to Latin rituals when I longed to be out in the fresh air playing with my friends. Reading books upside down at age five, I was indicating an inborn need to explore a world beyond the bounds of inherited belief. I am grateful, however, for the sheltering Catholic ethos of my childhood that acknowledged the divine origin of every human being. This predisposed me to follow my line of enquiry into the mysteries of Christianity later in life while simultaneously embracing a path of self-discovery. I never rejected the essence of the religion I was born into but simply outgrew its form as I became more willingly aligned with its principles.

The religious instruction I received as a child included a lamentation about the original sin of Adam and Eve, to which we are heirs. Their mistake, I understood, was to have partaken of the Tree of Knowledge when The Tree of Life was all God intended for them at the time. Ironically, this error, instead of being righted, was assiduously perpetuated in the classrooms of my childhood, where dogma seemed to take precedence over common sense. Children of my generation were induced—on pain of the humiliation anathema to a child—to learn by rote statements of theological import beyond the grasp of their innocent minds. Questions and answers spun out of the abstractions of theologians could, and often did, effectively subdue any spirit of enquiry. We were led to believe that only a card-carrying Catholic would be recognized by St. Peter at the gates of Heaven, the destination for which life on Earth served only to prepare us. For my father's generation, to be Irish was to be Catholic, a realization he devotedly sustained until he died. I had no quarrel with him in the end, having accepted that he would never understand how I could be religious and Christian without being affiliated with any official church. I still smile when I recall the questions he would ask—that were so irritating at the time: "Is that boyfriend of yours a Catholic? "Is that a Catholic book you are reading? The answer was always "No."

Nets spun out of restrictive dogma were cast around the souls of Irish Catholic children like me, "to keep them from flight," as James Joyce famously remarked. He unearthed the subconscious fallout from inherited attitudes in monumental literary feats and pursued a path of escape for himself by means of that "silence, exile and cunning" through which he forged what was termed by one of his characters "the uncreated conscience of his race." Only when I grappled with the effects of such conditioning in later life, did I actually become aware of its tenacious hold on my psyche, although all I could consciously remember was the kindness and perceived selflessness of the teachers in question.

As I go through life I realize that there are as many religious expressions as there are people, some of which hinder and some of which advance the individual quest for wholeness, and that these varied approaches have more to do with cultural circumstance than with fundamental principles. My Newfoundland in-laws had difficulty, for instance, in coming to terms with the rosary-in-one-hand, whisky-bottle-in-the-other practice of my home town, so far removed from the more austere version of Catholicism to which they were accustomed.

The promise of ultimate reward went a long way towards the acceptance of some fanciful beliefs, since retracted by the Church. Gone for instance is the notion of limbo, that no-man's-land to which the souls of babies who died in the womb or before baptism were relegated, "never to see the face of God for all eternity." Grieving parents suffered the intense agony of this belief to compound their loss. I used to have vivid imaginations of myself burning in hell until it finally occurred to me that I would not after all have a body at that point, for the literal flames to lick!

Henry Thoreau wrote that, like stranded vessels, the enterprises of one generation are abandoned by the next. Educated for the most part through the non-denominational Waldorf School movement, my children have had little experience of the prohibitive concepts of preceding decades. The Waldorf school year unfolds around the celebration of festivals, through which the students encounter sacred teachings of different cultures alongside

those of the Christian calendar. Its arts-centred curricu-
lum is ordered to reflect the natural phases of develop-
ment in the child and has no imposed sectarian agenda.
The Irish convent in which my daughter, Emer, aged ten,
was enrolled during a sabbatical year in Ireland provided
a contrasting experience for her. Turning to me in genuine
dismay one day, she enquired, "Mum—the nuns! What is
their problem? Why are they always talking about God?
Why don't they just live!"

Although I hugged her in delight at her assertion then,
I still had a soft spot for the nuns, who had nurtured my
own musical and literary aspirations. Many of the most
independent-minded and brilliant women of Ireland,
especially those with no inclination towards marriage,
had found fulfilment within cloistered walls, and were the
dedicated teachers and nurses of my generation. I have
come to feel great sympathy for the dwindling number of
convent dwellers, (one of them a friend who confides in
me), left to question the purpose of the now seemingly
anachronistic choice they made as young women. It can
be argued that the context in which convents flourished
has all but disappeared and the majority of nuns who
were young enough to make a change have left to find
other careers. The term vocation, a word oriented towards
community service, is all but obsolete, and immaculately
ordered convent mansions are now greedily coveted by
property developers.

Regardless of how well the traditions of the past have
served the life of a community, the human intellect seeks
out new paradigms to accommodate evolutionary change.
To be fully alive is to exercise an innate human capacity
in every moment—the freedom to make a new beginning.
My generation was marked by the desire for individual
autonomy in the quest for truth. The Catholicism I knew,
eschewing the private study of the Bible, did not provide

me with the whole measure of a religion that had tradi-
tionally sustained the community life of rural and urban
Ireland. Its sacred rituals were already losing ground in a
world that was changing beyond recognition for people
of my parents' generation. The religious beliefs I adopted
in childhood needed to be bolstered with a deeper under-
standing of the truths they served if they were to endure
for me as ideas to live by in later life.

My meeting with anthroposophy, the "wisdom of
man," in mid-life satisfied a deep longing in me, unlock-
ing many mysteries of the human spirit and provided a
context in which my fragments of knowledge and under-
standing could cohere. I had sensed from early childhood
that books held the keys to life's mysteries, and in Stein-
er's writings I realized the fulfilment of that promise. I
needed to understand the realities that lay behind tradi-
tions of the past, to go backwards in order to move for-
wards into the new mysteries of our time that presuppose
the integration of all that has gone before. I will share
with my reader in a later chapter how anthroposophy
came into my life. It provided a context in which to rec-
oncile the ambiguities of my Catholic education and con-
nected me with the Celtic Christianity that formed itself
around the apocalyptic writings of St. John, whose gospel
reminds us that God is love, a gospel central to the teach-
ings of Rudolf Steiner. These teachings were not to be
absorbed as theory, I discovered, but remoulded in my
soul into healthy traits of feeling and character. They also
provided me with an understanding of earth evolution
and our descent from a spiritual world, being as we are,
the children of ancient times. I gained a clearer sense of
my true worth as a human being, that I was, as AE had
termed it, "self ancestral," one of the spiritual links in a
human chain stretching through all ages of time. Steiner
made me aware of the invisible forces that order human

destiny and how I might direct my life in service to the greater good. I took comfort in some words written by Dr. Steiner to one of his esoteric students, in which he pointed out that inner training ought not to take anything away from her but only to add to what she already had: "Good health, strength in your life, security in your way of working, and inner peace, that human beings need, not for their own sake, but for the sake of others."

Goethe, whom Steiner often cited in his lectures, said of his epic character Faust, that he was a person "engaged in striving's eternal endeavour." *Faust* was a work begun by Goethe when he was only twenty-one years old and it became a metaphor of his own mythic journey. Faust's struggle is everyone's struggle to accept the ordinariness and imperfection of our human state while remaining true to the ideal of what we might become. Goethe himself gathered practical wisdom through consistent grappling with the complex problems of life. He had the imaginative power to envision the desired result as a *fait accompli* in each situation and to begin from that end, never once resting on his laurels. Imagination existed as a force of love in him that he exercised to the full in an exemplary way.

The religious identity we hold from the past, of whatever colour or creed, becomes more and more irrelevant in this striving towards ideals of universal human value. Imagination, on the other hand, is our best guide in the realization of such ideals. It takes all I can muster of wonder, reverence, sympathy and conscience to align with a force of love that pushes all my boundaries. It is love that impels me to do what I imagine I should do. To be led by love for the deed into a particular course of action is my definition of freedom. The expression of love is unique to every person and we are left to ourselves in the individual discovery of what love might be. Love is no more than action at the level of the physical body, idea at the level of the mind and meaning or beauty at the level of feelings. In striving to be free of everything that love is not, in overcoming possessiveness, I begin to experience what love is at every level. It can be regarded as the "moral" sun of the world, a sun that illumines all religions that come from the past and celebrates the divinity in all humanity. The more I glean of the wisdom of life, the closer I come to an understanding of love and realize its presence in my life. The promotion of love on earth then becomes the only wisdom, the real aim, to which I may devote myself and that is its own reward.

One of my guides on the journey, Christian Morgenstern, whose words I like to keep in mind, understood love as the true purpose of human life:

> I have seen man in his foremost
> formation,
> I know the universe in its
> foundation.
> I know that love, love is
> its utmost aim,
> And that to love, love more
> and more I came.
> My arms, as He has done,
> I open wide.
> Like Him, I'd like to hold
> the world inside.

Although I had come back to Ireland to deepen my spiritual journey, Ireland, at the time of my writing, was entering the most materialistic phase of its history and many of her people were losing the connection with the ancient springs of language, history and mythology that could carry its culture forward in a continuity of Christian identity, since every civilization builds on a previous one.

Yet there were several for whom those connections had never been lost, including one in particular, whom many regarded as a major writer. His style is dense and difficult but rewarding in its demands on the reader. Some have compared him to Yeats, Joyce and Beckett, and others have declared him a mystic and prophet who sought the rebirth of a Christianity that was inclusive of all religions and mythologies. "You really should meet him," I was often told. The meeting was to happen of its own accord.

I sometimes acted as night porter at Tinarana House. When the time came to bolt the front door one night, I noticed that the key to Room No. 2 was missing. Yet I had been told that all the guests had settled in for the night. I ran upstairs to find the door of the room unlocked. Peering into the darkness, I was instructed to turn on the light by a melodious male voice. A form I instantly identified with the mythological Irish sea-god, Manannáin Mac Lir, swam into view beneath waves of blankets. I recognized the leonine mop of hair and keen deep-set eyes of Ireland's reigning philosopher-seer. A man of encyclopaedic mind, his writing was often said to be impossible to understand but it was compared by literary critics to the works of Blake or Nietzsche. The friends we had in common sometimes shared anecdotes of his unusual ways with me. One had remonstrated with him, saying, "Get up John! They are only interested in your money!" when he prostrated himself before beggars on a Dublin street. His distinctive appearance was known to me from a TV programme I had recently watched, judging him rather overbearing in his discussion with others of a philosophical or religious persuasion. A broadcaster I admired had introduced him on radio as "the most extraordinary person I have ever met."

"You are the famous John Moriarty!" I exclaimed. He recognized my name and was familiar with my late husband's work in Celtic studies, having taught for several years at a Canadian university. "Come over here and sit on the bed so we can talk!"

Frieda's husband, a doctor whose unconventional medical practice would soon become the centre of controversy in Ireland, had generously invited John, a fellow Kerryman, to stay at Tinarana House. He had also offered him a free programme of treatment at his nearby clinic for what John described as his "wasting sickness," a pre-cancerous condition that rendered him incapable of working as a gardener any longer. We agreed to continue our conversation at the gate lodge over dinner next evening since he would be returning to Kerry the following day.

I often think that meeting a person for the first time is like dipping into a book. An intense encounter may keep one up all night, greedily savouring every biographical detail in laying common ground with a new soul-mate. This meeting however, represented a mere skimming of the surface of a nature whose depths I could not as yet have fathomed. It was as if I had put an important book aside, to peruse at a later date when I would be better able to grasp its meaning. Randomly picking over morsels of salad he had ordered in advance, John seemed weary to the bones of his massive frame that evening, displaying none of the talkative ebullience I expected of him. This face-to-face encounter had the quality of a dream that I would recall in years to come when the full measure of Moriarty's significance would be brought home to me and I would feel a sense of awe in having passed those few hours in his company.

John Moriarty's *Invoking Ireland* was published a few years after this encounter with its author and before he died of cancer. Written with an almost manic urgency, it calls for a rebirth of a Christianity that is inclusive of all philosophies and mythologies, one that acknowledges the "underworld" that exists inside us and around us, and that seeks integration with a metaphysical "overworld." A pilgrimage of soul, this writing invokes the spirit of Ireland by juxtaposing archaic texts, oral tradition and depth psychology to stir the conscience of the reader and reconnect her with springs of ancient truth. It begins with a question posed by the author: "How, working from within our tradition, might we reconstitute ourselves as a people?" At once paean and prayer, the book is also a prose-poem and parable; Moriarty's fingers appearing, like Blake's, to "emit sparks of fire" in a passionate exhortation that lays bare his longing for the restoration of Ireland's spiritual identity. His pure desire for wisdom over years of wandering, hardship and sickness led to a moment of mystic grace for the author, "when sight became 'pure wonder' in him." A life of complete simplicity, costing him Eliot's stipulated amount of "not less than everything" followed, when he made his final home amidst the mountain peaks of an untamed, glacial landscape in Kerry. "When you stand alone, as I have done most of my life, if you feel that you are at one with the mountains—if you are dreaming their dreams—it makes the solitude easier to live with."

Invoking Ireland demonstrated the importance of establishing the continuity of the Irish tradition. It kept me up all night and it revealed the soul of its writer. It also confirmed my conviction in the Christian identity to which I continue to lay claim with individual, feminine intent. John Moriarty demonstrated a power of deep blood-remembering and fierce commitment to his own destiny in this probing of the heights and depths of his psyche. To penetrate the mysteries and carry their message forward requires as many paths as there are people to pursue them, I believe. We can only be the truth we must speak when we have arrived at it by authentic individual effort. Moriarty's soul hoarded treasures of folklore, mythology and world religion and could thereby sustain the creative thrust of a divine world seeking to reveal itself anew. John Moriarty was a torch bearer in the dark night of a wintry world, a man of eager heart who proved by example that the recovery of experienced "at-oneness" facilitates an inner culture of self-discovery. In tracing the evolutionary roots of Ireland's mythological and Christian traditions he realized his own spiritual identity and carried the essence of this tradition forward in a gesture of love for the earth. Having braved his quintessentially Celtic "nine waves of initiation" and having lived in harmony with the music of what happens, "even when dreadful things were happening to him," John became attuned to the song which continues to name the land over which it sings.

Moriarty's work is bardic in scope and has a nostalgic edge because it is based in the memory of stories, faces and places and always centred in the heart. Bards are sometimes referred to as rememberers, cultivating a remarkable memory in the course of their travels. Scholarly pursuits led to a solitary monastic existence for John Moriarty. Remembrance leads other contemporary bards, like myself, to embrace the journey. (Rumi said: "Remembrance makes people desire the journey. It turns them into travellers.") A rich tradition of chanted lays and epics, incantations, songs and rhymes was passed orally from one generation to another in Ireland—a never ending self perpetuating stream. The task of the mystic bard in the old tradition was to present truths to society in a way in which they could be accepted, understood and assimilated, implying sensitivity to the spirit of the time, the zeitgeist. The bardic practitioner is also required to breathe new life into old songs, to acquire new repertoire on and for the road. I will share with the reader in my next chapter how, in my own small way, I have assumed the mantle of this tradition. Words uttered by the "sagaman" of the Finnish

Kahlevala (a mythological story) three thousand years ago, express a continuity of purpose with which I wholeheartedly identify to this day. I quote from an English translation by Eino Friberg:

> *... I am wanting, I am thinking*
> *To arise and go forth singing*
> *Sing my songs and say my sayings*
> *Hymns ancestral harmonizing*
> *Lore of kindred lyricking*
> *In my mouth the words are melting*
> *Utterances overflowing to my*
> *Tongue are hurrying*
> *So that we may sing good songs*
> *Voice the best of all our legends*
> *For the hearing of our loved ones*
> *Those who want to hear them from us ...*

4

To Go Forth Singing

Ireland is the best country to live out of...
GEORGE BIRMINGHAM

An Italian-American priest of my acquaintance who spent many years in Africa told me and a group of others who were listening to him speak how, in a particular tribe, the beginning of a person's life is traced back to the moment in which the prospective mother and father meet. The mother soon begins to hear the song of her unborn child. She teaches the song to her man and together they intone, calling the incarnating soul towards them in their love-making. During the pregnancy, all the villagers learn the song of the child. Everyone sings it during the birth. The song will accompany every life event. At the end of life this song will deepen into a keening, for its melody can effect joy and sorrow and reflect all the changing moods in the life of each unique individual.

"That tradition must mean a lot to the people of that place," I said.

"The song of life is in everybody. Listen to that song in your own heart. Allow it to guide you," he replied. Entering into the spirit of his words, I said: "Your story demonstrates how wisdom is passed from generation to generation. People everywhere have a great hunger for meaning. Poetry often satisfies that hunger in me. D.H. Lawrence once wrote a poem called 'Deeper than Love,' which identifies truth as a profound guiding force within each one of us." I recited the poem for the group which included the following extract:

...Oh long before love is possible
passion has roused in the soul
the primordial passion of truth
is awake, the passion for life and the passion to be aware
*   of life...*

The melody of truth is sustained in my heart by a growing capacity to hear it resonate in the hearts of people I meet as I pursue the path of bardic performer and workshop leader. Sometimes its echo is faint, at other times clear. Every speaking voice is distinct and resonant with the innate melody of the speaker. A poet hears his own song more insistently than most and gives it universal expression. Yeats's song called him to Innisfree, a lush island off the coast of Sligo where he spent his childhood summers:

...I will arise and go now, for always night and day
I hear lake water lapping with low sounds by the shore;
While I stand on the roadway, or on the pavements grey,
I hear it in the deep heart's core.

Even when walking the pavements of the bustling city of

celtic woman

London through the hum of traffic, Yeats could discern the gentle sounds of lapping waters murmuring his name and calling him home.

A similar yearning drew me into the well-established stream of bardic tradition. The brilliant, exciting and dynamic man I fell in love with and married was a professor in the field of Irish studies. He generously facilitated my interests and regularly invited me to share songs and stories with his students, who were eager to hear sounds in the Irish vernacular. The extraordinary richness of our native language is evident in every page of my well-thumbed *Dineen's Irish Dictionary*; sometimes the definition of a word can fill an entire page, which demonstrates that people placed more emphasis on meanings than on words, never using one adjective when they might use three, and frequently speaking in euphemisms. It was sometimes necessary to read a person's facial expression and distinguish where he came from to understand what he was saying. There was often a hilarious disparity in the dictionary explanation of certain words, demonstrated in the following example: a) a rare disease found in sheep; or b) a raucous noise made in an empty house by an unauthorized person.

I like to claim the lineage of *reacaire*, defined by Dineen as "an auctioneer, a seller, a reciter, a story teller, a gossiper,

I am in reacaire *mode here in one of a series of performances produced by Aidan O'Brien of the Winnipeg Irish Society in 1979. I am recounting a story told by J.M. Synge, the basis of his play* Shadow of the Glen. *It concerned an old man who pretended to be dead in order to catch his wife in the act of seducing a young man. I used the big stick to dramatic effect when describing how he resurrected himself to angrily chase the intruder off his property.*

a poet's repetitor, a ranting female." The *reacaire* ranked close to that of original *god sibyl*, from which the word "gossiper" emerged. The surname "O'Driscoll" supports the description of storyteller and reciter. "O'Drisceoil" not only includes the word *ceol* (music), but is also a name derived in old Irish from *Uidersceol* (between stories) and *Idir scéil* (an interpreter). Every name has its own vibration and, when assumed and not inherited, a name can often sit uneasily with a person's true nature. In my case, this surname called forth an innate talent, as did the whole way of life I entered into with my marriage and departure from Ireland.

Our home in Toronto became a kind of unofficial Irish embassy, a first port-of-call for Irish scholars, poets, musicians, and artists, a centre of hospitality where ideas were freely shared and animated discussion continued late into the night. We provided what little we had, pouring gallons of tea and whiskey for some of the finest talkers in the world. It was a phase of my apprenticeship when I acquired the skills of a good listener, which includes the ability to sense what will or will not hold the attention of an audience.

The *reacaire*, who accompanied the bard in earlier centuries, provided postprandial delight for revellers in the great halls of Irish castles. He was an acolyte and companion to the poet-seer, who supplied him with stirring lines for memorization. As musician is to composer, so *reacaire* is to poet. To recite is to "make present again." A Vancouver poet, Anne McMurtry, once attended a poetry evening I gave in that city and called me later to ask if I would coach her in the recitation of her own poems. It took only one session for her to grasp an essential key. I told her to "breathe deeply and become very relaxed. Recall the original idea or phrase that fired your imagination. What truth was being communicated to you? Give thanks for the meaning and wisdom that inspires you. Hold that focus as you recite."

The years I spent in Vancouver after my marriage ended afforded me opportunities to present my evenings of poetry, song and story throughout the breathtakingly beautiful province of British Columbia. I travelled to several outlying islands conducting workshops and giving performances. Once, following a presentation in Tofino, on Vancouver Island, a young man came to thank me saying, "I have just returned from Indonesia where I spent the last year travelling. Do you know that although what you do is unusual, there are a few women over there going from place to place raising consciousness, singing songs and telling stories in the way that you do."

I had come a long way—having been, to begin with, a painfully shy child, shrinking from centre stage as the periwinkle from the pin. A nun who taught me in sixth grade told my mother that she had to refrain from asking me questions in class, because my embarrassment was so acute it would cause even her to blush. It took me more than half a lifetime to overcome this handicap and to be less susceptible to praise and blame.

Paradoxically, I never showed any reluctance in singing solo, making my stage debut dressed as a sailor at age four in a kindergarten production entitled *The Doll's Wedding*. Competitive singing, which went with the territory of convent schooling, steeled my nerves. I would endure anxiety and discomfort for the sake of winning a medal because success always won favour. At any rate, I grew up with the idea that singing was a pleasurable and natural expression of heart. I did not have the kind of voice that would warrant serious training, but I soon found that singing in the Irish language, with all its soulful vowels, was what I loved, and I listened keenly to tapes and records of the Connemara singers I aspired to emulate.

The first song I made my own was "Anach Cuain," a lament composed by the blind journeyman poet, Raftery, in memory of eighteen young people who drowned in a boating accident in the mid-1800s, near the town of my birth. I had just learned it when my father invited me to accompany him on his annual pilgrimage to Lough Derg in Donegal, a little island in the middle of a lake, its ground hallowed by our patron saint and known as St. Patrick's Purgatory. I was introduced there to the joys of penance that my father so rigorously inflicted upon himself. It was a demanding three-day routine of fasting, sleep-deprivation and dogged circling of stone beds, barefooted, in pouring rain. All night church vigils, incessant prayer and those incidental foot reflexology treatments on sharp stone produced signs of glowing health and high spirits in survivors, who were ferried back to the mainland, purified and sanctified. We broke the long car ride home by stopping in a small town where a *feis*, or festival of music, was in full swing. My father admonished me to hop up on the back of the old lorry that was parked in the town centre as a temporary stage. In my state of induced holiness, I sang out "Anach Cuain" with all my heart. When I got back into the car I was the proud bearer of the first prize—a little silver cup, and the apple of my father's eye.

I have already alluded to my mother's musical background and her County Clare ancestry. My father, who hailed from County Galway and could always be called upon to make a speech, did not have a note in his head, so he assumed the role of impresario and installed a makeshift stage in our kitchen when I was growing up. My siblings and I could be assured of his undivided attention and occasional monetary reward when a freshly memorized or improvised poem, song, dance or story was trotted out.

I am wearing my Irish dancing costume, aged twelve, and holding a cup I won for singing at a Connaught feis earlier that day.

My initial experience of successfully holding the attention of an audience of one prepared me for gatherings that were wont to erupt in our town, where everyone was a performer-in-waiting. My memories of growing up in Tuam revolve around an unbroken melody of musical evenings. Nobody seemed to tire of the repetition involved and nobody dared to infringe on the party piece of another. I shall never forget the hush of dismay that once met my young ears when a visitor to our town pre-empted the performance of the charismatic Luke O'Brien by singing "She moved through the Fair"—before the man whose song it was had taken his turn! My father was in ardent listening mode when my mother, always a star turn, was called upon to sing. You could hear a pin drop.

Broadway made entry into our gatherings via musicals performed in the Town Hall, where my uncle P.J. Greal-

8 o

celtic woman

ish, who knew all the songs, was always cast for a part. The polished duets he performed with his friend Morgan O'Connell were voted the hardest of all acts to follow. My aunt Lil, an accomplished violinist, had played for every Gilbert and Sullivan operetta ever mounted in the town and could be counted on for accompaniments when she was not dancing a reel or jig.

I was invariably the one striking a blow for "old Ireland" in the programme, with *sean nós* laments in a singing style associated with earlier times and an almost forgotten language. Celtic was not a word in my vocabulary then, just like, as Gertrude Stein once remarked, "In China there is no china because in China everything is China." Only when the commercial potential inherent in Ireland's traditional art forms began to attract the attention of national and international marketing forces would the hitherto scholarly term Celtic be called into universal service, gaining unanimous approval as a word whose time had finally come.

My parents, whose formal education ended with primary school, had both entered the work place at age fourteen but had learned to speak and write in the Irish language of their own volition in later life. Through habits of frugality and an admirable capacity for saving, they succeeded in affording their children a university education. Since the apple never falls too far from the tree, my siblings found their calling in fields of arts, social sciences, care giving and insurance, all of which drew upon the leanings of mind and heart exemplified in our parents.

The marriage of my mother and father was deemed by all who knew them to have been made in heaven. I have a vivid early memory of entering a room without knocking—to witness a tender scene—my father with his head

I am sitting on my mother's knee, aged four, and three-year-old Ann is perched on my father's with two-year-old Frances in the middle. This was taken outside a chalet at Ireland's Butlin's Holiday Camp, my parents' favourite destination for our annual family holiday where children, no matter how small, were happily occupied all day with organized fun and games. Their elders could freely follow their own pursuits within a closed circuit, sometimes freezing in mid-waltz on the ballroom floor at night when their chalet number was called over the sound system to alert them that "there is a child crying in chalet number…"

on my mother's lap, she, stroking it gently as she sang to him quietly. This was the mood I always sensed between them, although they had their disagreements, mostly relating as I recall, to my father's reluctance to wear his good clothes when the occasion demanded. He exonerated himself in the end—the instructions he gave for his funeral, at the eleventh hour, were as follows: "Be sure to close the lid of the coffin. Don't spare any money on the party after I am gone. Tell your mother she can put the good suit on me!"

While I was the first of seven children to arrive, I was very slow in coming, my mother having given up hope of ever conceiving when she happily discovered she was pregnant at last. We played musical beds in accommodating each newcomer of the six more that followed me in quick succession. Our bungalow home even stretched to a live-in housekeeper who bunked in with us to add to the crush.

My mother would flee the cooped-up bedlam of rainy days, choosing to spend more uplifting afternoons communing with friends in a local hotel, and we were left to torment the "help" instead. A faithful friend of many, my mother was active in the Irish Countrywomen's Association, which fostered traditions of arts, crafts and good housekeeping in homemakers around Ireland and provided a meaningful social network for women of the day. She also kept her own record of the history of the town and, now in her nineties and still hale and hearty, she shared her recollections at the official opening of a new museum in Tuam a few years ago.

My father only appeared at intervals, being always "on the road" with his job as inspector for the Irish Life Assurance Company, travelling the length and breadth of Connaught and leaving no stone unturned that could yield an insurance premium for an agent. He had been one of the first to introduce people to the notion of a bounty that might follow the death of a relative if the premium had been paid up. So persuasive did he prove to be that the bereaved sometimes attributed the sudden windfall to his own good nature. It was not uncommon for me to receive a box of chocolates in the mail after I entered the boarding school that became my refuge from the bedlam. The enclosed card might have read: "This is to thank your father for all the money we received on the death of our beloved mother. We heard he had a daughter away at school and we thought she might be homesick and might appreciate this little token of gratitude," or words to that effect. "What is the purpose of life?" my father was liable to enquire from time to time and, answering his own question, to conclude: "To have a big crowd at your funeral!" This purpose was overwhelmingly fulfilled in his own demise when several hundred of his admirers paid their respects to his immortal spirit in the days and weeks after his passing.

Between the ages of four and nineteen almost all my teachers were nuns. Ireland was full of nuns then. I heard of a young English boy who spent a holiday in our town. When he went home somebody asked him, "What did you see when you were in Ireland?"

"Nuns," was his reply.

I am indebted to one nun in particular, for her comprehensive and impassioned instruction on the rubrics of English composition. Her religion classes were memorable indeed and usually focused on the theme of purity, a virtue calling for sexual restraint that was held aloft in every convent. Reaching fever pitch one day, she implored us to instruct our mothers to sew sleeves and skirts onto our bathing suits. The irony of this was that very few of us had bathing suits or had ever seen a beach, and it was unlikely that we would adorn the wind- and rain-swept strands of the Atlantic in any kind of scanty attire, then or later.

Most mornings she had us standing with arms outstretched, reciting rosary after rosary on our knees, in no hurry to get around to the three Rs. I later learned that this was common practice for Irish saints. Legend has it that the sixth century St. Kevin of Glendalough had mortified himself by standing so long in this position, knee-deep in freezing water, that some birds built their nest in his open palms. This dear nun later became ill and died but not before she had named the date for the end of the world, which we all jotted down in our note books, November 23, 1957. The dreaded day came and went and I have been inured to any such predictions since then.

When I was twelve, my name appeared among the first hundred listed when the result of a nationwide examination in Irish was circulated. This won me a coveted place in one of the four or five preparatory colleges located in remote *gaeltacht*, or Irish-speaking areas around the country. Thenceforth referred to as *ábhar múinteora* (the stuff of teachers), we were moulded to fit the national ideal: fluent in Irish, proficient in Latin, Catholic in orientation, well-versed in the musical and literary traditions of Ireland, with a good grasp of our history and mythology. It was expected, in return for a generous governmental subsidy, that we would pass our education on when we eventually assumed our secure and respectable positions as teachers.

Among the faculty at our college were authors of the text books we studied, inspiring and dedicated teachers who made learning enjoyable for me. They would move on to distinguished university careers when this experiment of De Valera's government ended, as it did in my final year. Over half the students were drawn from the Aran Islands and Connemara, to facilitate a total immersion in the Irish language. It became evident to me, for the first time, that a surprising percentage of people in my country whose fluency in Irish arose out of a racial consciousness at once foreign, exotic and deep, spoke only the most halting English as their second language. At the end of four years, a few opted for university courses but the majority of us proceeded as planned to Teacher Training College in Dublin, Irish continuing to be our preferred medium of expression.

Carysfort Training College had a strong "correctional" orientation, and senior nuns of an authoritative persuasion made excellent wardens. One in particular took unnatural pleasure in assemblies, during which students were subjected to public humiliation on the merest suspicion of wrong-doing, such as appearing at mass in a white veil on a day when a black one had been designated or displaying a tendency to run rather than walk along a certain corridor. There was always a potent force-field of Catholic guilt to draw on during these tests of endurance, so much so that I once confessed to something I had not done, becoming the butt of considerable wrath for the nun in question. (It had to do with a box of matches going missing from the kitchen, resulting in the students being deprived of a proper breakfast that morning...)

We were practically indistinguishable from the student teacher nuns who were our fellow inmates, because of the regulatory uniforms—unbecoming black serge dresses that concealed any hint of shapeliness and hung to the floor, set off with black or white veils for the seven o'clock morning mass. Slaves to the toll of bells and the elaborate concoction of rules and regulations—very little at all was actually permitted—we spent our waking hours cramming our minds with mind-numbing theories of education, with very little time devoted to the hands-on teaching practice we were so crucially in need of for the job that lay ahead. The curriculum, ordained by both church and state, represented a normal four-year university degree course, but for the hundreds of us aspiring teachers packed into stuffy auditoriums with severely nerve-racked instructors, the entire content had to be committed to memory in a two-year period. As an unwitting victim of this outmoded system, I could understand why the Irish educational system had once been referred to as "the murder machine." Aged only eighteen and overdue for adventure and romance, I was often in trouble because, even with the best of intentions, it was impossible for me to adhere to rules that made no sense and that seemed designed to subdue the current of life now bursting to express itself in me.

There was saving grace, however, in my being cast as the lead in an Irish operetta, *Nochtuirn sa Chearnóig*, performed in my final year of training. Tomás MacAnna, later artistic director of the Abbey Theatre, was in the audience on the opening night, and invited me to do a drama course with him in Donegal the following summer. This led to a stint at the Damer, a semi-professional Irish-language theatre where he also directed. *An Triail*, or The Trial, was the main dramatic offering of the season, with Fionnuala Flanagan (now a movie star) in the lead. MacAnna, whom I later came to know well when he directed for my husband in Toronto and stayed in our house, also cast me for the annual Christmas pantomime at the Abbey Theatre, which usually had a long run and that year (1964) included the young Donal McCann and Stephen Rea, who were destined to become Hollywood stars.

Before I could avail of this means of augmenting my teacher's salary by £6 weekly, I had to acquire the approval of Earnán de Blaghd. A friend of President De Valera's, he maintained quality control of the Irish language in our national theatre. I sang a couple of *sean nós*, or old-style, songs for him. To my surprise, he beckoned me over him and proceeded to examine my ears, and by the mystery of this yardstick I was hired. Maybe he was influenced by the old Irish saying, "the woman or the donkey who don't look at you with their ears are no good." It was in the course of this run that I encountered Robert O'Driscoll, my husband-to-be, on the stairs of a house in Rathgar, an upscale residential area of Dublin where we both had rooms.

When I had finished teaching each day, I would make my way by bus to the Abbey Theatre, where I performed my song and dance routines in the pantomime. It was an exhilarating but exhausting daily routine. Every morning I appeared bright and cheerful before my forty-three eager four-year-olds, although I hardly slept at all due to the raucous nightly revels of my flat mates. I was mulling over this annoying state of affairs as I walked along a Dublin street one day, when I came face-to-face with Rita King, a girl from my home town. She was also in search of alternate accommodation. Now on her way to inspect a vacant bedsitter, she encouraged me to join her. Such are the serendipitous occurrences of life! There were two beds in the spacious room, which we immediately decided to share.

I met Robert, who occupied the room below ours, soon after moving in. He was in the act of making a call from the public phone box outside my room and in dire need of the regulatory "three-penny bit," with which I readily provided him. I learned that he was a lecturer at University College Dublin, had a Ph.D. in English Literature, and that he occupied the room below ours. I was soon ensconced before a blazing fire in his cosy nook, sipping brandy and happily devouring Christmas cake. I said to Rita as I was falling asleep, "Please pray that he will invite me into his room again. I must have more of that cake!

The most delicious and unusual concoction of butter, brandy, dates, nuts, and molasses imaginable and made by his doting mother in far-flung Newfoundland!"

Before I could proceed any further with this tale, I had to take a break from writing...

Lynette, a competent typist, lived a mere country lane away from the gate lodge, faithfully welcoming the delivery of each new instalment of my handwritten book. After I had dropped the latest chapter off, I decided to drive to the village. My brother Pat had generously provided me with a batch of German-made ballpoint pens which had facilitated the writing thus far. The last of them had however run out and I hoped to find more of the same in a local shop. Having no luck in this venture, I made my way to a popular pub called Goosers. It was early summer by now, tourists were flocking to scenic Killaloe and there was no room for me at the outdoor tables that overlooked the lake. I found one empty chair inside the premises and squeezed in beside a man who, like me, was ordering the Irish stew that was my favourite item on the menu, offered in half portions that were more than adequate for the average appetite when it was not boosted by a full pint of Guinness in advance. We started to chat and I quickly gathered that he was a salesman, market bound for the city of Limerick.

"What do you sell?" I asked.

"German ballpoint pens," he replied. My eyes lit up.

"May I see them?"

"Certainly" he said, and opened a little suitcase full of the very pens I had been seeking!

"I have become accustomed to that particular pen but it is not available in the shops here," I eagerly informed him, adding a few details about the book I was writing. Bundling up a handful of the precious items, he placed them before me, insisting that I accept them as a gift, to mark the serendipity of our meeting. I find that whenever there is a true need it is invariably satisfied. I thought about the synchronicity and timeliness of my meeting with Bob many years before as I reflected uponthe story of our courtship which I would now pick up again at the gate lodge …

*The dream of love that was kept "on hold" in boarding school con*tinued to pervade my waking hours being finally satisfied in my romantic encounter with a "foreigner," although any man would have appeared foreign to me then, so remote was the mystery of the opposite sex from the sheltered life I had led to that point. Virginal and naïve, aged only nineteen, I deferred to Bob as an experienced man of the world. Disarming in his good and self-effacing ways, and hard working to a fault, he easily won my heart. I bore with the Henry Higgins/Eliza Doolittle dynamic that predominated to begin with until love overcame the divide and a more equitable balance of gender and temperament was established. The relationship seemed somehow "meant to be," although the concept of destiny was new to me and the life that lay ahead beyond anything I could have imagined at the time. Love is unconditional but I was soon to learn that relationship is conditional on a couple's skill in negotiating and intuiting individual needs and preferences that must be constantly reviewed. I was by nature disposed to value relationship for its own sake and held fast to a vision of peaceful companionship, however elusive the balance of opposites would prove itself to be:

… And yet all the while you are you, you are not me.
And I am I, I am never you.
How awfully distinct and far off from each others being we
*   are!*

Yet I am glad.
I am so glad there is always you beyond my scope,
Something that stands over,
Something I shall never be,
That I shall always wonder over, and wait for,
Look for like the breath of life as long as I live…
   "Wedlock" by D.H. Lawrence

Living out of Ireland

…And the best of all ways
To lengthen our days,
Is to steal a few hours from the night, my dear!
THOMAS MOORE

My education had better prepared me for the upcoming role of professor's wife than for the job I held during our period of courtship. My first day of school coincided with that of forty-three four-year-olds in search of a teacher, plunging me in at the deep end. Curriculum-driven and under imminent threat of an inspector's visit, I, to my subsequent regret, subjected these little ones to a harrowing daily round of Rs, with only occasional pauses for games or artwork. No visual aids were provided for us teachers—we had to purchase our own supplies with a meagre weekly salary of £11. I was not even aware, at that point, of the need for special kindergarten training or that a science of pedagogy existed through which faculties other than cognitive and verbal ones could be developed. I would happily discover Waldorf schools many years later when

I had children of my own of school-going age, but they were but twinkles in our eyes as yet.

After my exacting days with the children, it was a pleasure to relax with Bob. Besides being the soul of hospitality, he was the first man I had met who could cook, iron, wash and sew for himself. A model of discipline, order and industry, whose shirts and underwear were immaculately laundered, he was outrageously funny and a great mimic to boot—hilarious take-offs on Conception Harbour characters he had known inducted me into the colourful ethos of his childhood. Impeccable manners had been drummed into him by an exacting mother who had, almost single-handedly, reared nine of her own along with two adopted children. His father, who failed to find suitable employment in Newfoundland, had spent nine months of every year risking life and limb to build the bridges of New York, thus providing a university education for each of his children.

Bob's most appealing feature was the timbre of his voice, reminiscent for me of the quality of voice I had encountered among native speakers of Irish in Connemara. The rough and unrelenting fierceness of the landscape was reflected in many of the Newfoundlanders I would later meet, whose ancestors, like the Aran Islanders I knew, depended on the sea for their livelihood. I soon learned that his mother, besides being clairvoyant and a superb cook, had a turn of phrase that reminded me of characters in the plays of J.M. Synge. When I enquired how she was coping after the death of Bob's father, she replied: "I don't know whether I am a-sea or a-shore." I once heard her caution Bob: "Don't mind those obstacles that come in your way. Just think of them as dust on your path to prevent you from skidding!"

Bob had been one of the first graduates of Memorial

University in his native Newfoundland to be granted a foreign scholarship. He opted to study at London University, procuring a Ph.D. there by the age of twenty-three— his thesis explored the work of Sir Samuel Ferguson, a Northern Irish Protestant who had declared, "I am an Irishman and a Protestant but I was an Irishman before I was a Protestant." Ferguson was a poet in the epic style, whose scholarly exactitude and authentic translations from the Irish laid a foundation for the Celtic Literary Revival. Having studied the language, Ferguson avoided the stilted efforts of earlier translators and carried forward glimpses and gleams of a lost art, so that Irish poets might again evoke the "wavering, unemphatic rhythms" of the originals.

Ferguson's pioneering spirit found resonance in Bob, and his efforts to reconcile the religious differences of mid-eighteenth century Ulster were often cited by my husband-to-be in lectures. Here Bob pointed out that the struggle that had bedevilled Ireland for centuries was a fratricidal one, since Ulster Protestants and Southern Catholics shared a common cultural heritage. Ferguson had overcome a great aversion to Catholics when he began to comprehend the intricacy and sophistication of the literature in Irish. He had consequently substituted his litany of vices for the following virtues, which Bob used to quote with relish: loyalty, hospitality, openheartedness, idealizing of women, sanctity of place, love of tradition and a sense of wonder. They were qualities anyone who knew Bob could also ascribe to him.

Pat O'Flaherty, Bob's life-long friend, wrote the following tribute in *Books in Canada* in 1996, reminiscing on their early days together as Ph.D. candidates in London, twenty-year-olds fresh from the outports of Newfoundland:

Soon after arriving in England, we found ourselves one evening in the main hall of University College London, where a debate was taking place on the possibility of European union. The debate was in its finals stages; would-be Ciceros were orating from the floor in the odd accents of the British upper class. I could hardly pick out what they were saying. I turned to speak to Robert (Bob), but he had left my side. A minute later he appeared on the dais in front of the hall, and proceeded to address an audience of about three hundred, in an accent that must have seemed as peculiar to them as theirs did to me, on the virtues of continental federation. He knew nothing about European union, but this did not stop him from expostulating on the issue, without preparation of any kind and at considerable length.

Although Bob claimed it was love at first sight for him, there was a parade of other female flames to be appeased before intimacy was established between us. Our middle-aged landlady, who was painting his portrait at the time, began to resent our developing friendship and abruptly terminated my lease. In so doing, she fanned the flames of romance, inducing the period of separation that often proves decisive in the union of a couple. Rita and I found more spacious accommodation in the area, meanwhile, and Bob became a frequent visitor.

His friends were legion at the time, although he had only arrived in the city a few months earlier. It became a challenge to accommodate all the invitations in which I was now included. My Irish-speaking theatrical circle gradually merged with his academic set that intersected all factions of Dublin life. There was theatre to be found everywhere, and entertaining characters competed with each other in pub and drawing room. Social gatherings became the be-all and end-all for me.

Whatever one saw on stage had usually been enacted

Bob amassed a fine collection of first editions of works by W.B.Yeats
over the years. He displayed these prized possessions to visitors to
our home who had any appreciation for the poetry of Yeats. Bob
would proclaim his delight in an artful cover design, in the quality
and weight of a particular paper, in the handsome binding or gold
embossed Rosicrucian symbolism, before reading a favourite poem
aloud to dramatic effect. The look and feel of a book by Yeats had to
be commensurate with the lofty fruits of poetic imagination it con-
tained, nothing short of a sacred text for Bob. These were volumes
to be carefully handled or marvelled at from a distance. The pleas-
ure of reading was only indulged in the less costly modern editions,
some in paperback, that filled lower shelves of his library. I loved to
pore over Bob's annotated working texts that provided many clues
to occult meanings that would have otherwise eluded me. PHOTO
BY PAT CONROY

in real life first. No drama can grow out of anything other than the fundamental realities of life. I remember a lady of my acquaintance calling out, in a voice that all could hear, during the interval of her recently estranged husband's new play, "My lines are coming across very well." I grew up beside Tom Murphy, Ireland's leading playwright, and a busload of our townsfolk always arrived at the Abbey for a production of his, sure to know who amongst their ranks had inspired this character or that in the play, giving the peculiar traits of neighbours universal relevance.

The Dublin social treadmill of those days was not for the faint of heart and was severely challenging to anybody with a regular job, leading to the frequent repetition of a remark of Oscar Wilde's about work being "the curse of the drinking classes." But it was to be recommended in small doses for those with the stamina to endure high levels of merriment and indoor adventures of a mental kind. You could set out in good and sedate order with plans for an early night, attending a lecture or a Yeats play, proceeding afterwards to a pub for some scholarly discourse that might suddenly erupt into a singsong. Levels of conversation would rise in growing animation, and soon a mood of carefree abandonment would sweep the room, giving occasion for the barman's anxious cry over the din: "Have ye no homes to go to?" We would be shepherded out into the reality of the cold night air soon to be piling into cars, careening through highways and byways, because somebody had a friend somewhere who had a few bottles of whiskey and who could withstand an all-night vigil. In those days, you never got up to see the sunrise but often stayed up until the breaking of daylight brought the revels to a natural conclusion. A whole book might be devoted to these late night escapades and the stories that were embroidered out of them.

There was a classic tale in circulation about writers Briain

Ó Nualláin, alias Myles na Gopaleen (whose brother married a sister of mine), Brendan Behan and Patrick Kavanagh, who could not drink together in Dublin because one or other of them was barred from any given pub. They had the bright idea to hail a taxi and instigate a pub crawl beyond the confines of the city. At each watering hole they noticed a sinister figure in a corner, drinking what appeared to be a mug of tea. The sight of this solitary man gradually became a source of paranoia in one or all of them. Finally, now some twenty miles outside the city in a snug little bar, they approached him with the question: "Are you following us by any chance?" Innocently he looked at them—"Sure am n't I your taxi driver!"

Yarns were the fruit of all such episodes and gave excuse for more rounds of social drinking. I was introduced in this manner to poetry, song and story in the fast lane, the pace of which was guaranteed to steer anyone towards an early grave. There was a wealth of oral tradition to be imbibed along the way, but anything gathered in a state of inebriation was liable to be lost to subconscious memory only.

Extracurricular lectures became a great source of enjoyment, especially when the speaker was familiar, and passionate about his or her subject. Whatever theme was being sounded on the podium always seemed to be in context of some conversation to which I had been privy. I became aware of the importance of cultivating a natural style of delivery, and of never sacrificing the engagement of an audience to the temptation of pedantic vanities. Irish academics are well aware of the entertainment value that must attend even the most serious of topics, and they always add a good sprinkling of humour and sometimes an outburst of song or verse to their lectures.

Post lecture get-togethers were convivial and relaxed; a great hush fell when singing was called for and I was often put on the spot. It was in the warmth of these gatherings that I acquired the ability to sing from the heart in response to the receptive listening field that productive social encounter engenders. Copious drinking was part and parcel of the literary life in those days, and alcoholic poets growled from some corner of every pub. Although it did not escape my attention that Bob spent a lot of his money on rounds at the bar, I was too infatuated to read the shadow of coming events in such extravagant displays of generosity.

His generosity of spirit in coming to the practical assistance of friends and strangers in need had marked him always as a person apart. Any suggestion of injustice in the air had him drawing an invisible sword, and racing off in defence of the victims. Seeing some plainclothes policemen pull a young man by the ear and bustle him into a waiting car sent him charging James Bond-like after them to the Galway police station to demand an explanation, leaving me stranded meanwhile on the sidewalk.

Bob proposed to me within hours of returning from a working holiday in Rome. He, his close friend, Professor Lorna Reynolds, and novelist Kate O'Brien, all speakers at an international conference, had been guests there of Darina Silone, Irish-born wife of one of Italy's most important writers, Ignatio Silone. To begin with I felt very threatened by the intellectual credentials of such companions as these and it did not escape my attention that older academic women were very possessive of his time and attention. The proposal came as a great surprise to me but I accepted it without hesitation. I was only nineteen and could imagine no more glorious future for myself than to share my life with a man I loved, whose enthusiasms I shared, whose sense of fun was infectious and whose spirited approach to life and hard-working ways had won my heart and earned my trust. By coincidence, my parents were also in Rome and met Bob for the first time in St. Peter's Square. The liking was mutual and his great affection for my father grew over the years. We married a few months before he was due to begin teaching at St. Michael's College in the University of Toronto.

My uncle P.J. Grealish had that year purchased the only hotel in Tuam, a town with a population of 3500 at the time. Renovations were under way and geared towards a grand opening that would coincide with the lavish production of our wedding. This added to the excitement and festivity of the day and turned our church ceremony, and the reception that followed, into something of a spectacle for the townsfolk. Playing to the gallery as always, Bob cheerfully led me and our long bridal procession, with Rita as the chief bridesmaid, through the crowd congregated outside the church. I turned my head for a moment when, suddenly veering us off to the right, he swept the party through the gates that opened off the cathedral grounds into the driveway of the convent I had attended as a child. Nuns came pouring out of the "motherhouse" in responding to his clarion call, crying out: "I love you! I love you all!" Bob herded them into an improvised reception line, in a surreal Fellini-like movie moment. He had often spoken of himself as being "propelled by forces beyond myself," or "following the cry of the wind." Certainly, to be in his company was to experience how the inevitable never happened but the unexpected often occurred. I often overcame great embarrassment in accepting the theatrical flair of Bob's original responses to "the music of what happens" and often scolded him in private for incidents that compromised my sense of propriety. He would argue on those occasions for my need to escape the limitations of a conventional upbringing and the effects of having been too long subject to the authority of the nuns, and there was some truth in that. He claimed to have settled a score on my behalf in his wedding stunt outside the convent. Indeed, one of the older nuns confessed to my mother, when they met on the street a few days after the wedding: "I felt sorry for Treasa—going off to spend her life with such an excitable foreigner," before adding, "But the young nuns loved him!"

I was perhaps already pregnant with our first child by the time we returned from a sun-drenched honeymoon in Greece and Turkey. The rhythm method, a form of birth control favoured by Catholics, had failed me miserably in Istanbul—the shiny thermometer on which I was relying having disappeared from our hotel room the day we arrived.

Our holiday was punctuated by Bob's earnest attempts, by dint of gesticulation and facial contortions, to penetrate language barriers in establishing a rapport with people who just happened to be eating at tables near ours. This resulted in having total strangers sentimentally cling to us, when we would later attempt to extricate ourselves from their birthday parties or anniversary dinners. I had the impression of being restored to a long-lost family every other day. Getting me to sing for people was one of his favourite ploys in making these connections. The typical experience of the tourist was obviously not a feature on Bob's agenda although we approached the sacred temples with awe, entering the inner sanctum of the Blue Mosque, feet bare and eyes agog at the brilliant colour of the tiles from which its name derives. We haggled with sharp eyed vendors in the Grand Bazaar's labyrinthine web of vaulted arcades, who lured us into cave-like dens and plied us with delicious Turkish coffee until we succumbed to the purchase of a prayer rug or the tempting array of jewellery to be dispensed as presents for the folks back home. Everything was dirt cheap and we threw in a few extra dollars when a reasonable bargain had been struck. An industrious tailor made a figure-hugging, full-length leather coat to measure for me in twenty-four hours, for the paltry sum of twenty-five dollars!

Bob organized a strike amongst the holidaymakers on our bus during a trip to the Sea of Marmara, because it appeared that the tour operator had short-changed us. The money was all returned before he allowed the grateful passengers to return to their seats. Later that night, instinct led him off the beaten track, with me of course in tow, to a seedy district of Istanbul where we gate-crashed a circumcision party. The sounds of muted revelry among a group of traditionally clad Turks had not escaped his attention as we went for an evening stroll. We found men and women congregated at opposite sides of a large room, in the centre of which a bewildered-looking twelve-year-old boy, enthroned on a platform that was swathed in pink satin, stared at us with large mournful eyes that I can never forget. Not until I had danced with most of the men and Bob with the women were we inclined to take leave of this peculiar scene. Never a dull moment!

Returning then to Sligo for the annual Yeats Summer School, there was no end of celebration for weeks to come as we packed our respective belongings and sent them ahead to Toronto. Our first stop on the trans-Atlantic route was Gander, Newfoundland, where I met Bob's parents and a few of his sisters and brothers for the first time. I was overwhelmed by the feasting that ensued, but there was a great deal more of that to come. The entire O'Driscoll clan combined their considerable culinary skills in preparing a splendid buffet for our second wedding reception of the summer, held this time in Conception Harbour's modest community hall. Donning our wedding garments once again, we enjoyed the banquet spread out before us and duly enacted the cutting ritual on a cake that tasted remarkably like the one that had brought us together in the first place. I was invited to sing and then had the fun of identifying the legendary characters among the guests, for whom Bob's impersonations had already prepared me. Noting the rate of alcoholic consumption and the oddly familiar faces and accents with which I was surrounded, I knew I had found a home away from home. It was hard to believe that an ocean lay between the family I had left behind and the one I had now joined, in this rugged outport of itself that Ireland had forgotten.

This was to be the first of many visits to Newfoundland. The hospitality practised in the O'Driscoll household gave new meaning to the "hundred thousand welcomes" for which Ireland had once been famous and set a precedent that I would from then on observe. A few years later, when Bob and I acquired a house of our own, I would be fully employed in cooking, cleaning and making beds for a stream of visitors, many of them distinguished scholars, artists and writers. Those coming to stay in our first abode, however, a modest one-bedroom apartment near the university, were mostly young, temporarily homeless students from Newfoundland with their own sleeping bags. Bob was incapable of refusing any friend, or child of a friend, shelter. My pregnancy was in its advanced stages, and as I picked my way one morning over sleeping bodies in what used to be our living room, I knew in that moment that my best alternative was in jumping ship, notwithstanding the convenience of having a large modern hospital at my doorstep. Travelling back to Ireland only months after I had left it, I chose instead the peaceful refuge of my parents' home in Tuam and the familiar confines of the unpretentious Bon Secour nursing home located only minutes from our house. Bob arrived from Toronto on his own birthday, May 3, Briain having made his appearance the day before, a healthy baby boy proving the "gift of a lifetime" for his proud father. It is my firm belief that children choose their parents and that it is the spirit of their intent that fans the flames of desire when the eventful union occurs that leads to their conception. The momentum is great when mother and father gaze upon the child together for the first time, the force of love palpable between all three. I make a point of thanking my children for this great honour when they gather around me on Mother's Day.

Delivery rooms were out of bounds for fathers-to-be in those days and it seemed natural then to rely on my mother and grandmother, who remained close by me during labour and whose practical advice and reassuring hugs gave me all the comfort I needed. Like a mountain climber, pushed beyond bearable thresholds of endurance, in the reach for a distant summit that can grant him a lofty view of all that lies below, the experience of giving birth was an entry into the deepest mystery of human existence and one of pushing against boundaries of pain in defiance of my own physical frailty. My reality of space and time was altered in the process, a temporary loss of personal identity raising me to heights of joy and gratitude in which my spirit seemed fused with that of the child. A heavenly atmosphere, subtle as the delicate whiff of a rare perfume, seemed to surround each of my four newborn babies in turn as I observed them lovingly in sleep. Nobody can deny the promise of a more perfected humanity that a baby embodies...

I chose to return to Tuam two years later, for the birth of our second boy, Michael Robert, thus giving both babies the benefit of the Bon Secour sisters' inspired approach to maternity care. I could rest for two whole weeks after each birth in a pleasant room of my own, receiving visitors for only a few hours each day. This long

Here I am in July 1974, two months before the birth of my third son, Declan, against the impressive backdrop of Bob's first editions. PHOTO BY PAT CONROY

confinement facilitated the watchful, patient tranquillity required in coming to know the little being cradled in my arms. A baby can ease his way into what must appear an alien world at first, if he is welcomed into an atmosphere of stillness, solitude and silence, where the spiritual event that birth is can be recognized as such.

I relished every moment, feeling somehow closer to the heartbeat of time, not the time that is measured by the clock but the eternal quality of time that reveals itself in cycles of birth and death and in the unfathomable depths of human love it sustains. Adapting myself to the rhythm of feeding and caring for the baby, I rejoiced in simple tasks that seemed so meaningful. I loved to think that the milk of human kindness flowed into the life of the child in the intimate shelter of the breast, ensuring a healthy awakening for him to the sensual life of the body. Caring for a child means more than catering to its physical needs. This truly new beginning in my life aroused not only the protective instinct of the mother, but awakened forces of love and intuition in me that would foster qualities of soul in the child and help him find his tasks in life. Bob and I rejoiced together in the wonder of love made manifest in this new life. He kept company with me often as I was feeding the baby when we seemed, all three, enfolded in angel's wings. Knowing them now as adults, I can still recall how clearly the unique spirit of each child declared itself in essence from the very first day, and how each one keeps faith with the mystery of that holy presence that unites us for all eternity.

Now that I had children to care for, I could not attend to Bob's interests in the same undivided way I had before, living as we did for the most part in Toronto while maintaining a preoccupation with Irish affairs and visitors. We continued to commute between Canada and Ireland even though our children became more and more reluctant to leave Toronto during the holiday months.

They really belonged in the idyllic neighbourhood enclave of Summerhill Gardens. There a whole generation of children experienced themselves as members of one extended family, daily spilling out of rustic, rambling homes onto an equally hospitable city street under the watchful eyes of discreetly vigilant stay-at-home moms, of which I was one. The so-called "hyperparenting" that dominates modern child rearing was fortunately not yet in vogue. A more free ranging approach was favoured in which children walked on their own to school and rode the subway, often exploring the outer limits of an elaborate public transit system in adventurous defiance of boundaries, while curiosity, unstructured play, open green spaces and the absence of hovering adults fuelled their life of imagination. Einstein confessed that he approached the world in his growing years with a fundamental question: "Is the universe friendly?" and for my children and their cherished peers—growing up in Summerhill Gardens in the 1970s—it most assuredly was! Child care flourished of its own accord in an ethos of commonly shared family values, unlocked homes and cars, and social activity that had the natural buzz of a hive. The attractions of the annual Summerhill Fair called young and old into service when hidden talents were given a summer airing around neighbourly picnic tables under a blazing July sun. Rainy indoor Ireland could not compete with the attractions of this home ground in my children's estimation although my eldest son, Briain, would unexpectedly choose County Clare as his permanent home in later life.

As for me, while Canada is the country in which I now feel most at home, it took many years for me to shed my exclusively Irish identity. The privilege of my education,

50 Summerhill Gardens, our home 1968–1988, a spacious three-storey house with a basement apartment. Located in a secluded enclave, backed by the Rosedale ravine, it lay within easy access of St. Michael's College and Toronto's downtown core.

flawed though it may have been, imbued me with the spirit of Irish culture that my marriage to Bob advanced. In upholding the positive gifts of my country, I was fulfilling my obligations to the past while learning to move beyond my own personal preoccupations and prejudices. While our physical bodies take a recognizable shape in space, each one of us also has a profile in time that has its own contours and characteristics and patterns of evolution. Countries can be viewed by the same yardstick. Like a child, a nation learns from its environment and absorbs

Reading to the boys, Christmas 1974, an occupation that was as enjoyable for me as it was for them. They both took part in A Christmas Carol at the Colonnade Theatre (on Toronto's Bloor Street) that year. Robert played Tiny Tim and told me, after his first rehearsal, that the director had asked him to listen for the bells of heaven during his final scene, earnestly then declaring to me "…and mom, I listened…and I heard them! Mom, I heard the bells of heaven!" PHOTO BY ROBERT O'DRISCOLL

Declan's baptism, performed by Bob's faithful friend, Robert Mad-
den, a Basilian priest and professor of English at St. Michael's.
Father Bob was largely responsible for my husband's appointment
at the college since he had come to know Bob well when they were
Ph.D. students in London together. Zena Cherry, gossip columnist
for the Toronto Globe and Mail, attended this event, never willing
to miss a party in our house and, to our great surprise, ran a story
with this picture in the paper next day entitled "Home Christening."
This created an awkward moment for Father Bob with his bishop,
who, unbeknownst to him, had recently declared such "unchurchi-
fied" rituals beyond the pale for Catholics! Gerard O'Driscoll, Dec-
lan's godfather and favourite uncle and my very reliable brother-in-
law, is standing behind me. PHOTO BY PAT CONROY

the example of more advanced civilizations, often rebelling against the influence of its nearest neighbours, sometimes betraying a kind of egotism in extreme expressions of nationalism, eventually growing beyond that tendency in the interests of peace and prosperity or because of its growing harmony with the zeitgeist that guides humanity towards its highest fulfilment. In paying my dues to Ireland, I was also freeing myself for the embrace of a Canadian identity that developed quite naturally as I raised my children in Toronto. Canada represents a confluence of many nations and the day I accepted Canadian citizenship in the company of sixty other people of diverse nationality was a landmark one for me. Without renouncing the pride I have in my Irish origins, I was making a conscious commitment to the unique experiment in nation-building that Canada represents. It did not surprise me that Canada, according to a United Nations survey in 1992, ranked first among all countries of the world in its quality of life that is, I believe, reflective of Canada's potential for leadership and compassion in a changing and troubled world.

My fellow new Canadians and I were encouraged to freely contribute the essence of our hopes, dreams and talents, the qualities of character shaped in us by diverse cultural norms, to the vibrant ethos of a country in which the wellbeing of every citizen takes precedence over any reach for power by the few. In becoming a Canadian, I could acknowledge the common humanity and democratic ideals that fundamentally link me to every per-

Here we are, the O'Driscoll family, in the Rosedale ravine in the early Fall of 1976 after we returned from a four-month sojourn in Ireland. Briain (aged nine) and Robert (seven) are in front. Declan (two) is in Bob's arms, and Emer (six months) is in mine. PHOTO BY PAT CONROY

Bob, Father John Kelly (president of St. Michael's College), and American composer John Cage in an animated moment, February 1982. Cage remarked of Bob that "he takes the 'im' out of 'impossible' and puts the 'in' into 'infectious'!" Father Kelly hosted a reception at the college to mark the world premiere of Cage's ROARA-TORIO *which Bob presented at Convocation Hall, University of Toronto, to coincide with what would have been James Joyce's 100th birthday.* PHOTO BY ROBIN KNIGHT son on earth, of whatever colour, creed or background because so many national histories are included within Canadian shores. Its great open spaces are indicative also of the openheartedness of its people reflected in the spirit of universal charity and literary flair that imbues the many Canadians I have come to know and love.

The hospitality that greeted me when I arrived in Newfoundland set the tone that continued to sound for me over years of tentatively putting down my Irish roots in Toronto. I had been totally accepted for who I was and never had the sense of living in exile from Ireland, which I meanwhile discovered to be "the best country to live out of!" I look back on those early Toronto years with a sense of gratitude for the social context—its ideal balance of family, work and friends—provided me in the midst of child-rearing and mundane household chores. There was intellectual stimulation in the many dimensions of Irish and Celtic studies that spilled over into our home life, and I learned a great deal during lectures or in sitting with speakers around our dining table. I was all ears at the time, always gathering food for thought and further research. Bob was ever-generous in providing a platform on which others, sometimes of lesser brilliance than him, might shine. He would argue that visionary enterprises to which he wholeheartedly devoted himself, owed their inspiration to Samuel Ferguson, W.B. Yeats and AE, on whose pioneering shoulders he claimed to stand.

Bob appointed a Celtic Arts board of directors, drawing from the ranks of Toronto's high society, which included three outstanding women: Catherine Graham, wife of Bill Graham, who, in due course of a distinguished academic and political career, became leader of the Liberal opposition in Ottawa; Adrienne Clarkson, who went on to become Canada's governor-general; and Hilary Weston, who later served as lieutenant-governor of Ontario. Celtic

Actress Siobhán McKenna, her "uproarious" dog Rory, and Marshall McLuhan when the party held in his honour at our Dublin home in July 1981 was winding down. The time was 4 a.m.! PHOTO: SUNDAY PRESS

Arts has continued its work beyond Bob's death under the effective chairmanship of Dominican priest and historian Edward Jackman, who facilitated and funded the publication of *The Irish in Canada: The Untold Story*. This was a two-volume magnum opus of some one thousand pages, to which Bob devoted every ounce of available energy while pursuing a full-time teaching career, manic episodes notwithstanding. It fell to me to ship the many orders for this huge item from home. Emer, who was about twelve years old at the time, was helping me to stuff the books into envelopes one day. Pausing on the word "untold," she asked, "If it is an untold story, why would anyone want to read it, Mom?"

No sooner had Professor Robert established himself as a lively and reliable teacher—sure to be in alert attendance at every faculty meeting, a natural favourite of students, an entertaining and, at that point, only a mildly outrageous asset to staff parties—than he proceeded to bring his unique leavening to bear on a predictable and flat mix of university affairs. He found many allies among the erudite and distinguished company of priests who were his colleagues and whose counsel he often sought. They lauded his successes and tolerated his excesses to the furthest reaches of compassion when, with the passage of time, he no longer functioned as an asset to the institution.

Our downtown house was a hub of artistic and cultural life that could quicken the equally hospitable core of St. Michael's College, presided over by John Kelly, a charismatic Irish-American Basilian priest, and a beloved and abiding supporter of Bob's while his extra-curricular activities at St. Michael's were attracting an estimated thirty-five thousand people. Bob pioneered North America's first comprehensive undergraduate program in Celtic Studies, an innovative collaboration between universities

tReasa o'ORíscoll

Two of a series of photographs taken by Colm Henry in his Dublin studio in connection with the release of my album Farewell But Whenever: Love Songs of Ireland from the 15th Century *The earrings were adapted from two medals I won for singing at the age of ten that sport a typical Celtic design. My wardrobe was quite extensive in those days, devoted as I was to the Dublin social round which often called for the "stealing" of Thomas Moore's recommended "few hours from the night."* PHOTOS BY COLM HENRY

Rev. Edward Jackman in his Dominican robes posing with Bob, Emer, Declan, and me in 1981.

on both sides of the Atlantic. He gave Canadian students the opportunity to explore the full range of Celtic civilization and learn Irish, Scot's Gaelic and Welsh, under the guidance of some of the most distinguished scholars in the field. It is a program that still thrives today.

We maintained our connections with all our literary spalpeens or journeymen labourers during our annual summers in Ireland. These visits were extended to eight-

een-month sojourns every seven years. Marshall McLu-
han, in his autobiography, mentions a memorable party
we held for him and his beautiful wife, Corrine, when they
came to Dublin. A photograph of Marshall, as guest of
honour, appeared in the *Sunday Press*. In it, he is crouching
on the floor with Ireland's most popular actress, Siobhán
McKenna and her dog, Rory. The time, I remember, was 4
a.m. The caption reads "Uproarious Party," because Rory
barked incessantly while the revels continued until dawn.

It was during one of these sojourns that the Irish
recording company, Gael-linn, launched my record *Fare-
well but Whenever*, love songs in the *sean-nós* style, most
of them sung in Irish. This gave excuse for more parties
and a memorable two weeks spent in the luxury of Dub-
lin's Gresham Hotel, graciously provided by the record
company. One of the songs I recorded was "Mná na
hÉireann"—Women of Ireland—a tribute to the female
gender sung to an air composed by Seán Ó Riada, a song
which he had chosen to dedicate to me shortly before he
died. A celebrated Irish composer, I came to know him
well during the last six months of his life. He showed
a remarkable alignment with the Spirit of the Times in
establishing a community that would endure beyond his
own short life, in restoring Irish traditional music to the
popular consciousness of the people, and in the fusion
of traditional and classical idioms he effected in his com-
positions. My memory of his visit to Toronto, in 1971,
deserves a chapter in itself.

Seán Ó Riada at the piano, accompanying me during the concert at St. Michael's College. He knew all the words of Irish language songs from the oral tradition and his accompaniments revealed nuances of meaning that enhanced my interpretations in the sean nós style. This snapshot was given to me by a student weeks after the concert. The ghostly quality of this likeness seemed to cast a shadow of coming events because Seán died some six months later, not long after his fortieth birthday.

6

A Lingering Presence in Toronto

The longer one studies life and literature the more strongly
one feels that behind everything that is wonderful stands
the individual, and that it is not the moment that makes the
man but the man who creates the age.

OSCAR WILDE

Seán Ó Riada, a composer who lived from 1931 to 1971, was the
outstanding artistic figure in the Ireland of his time, his
music capturing the imagination of a whole nation. Seán
Ó Mórdha, who made him the subject of a posthumous
television documentary, wrote in the *Irish Times*: "Learned
and stylish, his presence could transform the most mun-
dane occasion into a memorable and celebratory happen-
ing. His boyish sense of humour—a concoction of word
play, literary parody and outrageous role-playing—could
keep a gathering in hoots of laughter throughout a lei-
surely afternoon."

I experienced the pleasure of hearing Ó Riada "live" for the first time in Kilkee, County Clare, during the Merriman Summer School of 1970. His wife, Ruth, who would herself die at a young age, introduced me to Seán after the concert. He took a step backwards when I held out my hand to him and later told me that he experienced a shock of recognition on seeing me. The meeting led to my husband's invitation to him to participate in a forthcoming conference to be held in Toronto in February 1971. This conference would mark the dual centenaries of the births of the painter Jack B. Yeats and the playwright John Millington Synge. Seán's eagerness in accepting overrode his reluctance to "cross the Atlantic in an aeroplane," and his amusement at the smallness of the fee being offered to all participants. "I wouldn't blow my nose for $150 but I will come anyway!" I agreed to sing a few songs in the course of the concert. Letters were subsequently exchanged and, because he took boyish delight in long distance telephone calls, he unravelled the few uncertainties relating to the final program with me over the wire.

He arrived at Toronto International Airport in the company of Anne Yeats. Toronto seemed to live up to his expectations. His fear of flying furnished him with a legitimate excuse for high spirits. He thus engaged me, when I deposited him in his hotel, in the first of many long chats into the small hours. The brilliant carpet of snow, spread in welcome before him, the cosmopolitan air of the city and the hooley-like (Irish party) atmosphere that surrounded the social events of the conference, all contributed to his sense of having come from home to home. He sat restless through the opening panel discussion on the theme of the conference, "Theatre and the Visual Arts," itching to add his insights to those of W.H. Auden, Buckminster Fuller, Marshall McLuhan, Norman Jeffares and Jack MacGowran. Had an opportunity afforded itself, he

*Marshall McLuhan and W.H. Auden conversing after the panel
discussion. Someone said Auden's face resembled "a ripe Autumnal
apple" that day. He had refused Bob's earlier invitations but decided
to come to Canada when Bob wrote for the third time: "Dear Mr.
Auden: If you are not willing to accept my final invitation please do
not reply to this. I simply could not bear to receive another refusal."
Auden wrote to reassure Bob that he was coming. Marshall was
highly amused when Bob let him know this, pleased to hear that
Auden would join the panel with him and Buckminster Fuller.*

undoubtedly would have had much to add to this closing
exchange between Auden and McLuhan:

Auden: *Tradition means giving votes to that obscurist class,
our ancestors. It is the democracy of the dead. Tradition refuses*

surrender to the small arrogant oligarchy of those who merely happen to be walking around.

McLuhan: This is what old Agnew calls the silent majority.

Seán whispered in my ear, "Auden stole that line from Chesterton." He knew about the democracy of the dead, having apprenticed to the native carriers of language and oral tradition, some of them of advanced age, living around him in West Cork. He had moved with his family ten years earlier to this Munster gaeltacht, settling down in the little village of Cúil Aodha, thus ensuring a continuity of cultural heritage that would endure, Seán hoped, for the next seven generations of his family.

Upon observing that I sang as "a person singing a song and not as a 'singer'" and that I had "the kind of mind that works in Irish," he extended me the full measure of his charm and wit, which cast its certain spell upon me. We spent less of the little time at our disposal practising, in the accepted sense of the word, for the concert than we did in exploring our mutual love of poetry and yarns. My choice of songs were all, by coincidence, favourites of Ó Riada's, "An Droighneán Donn," "Liam Ó Raghallaigh," and "Brídín Bheasach,"—he being drawn, as I am, to those moving expressions of unrequited love, which assumed more poignancy as we became aware of our attraction for one another. His sensitive chording reminded me, at every turn, of the essential meaning of the words I was singing and of the power of these melodies to embody the feelings that gave rise to them. He included me in the early part of the concert but it was Ó Riada the audience wanted to hear, and hear him they did for something like three and a half hours.

Seán established and maintained a jolly rapport with the crowd, subduing it completely in the first few bars of "Marbhna Luimní," the tune that a lone piper was to play at his own funeral later in the year. The famous bard Carolan and Irish language vision poets of earlier centuries were all affectionately referred to in the course of his introductions as though they were dear personal friends. He played "Port a' Phúca" as a composer, conveying to chilling effect the ghostly quality of the tune his friend Paddy Daly, alone in his hut on Inishvickillaun, had overheard late at night, when the elements pitched themselves in eerie harmony with the wild Atlantic.

The audience was allowed to draw their parallels between "Anacreon" (by Carolan) and "The Star Spangled Banner" and could not fail to hear echoes of "God Save the Queen" in "Robin is my delight, Ochone, Ochone." But he was deadly serious when he proposed "Mo Ghile Mear" as an appropriate national anthem for Ireland, conveying a sense of courage and daring in the playing of it, alternating between harpsichord and piano.

"Aisling Gheal," or "bright vision," was introduced by him as "a song from my own parish," and elicited from him a story that proves that he, like AE before him, had received the blessing of the Irish Folk Spirit:

> I once saw a vision when I was twenty-one years old. I was walking home from Kilmalloch in County Limerick. I really did see a vision, a most frightening thing. I had come from Dublin on the train that stopped at Kilmalloch. No buses were running. As usual, I was not in agreement with my parents, so they hadn't sent a car. When you go outside Kilmalloch, a long straight road stretches in front of you so that you can see clearly ahead for two miles. I had been walking for about fifteen minutes when suddenly I saw a woman coming towards me — she hadn't been there a second before. She was wearing a long red skirt, a white blouse and had a shawl around her shoulders. The hair stood up on the back

of my head. I was terrified. As she passed me, I followed her
round like a magnet. Suddenly she wasn't there any more.
That, I think, was a real vision, a real aisling.

He talked about his admiration for the poet Raftery, who played with his face to the wall when traditional Irish music was not at all fashionable. "I feel if one is living at all, if one is really living, one must be living with passion and Raftery was dominated by a real passion and love of life." His remark that laughter is the enemy of passion, was counterpointed by his altering the rhythms of such slow airs as "Bean Dubh a Ghleanna" to incorporate dance rhythms before returning to the original tempo he started with. He pointed out the Irish propensity of taking life with a grain of salt. "You must learn to laugh at your own emotion," he declared.

The audience joined him in "Óró Bog Liom í" ("I hope we won't all be put out for singing obscene Gaelic songs in Canada!"). "Róisín Dubh" (or "Dark Rosaleen") was requested many times. He began by playing the version he had first heard his mother sing as a child "not for patriotic reasons but for local parochial reasons" before going on to do full justice to the song he made famous in the score for *Mise Éire* (or I am Ireland), a film that brought him to national prominence. He made reference to his mother's singing of "The Suit of Green" and played it after reciting the words. A last call for "one of your own" brought the response: "No, I'll play you one of my father's—a lullaby he sang me, my earliest childhood memory, in the hopes that you will either go to sleep or go home." And thus the concert finished in moving tribute to his father with "Bog Braon don tSeanduine."

As the conference progressed, the kitchen of our house became the centre of action in the late evening. Seán forsook the elegant surroundings of the Windsor Arms

Hotel for a couch in our living room. Not much time was devoted to sleep in any case, and our home became a nightly hub of talk and music.

Along with the ongoing festivities that we played host to at this time, Bob and I had also agreed to host a reception in honour of the opening of *The Heart's A Wonder*, our Dublin friend Maureen Charlton's adaptation of *The Playboy of the Western World*. However, on the eve of the party disaster struck when our living room ceiling collapsed. Fortunately, the day was saved when Claude Bissel, the president of the university at the time, and his Scottish-born wife, Christine, leaped into the breach and offered their home for the event. I was able to thankfully deposit the food and drink already stored in our house in their stately abode, and the event went off without a hitch.

In fact, the evening was a huge success. The Bissels were famous during his fifteen-year term of office for their innumerable stylish parties free of academic constraint. Claude mentions only two in his memoirs: one that was carefully planned as a surprise to honour Marshall McLuhan on his return from the United States in 1968; the other a party that, he said, "erupted suddenly." In his memoir, *Halfway up Parnassus*, President Bissell described it thus: "It seemed as if a good part of the Toronto Irish community came to the house, and a fair number stayed on until first light, as if they were attending an enormous wake. We shall always remember gentle Seán Ó Riada, composer of austere, Schonbergian serialist music, fervent Irish nationalist, sitting at a battered piano in the recreation room, playing his Irish folk tunes while the hours rolled away and a mound of cigarette butts formed at his feet."

Seamus Heaney described his impressions of being in Seán's company on another occasion:

…As he stepped and stooped to
the keyboard he was our Jacobite,
he was our young pretender
who marched along the deep
Plumed in slow airs and
grace notes…

The day of Seán's departure was fraught with tragic glee. The actor Jack MacGowran, not long for this world either at that time (he died soon after Seán), was unwell and held court from his hotel bed. Anne Yeats, James Flannery, Bob and I, along with John Richmond (the literary editor of the *Montreal Star* with whom Seán discoursed mainly in Greek) and Ó Riada, were positioned around the bed. Plans were hatched for the mounting of the Yeats plays in Toronto, which my husband would produce and for which Anne Yeats would design the sets, Ó Riada write the music, with Jack MacGowran directing them "six inches above the ground." There would be a part for me.

Such diversions as the telephoning of the prime ministerial residence of Pierre Elliott Trudeau "just say that Seán Ó Riada called" were indulged in. Plans to rendez-vous with Seán Kenny and Siobhán McKenna in New York enroute to Shannon, were shelved as the fun continued. The piece of music he had agreed to write for *Here Are Ladies*, Siobhán's one-woman show had, he said, regrettably been lost in the snow. No doubt it had been completed in his head, but the fun and games had diverted him from the actual writing down of the music. He wept when his departure could be delayed no longer, and we all had a sense of the party's being over. In a thank-you letter to Bob, he toyed with the notion of putting an ad in a Toronto newspaper in which he might express his delight in the luxuriance of the snow, the warmth of the people, and the happiness his brief visit had afforded him.

He frequently called me from Cork and we exchanged letters. His were accompanied by words of songs he thought I might like, such as "The Suit of Green" and "The False Hearted Lover." His exquisite penmanship in the old Irish script—worthy of the finest calligrapher—and loving sentiments expressive of the poetic mode of an earlier century, revealed a vulnerable sensitivity of heart and mind. Most of the calls were short and conveyed his "urgent need" to hear my voice. Our next meeting took place in Galway two months later. Professor Lorna Reynolds had arranged a concert with Ó Riada as the star attraction. Seán Mac Donncha, the brother of my former teacher Mairéad, and I each contributed a few songs. Standing in the wings with Ó Riada before the curtain came up, I confessed to being nervous. Squeezing my hand he said, "Don't worry *a stór* (my treasure). Sure they are only people out there. Why would you be afraid of people?"

His accompaniments that night were truly inspired, and I realized that because he knew the words of the old songs, their meaning was relayed into every melismatic nuance. Sometime during the concert, Seán's close friend, Garech de Brún, a Guinness heir, arrived. Garech is owner of Claddagh Records and often travels with an entourage. At the time, his entourage often included the likes of Mick Jagger, Marianne Faithful and an exotic titled lady or two, but on this occasion it included Paddy Maloney of The Chieftains. Paddy sprang nimbly up on stage at Seán's invitation and a good-natured rapport between piano and tin whistle developed into something of a competitive joust.

I was also present at the last concert Seán ever gave, in Liberty Hall on July 14—Bastille Day. Like Joyce, he had an exaggerated attachment to certain dates of the calendar. He presented himself on stage that night in deference to his audience. Despite his involvement in a car crash three days earlier—from which he had walked away having spat out most of his teeth on the side of the road—Seán refused to disappoint his fans. Had a leading music critic realized the pain he was in, he would likely have been more kind in his review. His shattered appearance and his despair were evident later that night when we could spend some time alone. The implications of an enforced liquid diet now marked the beginning of the end for him. The liver he claimed was damaged from birth rendered alcohol a poisonous substance for him. His social imperative to drink was not easily overcome however and his early death was medically attributed to cirrhosis of the liver.

He celebrated his fortieth birthday on August 1, 1971. It was to be his last. He arranged recording sessions soon after for his final album, *O'Riada's Farewell*, to coincide with my last days in Dublin before I would return with my husband and children to Toronto. When I saw him in Dublin's Shelbourne Hotel, I was shocked by his gauntness. His greatest fear, he confessed, was that he had lost his musical gift and would no longer compose. It was clear that he was very ill. I sat with him in his room and sadness filled the space between us. There was a depth to this moment that has more reality in memory than many other experiences of my life to that point. We were soon startled by a very loud knock on the door to which I immediately responded, but there was nobody outside in the corridor. "It's 'the knocking on the door,'" he said, "my time is not far off," referring to one of the traditional warning signs of imminent death in a family. I was regrettably too young and too absorbed in subjective emotions to speak the words of consolation he needed to hear but I knew I would never see him again. Although obviously something of a sybarite, an air of other-worldliness hung around him always and never more than in this moment of parting.

That he was a man of many masks has been disclosed in the various accounts given by his friends since his death. All agreed about how complex a man he was and how brilliant a companion he could be. The late Seán White described him to me as "the André Gide of our student days in Cork." Louis Marcus, a close friend and film-maker with whom Ó Riada collaborated, wrote about him in *The Celtic Consciousness*: "There were too many of him to be contained in one frame, however wiry. One day he would insist on speaking French, another only Irish. Sometimes he would be a Montenotte Corkman, other times a Viennese academic, and yet others a West Cork peasant." George Morrison, another film-maker, whom I met once, remarked on the Edwardian pose Seán adopted so effectively in manner and dress. A man sitting in the Ó Riada kitchen after the funeral was overheard by poet John Montague to say: "Ah sure, we were nothing at all until he came along. He was our great Chieftain, our great Chieftain!"

He was indeed buried as a chieftain of old, his funeral procession stretching for miles as though he himself had stage-managed the ritual. His propensity in life to function as a kind of barometer in sensing or in altering the mood of a group at large pronounced him a natural leader. He had access to corridors of power. Being a natural aristo-crat, he could transcend all social barriers. He felt a sharp personal pain in the divisive forces sundering Northern Irish society—any threat to his country was experienced as a threat to himself.

The position of national composer was created for him in a country that had only conferred popular laureateship on writers up until then. He not only strove to fill a gap of centuries in Ireland's musical development, he succeeded in fusing Gaelic modalities into a European classical mode with, in the words of Louis Marcus, "a grace that con-

quered any possible incongruity." Marcus who worked
closely with him in the sixties points out that, more than
any Irish artist since Joyce, the current zeitgeist of Europe
was of urgent importance to Ó Riada. "Like Joyce, he had
to integrate all of what he was in an artistically success-
ful pattern. And, like Joyce he had to create a language
in which to do it." To my mind, his Nomos No. 2, which
moved me deeply in a performance I attended several
years after his death, was his most successful attempt in
finding form and idiom for a profound musical expiation
of his inner anxiety and general unrest about the future. It
presented both a brilliant synthesis of the European clas-
sical tradition while signalling its demise, a no less intel-
lectual and far reaching artistic feat than that achieved by
T.S. Eliot, who had also juxtaposed the emptiness of the
present with the classical glories of the past.

In forsaking Dublin life for what many of his friends
regarded as a rural backwater, Seán introduced an equally
dramatic juxtaposition of elements into his family life.
He urged his beloved English-speaking wife and children
to embrace the Irish language as he had done—becom-
ing extraordinarily fluent in a matter of months—before
departing the capital city. He knew, as Yeats had known,
that the literature of Ireland sprang from the rhizome of
an oral culture in which music and speech were interde-
pendent, the music being our language where language
ends. As Yeats was drawn to Celtic myth and mysticism,
and as Synge discovered the life of the Aran Islands to
be the outward expression of his inner being, so was Ó
Riada drawn to Cúil Aodh in West Cork. Synge sights
a moment of epiphany in his life when everything Irish
became precious and had a charm that was neither quite
human nor divine, "rather perhaps as if I had fallen in love
with a goddess." Ó Riada had his own vision to which he
attached a significance of similar magnitude. When he

turned to what he termed the rich and comparatively untouched pastures of Irish traditional music, he was responding to his own spiritual needs. He clearly understood the centrality of the Irish language to the musical idiom he adopted. He knew, as Patrick Pearse who led the uprising in 1916 did, how close the unseen powers have always been to Irish-speaking men and women. He too aspired to the true Irish mysticism of Pearse, the mysticism reminiscent of an esoteric Celtic Christianity that recognizes no substantial divide between visible and invisible reality.

When Seán's commitment to his vision was total, he sought an exterior landscape and environment, as artists often do, which might reflect his own psychic geography. He thus kept close to the nerves of ancient tradition, which his creative alchemy transmuted into patterns that would always sound recognizable to Irish ears and, at the same time, strange. In him, man and artist were one, exemplified by his lifelong commitment to reconciling the diverse leanings of an original and creative spirit with an instinctive return to all that was pure and rooted in Irish tradition. He demonstrated in this return, as only a great man could, that a man without a community behind him is no great man at all. His preoccupation with spiritual matters and the pathos with which he was often overcome, became more marked in the last months of his life.

Because he understood the intimacy with which Christ Jesus and Mary have been incorporated into the Gaelic clan, he understood the importance of his masses as the indigenous ritual of his faithful community. He told me of his pride in his Cúil Aodh Mass when I met him for the last time, on August 19, 1971. He pressed a copy of the mass into my hands as a parting gift, with a reminder that I should be hearing from him on my birthday, October 4. Garech de Brún's telegram bearing the news of

Seán's death arrived on the morning of that very day. He also promised that friends of his, including Siobhán McKenna, Sean Kenny, and Garech, would be coming through Toronto, as so they did, one by one, during the months following his death, when we could commiserate with one another in the loss of our beloved Seán.

Bob's generosity of spirit was evident in allowing me whatever time and space I needed in grieving this loss and this gave me great comfort. It had been painful for him to accept that I could be so passionately drawn to another man. However few and far between our meetings had been, given the fact that we lived for the most part on different continents, we were often in each other's thoughts during the last six months of Seán's life. As a true artist, Ó Riada had the sensitivity to feel accurately and creatively and to communicate true feeling through the spiritual language of music. I, being predisposed to the artistic exploration of feelings, tended to fall in love with what needed to be understood about people, always sensing that loving interest is my surest means of opening to the world, and of intuitively knowing the world of another. I did not realize at the time that while love is unconditional, relationship is not, and that robbing Peter to pay Paul is ultimately self defeating. It took me years to learn that the quality of a committed relationship is conditional on many complex factors of human nature and circumstance and is not determined by feeling alone but based in mutual choice, commitment, negotiation and compromise. It does not flourish of its own accord and demands wakeful attention and responsibility. I had not learned how to distance myself from infatuation at that time, being young and self centred, nor could I rationalize a powerful attraction into thin air that was not simply a fantasy of my own making. Robert Frost wrote, "Earth's the right place for love. I don't know where it is likely to go better." Certainly the elusive balance between intimacy and right relation that love demands of me has proven to be a life long and often risky endeavour. The shadow of Seán Ó Riada's imminent death hung over us from our first meeting and I know, in retrospect, that he needed the love of many people, of whom I was one, to ease him over that threshold.

We are told in the Song of Songs (VIII, 6-7):

... For love is strong as death ...
Its flashes are flashes of fire,
A flame of the eternal ...

Ó Riada succeeded in putting art into life. He exuded a reverence for natural wisdom and a joy in the company of others. He taught me that learning is an end in itself. A greater understanding of the life that animates us all might be brought about through an intensive probing into the spirit of Seán Ó Riada and the reason for this spirit's having manifested itself at a particular time in the history of Ireland. I had the opportunity to share some of my reflections about the composer on a CBC radio programme, aired in Toronto after his death. This led to my being invited to present a series of programmes on classical Irish composers and an *Ideas* series on "The Myth and Music of Ireland" for Canadian listeners for which I drew on the inspiration of my fateful encounter with Ó Riada.

Some fifteen years after the death of his father, Seán's eldest son, Peadar, a composer and *gaeltacht* man who has remained true to his father's legacy, came to visit us in Toronto, ostensibly to join me and American composer Steven Scotti in a series of performances. The outcome of that six weeks sojourn was that my two older sons, Briain and Robert, developed a great admiration for Peadar, who began to instruct them in the art of *bodhrán* (Irish drum)

My second son, Robert—poet, actor, woodcarver, teacher, and the father of Anwen, Tyrnan, and Ilan.

making. He led them on the successful mission of finding goatskins and sheep urine in the city of Toronto that they carried home with them on the subway, all the while holding them in thrall with his stories of life in his magical Cúil Aodh. He became such a mentor during this period that Briain, who had just finished high school, followed him to West Cork. In the course of his two years spent in the Ó Riada household, Briain became a member of the men's choir, which Seán had formed for the singing of his masses, and perfected his technique on the traditional flute, adding many new tunes to his repertoire under Peadar's tutorship. As a gifted teacher of music and metaphysics, Peadar made a deep and lasting impression on both my sons, much as his father made on me.

My eldest son, Briain, has now restored himself to the County Clare origins of his ancestors as if the continuum between his great-grandfather's life and his had never been interrupted, like an unbroken melody. Because it was his instrument of choice, he inherited my grandfather's flute, manufactured in 1780 and on which he perfected his musical skills. Briain decided to purchase a plot of land in County Clare with an inheritance he received from his father who died in 1996. The option of buying a few acres within miles of my grandfather's birthplace serendipitously arose for him. He was soon well-established in a community of small farmers, many of them of German, Dutch or American origin. They brought new energy and muscle to a dying art of farming in this remote rural setting, and Briain was welcomed amongst them as one of like ilk—a hard worker. Soon also in demand as a flautist, he joined a traditional dance band, since travelling the length and breadth of the county for weekend gigs.

In the course of these travels, he met an old man who admired his musicianship and invited him into his smoky, two-roomed cottage for a cup of tea. Noting his host's advanced age, Briain inquired if he knew anything about a fife and drum band that flourished in the Ennis area at the turn of the twentieth century. My uncle P.J. Grealish had shown him a photo, dated 1899, which included his late father Paddy as a prominent member of the band.

"By Jove, I do!" said the old man, jumping to his feet. "You know the band's instruments were confiscated by the Black 'n' Tans in 1920? But my people held on to a few of the fifes. They are still hidden in the back room."

He disappeared into the shadows and emerged a few minutes later clutching a long narrow object smothered in dust. "See if you can get a note out of that," he challenged.

"I'd better remove some of the dust first." Briain's fingers carefully explored the instrument. Feeling some embossed lettering on the underside, he brushed off the dust of ages, turning the fife towards the light. The original owner's name was—Paddy Grealish!

"This fife belonged to my own great-grandfather!" Briain exclaimed excitedly, as he stared at the instrument in disbelief.

"'Tis yours now, young man! Take it home with you and come back when you can raise a tune out of it!"

This fife remains one of my son's most prized possessions, another link with his ancestral line, which his friendship with Peadar Ó Riada had helped to revive. My son Robert, in the aftermath of Peadar's visit to Toronto,

My eldest son, Briain, was about to play a tune on the flute for me and my friend, Kate Somerville, who took this photo. Briain is sitting on one of the many walls, some over twelve feet high, that surround his property. He built them all himself with the reddish-ochre stones associated with the area of Ballinruan, County Clare, where he lives, farms, and makes music.

treasa o'driscoll

paid the following tribute to his father who had enlivened the cultural life of Ireland and left his mark on the city of Toronto and on two generations of the O'Driscoll family:

> *Ó Riada did*
> *St. Patrick's work,*
> *making masses for the people*
> *that the spirit would touch their souls*
> *more directly,*
> *with notes more telling than words,*
> *chords that were prayers…*
> *I'm sure the old voices had warned him*
> *that the battles would be fought in the soul.*
> *the voices of the ancestors*
> *were always clear to him,*
> *the communication liquid crystal,*
> *the kind that gleams within.*
>
> *the wireless of his harpsichord*
> *was his direct link to the other side,*
> *and being a true representative*
> *of the silent hierarchy,*
> *he knew that the only weapon a man has*
> *in the realm of the unseen*
> *is his art…*
> —ROBERT O'DRISCOLL, JR.

Household Names

*...Think where man's glory most begins and ends
And say my glory was I had such friends.*
W.B. YEATS

My daughter, Emer, came to visit me in County Clare at this point of the writing, making a getaway from bustling Toronto in order to prepare for a forthcoming CD recording of her songs. After a few weeks of refining, arranging and practising in the peaceful atmosphere of the gate lodge, she agreed to accompany me on a trip to County Kerry. A Sunday newspaper had recently run a feature about me, which elicited a generous invitation from a reader named Leo O'Shea. He was urging me to avail of a holiday cottage he had built next to his home, in the picturesque Atlantic setting of Ballinaskelligs. Claiming to have once enjoyed a party in our home in Toronto, he wished to return the hospitality. I had a longing to travel to this Irish-speaking area, a peninsula of breathtaking beauty and historical interest. Once again a wish was being serendipitously

granted me during a spell of sunny weather in early May, when we could enjoy it at its best.

Rev. Edward Jackman had written from Toronto only a few weeks before on behalf of Celtic Arts, an organization he and Bob had founded together. It had been decided that he would commission a memorial sculpture, to be erected in Ireland in memory of Bob. He was enlisting my help with the practical details of the project, which Emer and I planned to further as we made our way to Kerry. Nearing our destination, we drove through the small town of Waterville. A life-sized statue of Charlie Chaplin, a long-time hero of mine, dominated the pavement opposite the local hotel. Photographs attesting to the great actor's fishing expeditions in the area adorned the walls of the foyer. I enquired about the sculptor at the reception desk and learned that the artist, Alan Hall, lived locally. Later that day, I was introduced by my host to members of the Main family that was prominent in the area. The two brothers I met were nephews of the late John Main, a revered meditation teacher whose books I had read, and who had been the abbot of a monastery in Quebec. Friends of Hall, they offered to take us to meet him next day on Valencia Island, which was linked to the mainland by a bridge.

They picked us up, mid-morning, at our cosy and comfortable cottage. Our first stop was the once derelict famine village of Cill Rialaig, now converted into a colony of creativity. An international roster of professional artists

This photo of my daughter, Emer, appears on the cover of her first CD. Entitled Lucid Dreams, *the CD features several original songs she arranged for her band. She accompanies herself on piano and guitar and her husband, drummer Craig Halliday, provides a superb backing on every track. I have often remarked that his drumbeat is synchronized with her heartbeat!*

occupies the well-appointed cottage studios for designated periods, all of them donating a finished work in gratitude and in support of the project. These works are on sale in a nearby gallery, which we visited. The first thing that caught my eye was a length of the original underwater cable that extended from Newfoundland to Ballinaskelligs, displayed in a frame by the entrance. Bob had spoken to me of this vital connecting link between our two countries and, like me, he had hoped to visit the spot where the cable, facilitating the first technological communication between Ireland and North America, had reached shore. "This house originally belonged to O'Driscolls, and many people on the island have your surname! You will be very much at home here!" Alan Hall declared, when we arrived at his door.

Gladly noting the chain of coincidence I was meeting, I stated the purpose of our visit as Alan led us on a tour of his studio. Proffering a copy of Bob's weighty book, *The Celtic Consciousness*, I asked if he was willing to make a bronze replica of the unique Celtic cover design. Hall's enthusiasm for this commission and his interest in the details of Bob's life convinced us that he was our man. I explained to Alan how central Yeats studies had been to Bob's teaching and writing career. Amongst the poems by Yeats that he had been ever wont to recite were the following lines from "The Tower", which Alan agreed to engrave on the completed cenotaph which now stands at the entrance to my son Briain's property, in Ballinruan, County Clare:

> *...Death and life were not,*
> *"Til man made up the whole,*
> *Made lock, stock and barrel*
> *Out of his bitter soul.*
> *Aye, sun and moon and stars, all*

And further add to that
That, being dead, we rise,
Dream and so create
Translunar paradise ...

When Emer and I returned to the cottage, I thanked our generous host for facilitating this turn of events with his timely invitation. I told him that I felt the guidance of Bob's star in what had unfolded. Leo had followed my husband's career from a distance and we talked long into the night of our eventful home life in Toronto, the memorable party that he had attended, and Bob's devotion to the poetry and public accomplishments of W.B. Yeats. Literary interests and home life were so interlinked for us at the time that our family's household names included those of Yeats, AE, James Joyce, and Sean O'Casey, their accumulated wisdom of enduring relevance in the midst of the usual daily concerns. My conversation with Leo awakened memories of my life with Bob and I was itching to return to my desk in the gate lodge to record these reflections while they were still fresh in my mind ...

George, the widow of W.B., once cautioned a Yeats critic who came to interview her, "Do not spend all your life on Yeats." A good deal younger than her husband, she outlived him by some thirty years and had ample opportunity to observe the growing phenomenon of Yeats scholarship, taken up with the fervour of a religious vocation by academics worldwide. My husband numbered among them and I was an easy convert. Yeats studies were part and parcel of the life that opened up to me when I became engaged to Bob, who was always, from the day I met him, at work on one manuscript or another. All arrangements between us had to be laid before a Yeats tribunal. My husband's oft-repeated quotations soon lodged mantra-like in memory. Whenever he proved obstinate in argument, I could let the following line roll off my tongue: "Bob— didn't Yeats say, at the age of eighty, 'I have felt the convictions of a lifetime melt in a moment,' and here you are stubbornly refusing to concede a point." His arsenal was more heavily loaded, and if I ever suggested that he might begin to curb his workaholic tendencies, he had the following quote at the ready: "Excess is the vivifying spirit of the finest art and we must always seek to make excess more abundantly excessive."

Some of the finest minds and most delightful people were drawn to explore the labyrinths of wisdom Yeats had explored, the rich yield of interests he harvested in friendship with his peers. His contemporaries had led him into the study of French symbolism, Rosicrucianism, the Upanishads, Japanese Noh, hermeticism, magic, mythology and folklore. This poet, dramatist, senator and public man had, moreover, an endless fascination with himself, his own moods and idioms. James Stephens had to ask about Yeats: "Has he the right to saddle carefree citizens with his politics, his aristocracy, his philosophy, his love affairs—all his whatnots?" before concluding that time would tell whether or not Yeats had hung around too often in his poems, endlessly "clanked about in his rhymes."

Time brought a positive judgment to bear in the form of an annual Yeats Summer School, to which aficionados flock for two weeks every August, and which has continued without a lapse since the early sixties. For a period of nine years, Bob was among the speakers and teachers who approached the mecca of Sligo and its environs, ground hallowed by Yeats for all time, its litany of names sounding through the poems: Ben Bulben, Knocknarea, Innisfree, Lissadell, Coole, Tower Ballylee. It was thrilling to accompany Bob on trips to these landmarks. Returning

W.B. Yeats already had the appearance of a poet even in youth. A myriad-minded man, his life was devoted to resolving his own inner contradictions, creating his own unity of being out of a richness of esoteric knowledge and practice. Although he once confessed that "a hundred needs have lain upon my heart" he learned to rest in inner truth, becoming lord of his own destiny. He played an active role in Irish life, shaping its role in a social and historical sense with informed spiritual intent. He was Ireland's greatest poet, whose ardent nationalism, plays, preoccupation with mysticism, friendships, and fully lived life continue to fascinate and absorb the reader of his works.

from our honeymoon in time for the summer school in 1966, we were warmly welcomed by the director, Professor T.R. Henn. He remarked that participants had learned to love me, for "herself alone, and not her yellow hair," a reference to a short Yeats poem I had set to music and often sang.

There was always a great hush of expectancy as a speaker mounted the podium to deliver manna extracted from the poet's comprehensive theory of aesthetics or from his fertile exchange with contemporaries Ezra Pound, Rabindranath Tagore, Lady Gregory, AE, and John Millington Synge, to name but a few. A great interplay of influences from both past and present brought about the powerful self-development that Yeats's genius demanded. There was endless speculation in the afternoon seminars on such topics as W.B.'s epitaph and what he really meant by it.

Cast a cold eye on life
on death
Horseman pass by…

Bob and I travelled together to Drumcliff Churchyard to meditate upon these words or ponder the apocalyptic significance of an image from "The Second Coming," that arresting "rough beast" that was "slouching towards Bethlehem to be born." Bob would engage me for hours in his Sherlock Holmes-like probing into these conundrums. He also liked to claim that our first son was conceived at one of Yeats's favourite haunts. It is true that I gave birth nine months after the 1966 school and that his father had inserted William Butler after the name Briain on the child's birth certificate, despite protests from me.

Romance often blossomed amongst Yeats devotees; a certain licentiousness had the sanction of Yeats's purported sexual exploits in later life. Yeats had worried about love, making it the source of passion and drama in his life, writing about it as if it were an "almost–crime," thought James Stephens, who conceded that the great poet approached love as a violent kind of thing "that doesn't really brood about chickens, but is passionately concerned about the mice." The extracurricular bed-hopping at the summer school would have done Yeats proud. Crazy Jane's remonstrations gave bold directive to the poet's aficionados:

> ...A woman may be proud and stiff
> When on live intent
> But love has pitched his mansion in
> The place of excrement;
> And nothing can be sole or whole
> That has not been rent.

Bob had a profound scholarly interest in the Celtic Literary Revival that flourished at the turn of the twentieth century, due to the collaboration of Yeats and AE. He often lectured on the subject, pointing out how several factors had contributed to it—a mingling of two languages, a mysterious hearing of ancestral voices, the revival of bardic and antiquarian pursuits. These combined to bring about a moment in Irish history in which personal, national, and universal interests could find common ground. I had been profoundly moved by the first lecture of Bob's I attended. I learned there that the translations by Sir Samuel Ferguson from Irish to English of poems I knew by heart had provided a cornerstone for the development of Yeats's art, rooting it in the fertile soil of folklore. Bob hoped to one day found a centre for Celtic Studies that would integrate a confluence of elements—linguistic, literary, mythological, historical and spiritual—to stir the imagination of modern students and prepare them to actively engage the challenges of modern life as Yeats and AE had done.

Love for the teacher is a great stimulus to the brain and my rapt attention during my new husband's daily seminars would easily have earned me an "A". Bob's focus was exclusively on the poems, which he and I took turns in reading aloud in the group. Ignoring the exhaustive critical commentary that could overwhelm students of Yeats's work, Bob's tutorials encouraged the students to think for themselves. He conducted lively debates on the complex and often ambiguous nature of key poems, which sometimes carried over into nearby pubs when classroom sessions ended.

All speakers and spouses gathered in Sligo's Imperial Hotel, an establishment once frequented by Yeats himself, which at that time boasted, some would argue, the same mattresses of Yeats's day. Whether that was the case or not, they were certainly uncomfortable enough to feel like they had been in use for the better part of a century. Indeed, when the distinguished Canadian academic Northrop Frye, having driven with us from Shannon to Sligo, took a room next to ours there, the bed proved itself so detrimental to his ailing back that he moved to another hotel to prepare for his lecture.

Speakers who had held forth that morning could bask in the reflected glory of luminaries such as Richard Ellmann, Norman Jeffares, and the director himself, T.R. (Tom) Henn, at the large round mahogany table in the dining room. It was on those occasions that I first became aware of the searching insight and poetic vision of Kathleen Raine, who was a respected presence among us every year. I was much in awe of her and held back in conversation, but she later honoured me with letters of encouragement as Bob's illness progressed, always urging me to be happy in spite of circumstances. Late-night drinkers conducted critical post mortems on the day's academic offerings. These were sessions I rarely enjoyed, especially since they often included bursts of song from scholars who frequently could not hold a tune. Emotional immaturity often mixed with precocious intellect at these sessions, I noticed. To have a starring role in this scholarly exhibition was a mixed blessing; on the one hand, there was the recognition that one was amongst the elite, but, on the other hand, there was the recognition that that fact made one a sitting duck for all the "begrudgers" present. I was often led to understand that my naive enjoyment of the lectures was due to my lack of a critical faculty, and I could not argue with that, although I believed then and still do that praise never goes astray in any situation.

Most speakers came very well prepared. Francis Warner, genius extraordinaire and the youngest ever don at St. Peters College, Oxford, took a more daring approach. He could be heard hammering away on his typewriter when the day for his display of dazzling erudition dawned. He and I had struck an instant rapport and he subsequently wrote a part for me in his first play, entitled *Emblems*. It depicted two brides on their wedding day, of which I was one, about to marry the same man. Full of psychological complexity and ironic, witty dialogue, it had distinct autobiographical overtones for anyone who knew Francis well. This play afforded me the delight of spending six weeks in Oxford with my second infant son. Robert would become an actor himself when he grew up, having had his first whiff of greasepaint in the Oxford Playhouse at the age of two.

Francis used to stay with us in the tiny Toronto apart-
ment that was our home during my first pregnancy, launch-
ing forth from there into the city's high society, often with
us in tow. Millionaires such as the Eatons and Latners were
happy to host him and further their associations with the
hallowed institution he represented. Building projects at
St. Peters were funded through these channels. Ever dash-
ing, Francis always dressed in those days, as did Bob, in
finely tailored three-piece suits, his jackets revealing a
flash of crimson lining. More recently, I noticed, when
he showed me round his house a few years ago, where he
now occupies T.R. Henn's old chair at Cambridge Univer-
sity, that the same siren red adorned the opulent bedroom
Francis shares with a beautiful young wife.

Glamour always attended Francis—he was our first
link with the rich and famous. Either Richard Burton or
Lawrence Harvey, close friends of his, would fill in for
him at Oxford, whenever he made fund-raising forays
abroad. As Elizabeth Taylor's poet chronicler, he gave
us vivid account of her fortieth birthday party. Proceeds
from his plays were earmarked for the Samuel Beckett the-
atre he had promised his friend Sam he would build. To
that end, he engaged the services of another of his friends,
Buckminster Fuller, who planned to suspend the build-
ing embryo-like underground. But this proposition was
shelved when the initial excavation unearthed an abun-
dance of skeletons of long-dead parishioners beneath the
quadrangle of St. Peter's College.

In 1970, I travelled with the Oxford cast of *Emblems*
to Edinburgh, where we were listed in the festival fringe.
Affairs took a dramatic turn in true Warner style when
the leading man, Jeremy Treglown, who had finished his
studies and had taken up a teaching post in Southamp-
ton, made the nightly journey to Scotland by helicopter.
Francis was always on the runway to meet him, reputedly

flagging down large jets to clear a landing spot for Jeremy, while we all waited on tenterhooks backstage. One evening his arrival was in fact delayed, and I was nudged onto the stage to entertain the waiting audience.

There had been a great hue and cry about the nudity, for which Francis claimed artistic licence, that was featured prominently in *Emblems* and which would distinguish most of his subsequent plays. We discovered one night, shortly before the show was to begin, that the police "morality squad" had chosen to infiltrate the audience. It was elected that I would appear on stage to throw the officers off track, and to appease the waiting audience. Imagine their bemusement and perhaps disappointment, when all they could witness was a fully clothed woman singing songs in the Irish language. They departed before Francis and the actor who would bare it all finally arrived! It was this production that led to our touring the U.S., by which time Alan Schneider, Samuel Beckett's favourite director, had joined the team and we added *Come and Go* and *Breath* to our repertoire.

Breath was the shortest play in history, lasting the length of a protracted death rattle that gives way to a baby's cry— it required no actors, just a heap of rubble on the stage, but it was guaranteed to keep a stage manager on her toes! *Come and Go*, in which three woman came and went from the bench on which they were seated, was also a matter of timing more than acting ability for me and the other two actresses involved.

Samuel Beckett's plays and novels have provoked lively debate amongst critics, philosophers and readers who often misunderstand his message. He transmits a keen grasp of the uncertainty of the human condition, and arouses corresponding emotions of discomfort in theatre-goers to those enacted in his plays. To attend a Beckett performance is to experience claustrophobia, helpless-

Sorel Etrog gave us this photograph of Beckett. He looks exactly as I remember him from our all-too-brief meeting in Paris in 1972.

ness, confusion, frustration, anxiety and compassion first-hand. He was acutely conscious during his lifetime of the poor, the forgotten and marginalized, the reality of whose lives has little entertainment value. Yet there is comfort and mental stimulation in Beckett's work, as well as humour and literary elegance. Although he shunned publicity and only accepted a Nobel Prize because it would provide him with money to share amongst his friends, his readers are legion.

His close friend, the late Alec Reid, godfather of my daughter, Emer, and a welcome guest in our Toronto house in the late seventies, bemoaned the general perception of Sam as an inhuman, gloomy intellectual, a view Alec believed had affected the general appreciation of Beckett's work. Alec wanted to set the record straight and wrote a short impassioned book called, *All I Can Manage, More than I Could*, in which Beckett is acclaimed for the humanitarian he was.

I have known at least five other close friends of the writer who extol his virtues with equal fervour. When I accompanied Bob and actress Siobhán McKenna to Paris in 1972 for the express purpose of meeting the great man in the pub he had frequented with James Joyce, La Closerie des Lilas, I could appreciate the tributes of mutual friends. Lucidity, modesty, nobility and goodness were qualities I could recognize; also his shyness and penetrating blue eyes. He put me immediately at ease, interested to know I had grown up in Tuam, since he had once courted Nuala Costello, a neighbour and friend of my mother's. In her Paris days, Nuala had been the favourite companion of Lucia Joyce, the daughter of James and Nora, in whose home he had met her. Samuel Beckett's celebrated gift of companionship lay in his remarkable ability to make anyone feel the richer for having been in his presence. I remember the feeling of disappointment I had when the moment came for him to catch his train back to the country. Bob, Siobhán, and I followed him to the door, reluctant to part, and watched him disappear into the crowd, as athletic and eloquent of movement as he was of words. He left a vivid impression of deep humanity and great compassion. I can vividly recall his piercing blue eyes. "He reminds me of a one-eyed seagull," Siobhán remarked as he receded from view.

James Joyce, whose secretary Samuel Beckett once was, also occupied centre stage in our household from time to time, particularly in February 1982. My husband, with the assistance of my brother Tomás Hardiman, and a team of students, mounted a festival to celebrate what would have been the great man's hundredth birthday, February 2, the Celtic feast of Imbolc and a day after the feast day of St. Bridget, goddess cum Christian saint. Joyce had a superstitious attachment to dates of the calendar, not least his birthday, and he would, I think, have approved of the revels that erupted in Toronto. To an admirer he once said, "Don't make a hero out of me. I'm only a simple middle-class man."

Although his book *Ulysses* is, as he predicted, keeping professors busy for generations, several admirers of his writing who attended the festival were not overly burdened by learning. It was fitting that his "ordinary" readers abounded in our audiences, the kind of people Joyce had designated the true authors of *Ulysses*, which he said "was written by those I have met or known." He was referring to the undistinguished company of tailors, waiters, fruit sellers, hotel porters and bank clerks from whom he garnered his treasury of phrases. When an Irish relative complained that *Ulysses* was not fit to be read, Joyce had declared, "If *Ulysses* is not fit to be read, life is not fit to be lived!"

Some of Joyce's fans, I observed, took a voyeur's delight in Joyce's sexually explicit references and could quote, verbatim, lines from Joyce to his wife Nora that displayed

a fetish for her underwear. I knew all about this corre-
spondence myself, having once taken the part of Nora
part in a dramatic presentation of Joyce's letters, at the
University of Toronto's Hart House Theatre. I knew then
that his were not the kind of love letters I myself would
have relished and felt sorry for Nora, who, like me, was
a simple person and hailed from County Galway. When
she wrote a rare reply, she did so with a carefree absence
of punctuation or exaggeration.

Maureen Charlton, a Dublin playwright, wrote a musi-
cal entitled Nora Barnacle to mark the centenary, with
me in mind for the title role. Having memorized all the
songs, I was looking forward to the challenge of this part
but due to the demands of our Toronto festival, I had to
bow out of this engagement. The play was panned by a
critic during the Dublin Theatre Festival that year. It drew
a large crowd anyway, owing to the publicity generated by
Maureen herself when, in a fit of rage, she threw a pint
of beer over said critic's head during the press conference
held after his review appeared.

Many academics idealized the relationship between
James and Nora, who had been employed as a chamber-
maid when Joyce fell in love with her. It fascinated them
that their idol could have elevated so lowly a person, say-
ing to her, "No human being has ever stood so close to
my soul as you stand." Nora was unschooled but had a
rare gift of being natural and unpretentious in a world
of literary posturing. Her direct and spontaneous speech
lent authenticity to her husband's writings. A hundred
cares, a tithe of trouble, might have been Joyce's epitaph
for him and Nora. Theirs was a nomadic lifestyle, often
beset by sickness and creditors. Demons dogged Joyce in
the form of drink, debts, anxious publishers, and chroni-
cally failing eyesight; his deepest source of grief, however,
was the apparently incurable mental illness of his lovely

daughter, Lucia, for which he blamed himself. The shadows of some similar troubles have been sufficiently cast over my own life for me to feel deep empathy for the life led by the Joyces.

John Cage's Roaratorio, *an ambitious acoustic interpretation of* Joyce's *Finnegans Wake,* was a high point of the Toronto festival. Cage had sent technicians all over the world gathering up the aural phenomena referred to in the book, whether it was the cry of a newborn in Dublin's Hollis Street Hospital, snippets of songs, or the shrieking of seagulls over the rock of Gibraltar. The technical challenges of wrapping a cacophonous soundscape around an audience in the university's circular Convocation Hall while Cage simultaneously intoned the text would have daunted a less daring impresario than Bob. The avant garde composer also randomly conducted fragments of tunes by Irish traditional musicians, who were on hand at enormous expense along with the Canadian percussion group Nexus. "Sing anything you like for no longer than twenty minutes when I beckon," Cage had instructed Seosamh Ó hÉanaí, known also as "the king of song."

On the following evening I took part in a concert with Irish traditional musicians Liam Óg Ó Floinn, Paddy Glackin, Seamus Tansey, and Mel Mercier, all chosen by Cage for his production. An album entitled *Bloomsday* was later compiled from the singing and speaking of the great Connemara storyteller and singer Seosamh Ó hÉanaí and me on that occasion. I had raised the eyebrows, if not ire, of my fellow musicians, who were all very casual in their attire, by appearing amongst them in a very elaborate gown of flowing cream silk, which I had purchased that day after my attention was alerted to a sale in one of Toronto's leading costume rental stores. The figure-hugging dress had featured in a movie called *The Brides of Dracula*, and was going for a song, so I resolved to sing my songs in it that night! I shall never forget the look of surprise I got when I appeared on stage!

Sorel Etrog, one of the foremost Canadian sculptors and a close friend, wrote a dramatic piece entitled *Dreamchamber*, which Jim Sheridan—later the Oscar-winning the director of *My Left Foot*, but then an unknown genius at large who was living at the time in Toronto, and was a frequent visitor at our house—and I performed in Convocation Hall a few days later. It evoked the creative and iconoclastic climate of the period when Joyce and the Dadaists lived. It was an exercise in speaking mumbo-jumbo and keeping a straight face for us *reacaires*, enunciating such a passage as the following, said to feature the longest word ever printed, a mixture of English and Irish. Jim could manage it better than I could: Pappapapapparrassannuaragheallachnatullaghmonganmacmacmacwhackfalltherdebblenonthedubblandadadddydoodledand.

There was so much talk about James Joyce in our house at that time that when a neighbour, film-maker Joyce Weiland, happened to call to the door one day, my little daughter, Emer, then aged five, emerged from behind me to shyly enquire "Are you James Joyce?"

I enjoyed Cage's visits to our home, once in the company of Merce Cunningham and always with his basket of macrobiotic delicacies in hand. He memorably said of Bob, "He takes the 'im' out of impossible and puts the 'in' into infectious." This production had a profound effect on me. I could not sit in a restaurant or public place for weeks afterwards without being alert to every conversation and random sound in the air around me.

My love of Joyce led to encounters with some remarkable people. Joseph Campbell said my interpretation of a few passages from *Finnegans Wake* was "music to my ears," when he attended a performance I gave in New York at the home of Dean Morton, on the strength of which he invited me to sing and recite at his eightieth birthday party at the Princeton Club a year or two later. I was to represent his Irish ancestry, Martha Graham would dance, Isamu Noguchi was to create a sculpture, Jamake Highwater would honour Campbell's childhood fascination with the American Indian tradition.

I had watched this "Robert Redford Indian" in a TV series on PBS and I marvelled anew at his colourful regalia and imposing presence as I stood behind him in order of appearance. I did not know that he was now being exposed as a fraud by the various tribes with which he claimed ancestry. He would soon have to abandon his "Indian" persona due to public outcry, his string of aliases having already been uncovered. The melodious tones of his eloquent tribute to Joe Campbell that night betrayed no hint of this imminent fall from grace.

Other motifs from the symphonic reach of Campbell's interests and accomplishments were sounded by contemporaries and friends in glowing celebration of a life well-lived by a man well-loved.

"Follow your bliss" became a catchphrase for many after Joseph Campbell died, one invoked by him in conversation with Bill Moyers on PBS a few months earlier. "If you do follow your bliss," he famously said, "you put yourself on a kind of track that has been there all the while, waiting for you, and the life that you ought to be living is the one you are living. When you can see that, you begin to meet people who are in your field and they will open doors for you." That he was referring to the example of his own life was clearly to be seen on the night in question when

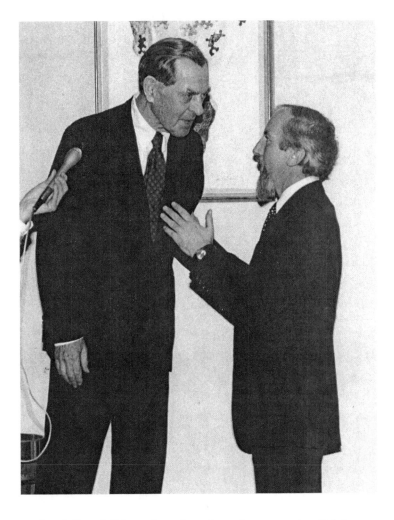

*Joseph Campbell leans down from the podium to speak to Bob just
before he officially opened our international symposium on The
Celtic Consciousness in 1978. He entitled his talk "Indian Reflec-
tions in the Castle of the Grail." Marshall McLuhan introduced
Campbell, remarking that ideals embedded in his writings were
becoming manifest in events presented by Robert O'Driscoll. Joseph
was very fond of Bob and later invited him to write a foreword to a
book he was writing about James Joyce.*

happy octogenarians of his own ilk clustered around him, an aura of bliss encircling them all. Sensing its contagion, I hovered close to their circle, Campbell drawing as ever from the established contentment of his happy marriage to Jean Erdman who had been one of his first students at Sarah Lawrence College. She was in her sixties then but still dancing with grace and poise when I attended a performance of hers that Bob arranged in Toronto, with Professor Campbell as my escort. "How beautiful she is...how beautiful!" he whispered into my ear.

Anthony Burgess also voiced his approval for my interpretations of Joyce when he heard me in a small theatre in Cork, "but you should be in a bigger hall!"

Another intellectual heavyweight of the three I knew who intuitively cut their critical teeth on the complex substance of the *Wake*, was Marshall McLuhan. A colleague of Bob's at St. Michael's College and a champion of all his efforts on behalf of Irish studies, Marshall McLuhan made *Finnegans Wake* a prominent part of the curriculum in his teaching and he often invited me into his classes to read or recite passages.

He and his wife, Corrine, were very dear to us and they were always concerned for Bob's health. Once when he had been taken into hospital from the university, I phoned Marshall to break the news to him. He listened compassionately and then said: "Now we will hang up and I will kneel down and say the rosary for Bob." As a convert to Catholicism, Marshall's deeply Christian perspective lay behind his pronouncements on the culture of the day. Ironically, this guru of communications was struck dumb for the last year of his life, having suffered a stroke. Two nights before his death he indicated his desire to visit us. He sat with his family around our dining room table and we wondered how much the benign, smiling but silent Marshall could understood of our thoughts and feel-

ings. Some weeks later we all met again, joined by Basil-
ian priest friend, Father Schook and Sorel Etrog, to lay a
plaque on his grave. It read: "The truth will set you free,"
which struck me at the time as a phrase worthy of Mar-
shall himself because the purpose of his famous epigrams,
ever reverberating in the global village, is the uncovering
of truth in all its facets to which he devoted his life.

We also engineered the first North American performance by the
Irish group The Chieftains, and the production of nine
Irish plays, including an acclaimed production of Sean
O'Casey's *Juno and the Paycock*, directed by Sean Kenny
not long before his sudden death, aged only forty-two,
and starring the incomparable Siobhān McKenna. The
opening night was marked by one of the now legendary
after-performance parties at our home in Summerhill
Gardens. Paddy Maloney, Sean Potts and Martin Fay were
there—the core members of The Chieftains. They were
known to me since my days in the Damer theatre, and I
had sung with them on various occasions. It was a strug-
gle to garner a small audience for their first Toronto gig.
I remember the night they arrived from the airport. We
wined and dined them until the small hours. After they
repaired to their hotel I was clearing away empty bottles
and glasses and airily tossed a piece of paper into the fire
with the heaps of cigarette ashes. I smiled as I read, "The
O'Driscolls have sole rights to the Chieftains in North
America—signed, Paddy Maloney." It would be another
year before they acquired an assertive New York agent and
began to truly blaze a trail around the world, succeeding
in a way that only real genius does.

The plays of Sean O'Casey captured the imagination of
Toronto audiences, amateur performances at St. Michael's
College and elsewhere in the city paving the way for the

more lavish professional productions that Bob would mount. Coming events cast their shadow when he and I played Mr. and Mrs. Grigson, a stereotypical drunken husband and long suffering wife, in *Shadow of a Gunman*, in which Clare Coulter, later to become a leading light in the theatrical life of Toronto, upstaged us all. Eileen O'Casey, widow of the playwright came to stay later, when *Juno and the Paycock* was in rehearsal, to the joy of our household. Many nights of rollicking fun ensued in the company of the professional cast—all leading interpreters of her husband's work. Eileen subsequently lectured around Ontario and made our house her base for several weeks. In her late seventies she was one of the most beautiful and gracious women I had ever encountered. Possessed of a flawless complexion, every fleeting expression registered on her mobile features. Content during his lifetime to bask in the reflected glory of her husband, she had "star presence" and was charismatically herself in every gathering. She evoked peals of laughter in the hilarious slant she had on every event of the day. We were so attuned to one another that I was taken for her daughter during one of our shopping forays in Toronto.

Michael and Gráinne Yeats were other welcome visitors to our home. Michael Yeats inherited his mother's level headed practicality and his marriage to Gráinne, daughter of the nationalist historian, P.S. O'Hegarty, led to a fundamental shift in the Yeats lineage from Anglo to native Irish roots. With a country house set in the Connemara *gaeltacht*, theirs was an Irish-speaking household and Michael shared a musicological interest in traditional music with Gráinne, an accomplished harpist and singer. As executor of his father's estate, he was endlessly patient in his shrewd handling of the demands of Yeats scholars, besides pursuing an international career in politics and holding a seat in the Irish Senate. As one who has had

My Aunt Lil (left) at the Sligo Yeats Summer School with Professor Lorna Reynolds, who lived at our Toronto house for months on end when she was collaborating with Bob on one of their book projects. Lorna is conversing with Tom Kenny of Galway's popular Kenny's Bookshop and Art Gallery. Standing beside him is Anne Yeats, daughter of the poet.

greatness thrust upon him, he appeared to take it with a grain of salt. When I first heard him speak publicly in Sligo, he began with a story about a remark overheard when two locals in a rural town were reading a notice that said, Lecture on Yeats. Speculating that it might be some new class of vegetable, one said to the other, "What, do you suppose, is a Yeat?" They pronounced the name to rhyme with "beet" as many country people did.

Gráinne, Michael, and his sister Anne—who celebrated her fifty-sixth birthday in our home—became good friends of ours. They admired Bob's drive and the eager-

ness with which he involved them in many of his extrav-
aganzas. Bob once lured Gráinne and Anne to Toronto
along with Jo and Liam Miller of the Dolmen Press, so
that they might confer together on the ideal mounting of
the production of W.B. Yeats's Cuchulainn cycle of plays
(that had been cooked up during the Ó Riada visit). James
Flannery, renowned as a fine tenor and for his work on
Yeats's drama, was their unanimous choice of director.
James bore the brunt of Bob's maverick ways, having to
coordinate a multimedia production that was top-heavy
with celebrities—a task made especially difficult because
Bob would periodically intervene to stir up some issue of
contention amongst cast members. However, the natural
diplomacy of Gully Stanford, Bob's able executive assist-
ant, often saved the day. Gully had forsaken Classics at
Oxford to pursue a theatre career in Toronto and live in
our house. "Bob seemed to revel in setting the cat among
the pigeons and then take perverse delight in sorting out
the mess himself," James recalled when I saw him recently
in Atlanta.

The reality of Yeats, the man, became more immediate
for me in the proximity of his offspring. Anne related
how the poet, who only became a father in his fifties,
sometimes failed to recognize her on the street as a young
girl, so engrossed was he in thought; indeed, he once
enquired of her as she boarded a bus with him, "Do I
know you?" On another occasion, he arose from the table
after a five-course dinner, with the query, "Have I eaten?"
I was delighted to come across James Stephen's account
of a visit he paid the great man, to find him complaining
bitterly about how difficult it was to write when his hands
were frozen with the cold. This endeared me further to
W.B., coping, as I write, with this damp and draughty cli-
mate.

"I've found out how to conquer cold feet," Yeats

declared. "My feet are never cold now. Come over to the bed, Stephens," he said, "and I'll show you." He threw the coverlets off. He was fully dressed under the bedclothes, and had a dressing gown on over his ordinary clothes. But it was his legs that delighted Stephens. "There," he said, "you can't get cold feet if you wear these." He had on a pair of huge rubber fisherman's boots that reached to his thighs. "Inside these," he said cunningly, "I have on a pair of woolly slippers, and I'm as warm as toast.

We did not, however, encounter many contemporary followers of the mystic AE, who had been as prominent a figure as Yeats, Joyce, and O'Casey at the beginning of the twentieth century in Ireland. AE lived according to a vision he had of a greater life, saying, "I know that the golden age is all about us and that we can, if we will, dispel that opacity and have vision once more of the ancient beauty." AE may have had his head in the clouds when he painted the fairies he saw in the woods, but he had his feet on the ground as he led a farmers' cooperative movement that ensured the prosperity of rural areas and fostered a communitarian spirit in country people. He cycled around rural Ireland and farmers would gather at the crossroads to hear him speak. What he had to say was often above their heads and it was fortunate that a parish priest was usually on hand to put it into plain language: "What Mr. Russell would like you to know, lads, is—if you want a pig you will have to pay a shilling!"

Bob had devoted himself to the vision of AE and for a time a painting by AE hung in our living room; entitled *Meeting with a Celestial Being*, the painting depicted a luminescent archetypal being that seemed to preside over people and landscape. My husband had introduced me to the works of AE, but I only began to appreciate such paintings when I learned about the nature forces he portrayed, invisible to most people and most certainly to me.

I memorized two pages of a 3000-word poem entitled "Natura," written by Brunetto Latini, who had been a teacher of Dante's in the thirteenth century. His description of this magnificent being corresponded, I thought, with visions of archetypal spirits recorded by AE. Goethe reinforced this description for me as well, perceiving nature as a supernatural being who, paradoxically, is "always changing while always remaining herself," while conducting a continuous metamorphosis of dying and becoming in every plant that grows. Rudolf Steiner's writings later shed a more scientific light on the unifying activities of archetypal and elemental beings in nature that were so often the subject of AE's musings and works of art. The more I studied these phenomena the more my wonder grew and the more attentive I became in observation.

The benign spirit of AE made its presence felt in our household when Pamela Travers, author of *Mary Poppins*, came to stay. She described herself as an apprentice file or poet to AE at a time when he was growing old and she was quite a young woman. They shared a sense of "the secret but communicative life of trees," and when she, an Australian, came to visit him in Ireland, AE would take her with him into the woodland, setting up his easel

This photograph appeared in London's Evening Standard *newspaper while I was staying with Pamela Travers. It accompanied a favourable review of my one-woman show by Stan Gebler-Davies, a well-known Irish journalist who had introduced himself to me after the performance the night before, which Pamela Travers had also attended. It was one of the many Irish events held in London to mark the Sense of Ireland festival in 1981.*

where he felt the strongest vibrations. And even though AE declared, "It is not now my time to burst into leaves and flowers," he was a prolific artist who completed at least one canvas every week of his life.

Mrs. Travers talked to our children about *Mary Poppins* but delighted us adults with her memories of AE, whose name was always on the tip of her tongue. She described his weekly "at home" gatherings when fellow writers came "to drink from his generous chalice" and where conversation always blossomed. She said it was like a crossroads, where meetings took place between people who were on a quest to find one another. AE often reminded her that, "your own will come to you." She read us a passage from AE's *Candle of Vision* about the attraction of affinity: "I need not seek, for what was my own would come to me. I knew that all I met was part of myself and that what I could not comprehend was related by affinity to some yet unrealized forces in my being."

I was reminded of some useful advice I had picked up from AE's writing; that we could cancel out negative thoughts by thinking of their opposites. He believed, as I do, that human energy and human experience always reflects whatever is most present in consciousness and that we cannot make changes on the outside until there has been a positive inner change to begin with. I had also taken great comfort in something he said about our being able to love only what is our own and that what is our own could never be lost to us.

AE had sent for Pamela when he was dying in Bournemouth, and she had cared for him while other friends gathered on the lawn outside the nursing home awaiting their turn for a last farewell. She noticed that the full moon reflected the sun on its northern journey on the night he died, a sign given in the *Bhagavad Gita* to mark the passing of a great spirit. "Never before or since had I seen such a moon. It came up slowly out of the sea, full, golden and enormous, dazzling as the sun." He had told her once that he could hardly tell where his being ended and another began. "We are haunted by unknown comrades in many moods, whose naked souls reveal themselves in an unforgettable instant." Some years later I stayed at Pamela Travers's Chelsea home and was amused to hear her housekeeper remark, as she noticed the self-portrait of AE on the cover of a biography of him I was reading: "Why, that is the gentleman who often stands behind the rocking horse in the hallway!" She didn't know his name but saw his ghostly likeness in the picture.

I promised my hostess that when I returned to Ireland, I would go with my husband to Mount Jerome, one of Dublin's largest and most famous cemeteries, and then report back to her on the current state of AE's grave. We found him buried amongst 275,000 others on the forty-seven-acre site. His grave—set among highly ornate crypts, romantic broken columns, weeping angels and imposing memorials—was entirely overrun with weeds. Bob began a campaign to restore this sacred burial ground. Soon money poured in through our mail box, the donations of several friends and acquaintances of the great man who were still living, including Lord Moyne, Lord Dunsany, and Monk Gibbon, who had been a young protégé of AE's and who had written a poem as a tribute to the rare spirit who had brought so many to the realization of their own divinity.

> *I have known one great man,*
> *One man alone to rise*
> *Shoulder and head above*
> *All his contemporaries ...*

With the help of our friends Maurice Henry and Anthony

Cronin, Bob succeeded in raising enough money to erect a bust of AE in Merrion Square and to surround his grave with fine green Connemara marble. He was in daily contact with Pamela Travers and together they decided on the following epitaph to be carved upon AE's headstone:

> I moved among men and places, and in living I learned the truth at last. I know I am a spirit, and that I went forth in old time from the self-ancestral to labours yet unaccomplished.

The literati and glitterati of Ireland were there for the unveiling of the headstone, the occasion marked by Anthony Cronin's reading of a passage from the *Bhagavad Gita*, as Pamela had instructed. It had been a lovely sunny day and many were out in their finery. However, at the mention of the word rain, the heavens had opened and the assembled gathering had to run for cover to the nearest pub, where a generous American friend provided refreshments for all and sundry. A very old woman emerged from the shadows of the pub to inquire of me if the celebration had anything to do with "a man who lived some years ago by the name of AE," explaining that her sister had been his housekeeper. Her face was radiant as she extolled his virtues and his kindness to her entire family; so vivid was her memory of him that one could hardly believe that fifty years had elapsed since he had passed away. I took her appearance as a sign that the beneficent being we were honouring was giving us his blessing.

AE visited America a few times at the request of the government, as an advisor on the question of rural civilization. He greatly impressed the experts in Washington. Monk Gibbon reports: "On his last visit there, a question arose in a Washington discussion on the contest that was then raging between property rights and personal rights.

The bust of AE sculpted by Jerome Connors, erected in Merrion Square in 1981 thanks to Bob's fundraising campaign, here lamentably obscured by overgrowth as his grave once was.

He reached for a piece of paper and pencil and said he thought he could 'make a poem' about that, scribbling on it some lines":

All that fierce talk of Thine and Mine,
If the true Master made His claim
The world he fashioned so divine?
What could they answer did He say
When did I give My world away?

In obedience to Pamela Travers, Bob and I had gone in search of a particular translation of the *Bagavad Gita*, that of the American theosophist William Q. Judd. We did not find it in the library of the Irish Theosophical Society although we engaged in a lively exchange with alert older members of the society there. We were eventually led to a retirement home where we met Miss Emerson, former teacher at Alexandria College, a posh Protestant girl's school. She was a direct descendant of Ralph Waldo Emerson. Now in her nineties, she was as lively and bright eyed as a person half her age. She had the coveted book and could pinpoint the passage that mentioned the rain, which Pamela had instructed we read at the graveside unveiling. As we left the building I remembered a quotation from Emerson that I had recently jotted down about there being nothing of more importance in the end than the integrity of a person's own mind, a quality much in evidence in his descendant with whom we had spent the previous hour.

My keen involvement with Bob's extracurricular activities ensured that I was following my bliss as Joseph Campbell recommended. It would take time for me to synthesize the glimmers of understanding that stirred my heart and mind as

I pursued a unique course of study in the open university of life. Drawn as I was to the fruits and blossoms of esoteric thought, my immersion in the creative imagination of the great writers I have mentioned, sowed seeds in consciousness that would continue to ripen throughout my life. What effect concepts derived from books had on me would have to be tested in more exacting ways before I could myself lay claim to an integrity of mind. The authors referred to in this chapter laid bare the contents of their souls, either directly through poetry or through the characters of their novels and plays. Because their senses remained alert to everyday passing impressions, they could draw on a rich treasury in recollection. Only experiences that have made an impression on the senses can be so vividly recalled as images to enrich the soul and provide ground for further contemplation, as Wordsworth so clearly demonstrated with the daffodils. I wanted to be fully present in and for the world and to appreciate the mystery inherent in every new encounter.

All the significant contours of my biography have developed through meeting a particular person. There are those who appear to work "in time" for the sake of the "timeless," implanting seeds of fresh development in the social order as they move through life. New cultural impulses sometimes come dramatically to light in a particular human being and in the next chapter I will introduce my readers to one such person.

8

On the Road to Meikle Seggie

*When the artist is alive in any person, whatever his kind of
work may be, he becomes an inventive, searching, daring,
self-expressing creature. He becomes interesting to other
people. He disturbs, upsets, enlightens, and he opens ways
for a better understanding.*
ROBERT HENRI

My first meeting with Richard Demarco took place in a lecture
theatre of the University of Toronto's Faculty of Archi-
tecture in the late seventies. The room was plunged into
darkness as a dynamic man of slight build gave voluble
testimony to accompany a display of slides, which were
being shown in support of his thesis that some contem-
porary art was beginning to resemble that of prehistoric
cultures and artifacts. His radical views were vividly
expressed as we feasted our eyes on these new and excit-
ing images. Waving his arms to great effect he declared:
"Our world is contaminated with too much art, and
modern art cannot remain in one place long enough so
as to become acceptable to future generations. There are

too many art galleries, too many self-styled artists con-
cerned only with aesthetics and with buying and selling
easily transportable artifacts!" He mentioned his friends,
famous artists Joseph Beuys and Paul Neagu a lot—they
had demonstrated to him the futility of trying to contain
art in a gallery. "The art world is the most dangerous place
imaginable if you want to search for truth," he cautioned
the audience, "because what you can end up searching for,
if you're not careful, is so-called success! Art should be
about risk and renewal, not about the shelter of an art
gallery!"

It was a fascinating performance, a delivery seasoned
with hyperbole, anecdote, aphorism and paradox, charged
with high voltages of energy. After about two hours, my
husband nudged me, reminding me that it was time to
leave. We were slinking out of the hall in the darkness
when Demarco took a leap off the platform in our direc-
tion. "Wait! Who are you and where are you going?" he
demanded. "Our names are Robert and Treasa O'Driscoll
and we are on our way to the Colonnade Theatre, where
my wife will perform a one-woman show tonight..." my
husband obediently murmured.

"I'll be there!" he cried as we scrambled to find pen and
paper in the darkness to jot down the Bloor Street address
and time of performance.

True to his word, Demarco did turn up later at my per-
formance. His force of presence was palpable; he was the
most visibly and audibly appreciative audience member I
could hope for. When I left the stage after taking a final
bow, a firm hand grasped my shoulder and I heard his
insistent whisper in my ear, "I invite you to perform in my
gallery during this year's Edinburgh Festival!" So an asso-
ciation with Richard began that would gather momentum
over many years.

An Italo-Scot, with a devastating combination of Latin

and Celtic fire, Demarco burst upon the consciousness of the art world in 1967 with his prodigious First Edinburgh Open 100 Exhibition, and thereby established his newly opened gallery as a bastion of contemporary art in Britain. By 1973, newspapers glowed with reviews of his endeavours. I memorized the following description in a daily I was reading during a visit to him in Edinburgh: "He is Scotland's Dionysus, its Mars, its Mercury, its Vulcan, one of the great, charming, difficult, recklessly expansive, priceless visionaries of the world."

A kind of blood brotherhood was forged between him and Bob. Richard, intrigued by the fact that Bob was in the throes of creating the Centre for Celtic Studies at the time, was determined to draw the world's attention to the Celtic origins of Europe, to a prehistoric culture that, he believed, made the Renaissance seem much more a sunset than a dawning. The re-awakening of interest in places of pilgrimage is significant because, in Richard's opinion, it puts modern people off balance, causing them to revert to intuition and imagination. Demarco's inspiring philosophy, his magnetism and vitality won our hearts when he made his first visit to our house in Toronto after my Colonnade show, deciding there and then to make it his Canadian home. He was on a whirlwind tour of North America, seeking to attract participants, and artists in particular, for a forthcoming Edinburgh Arts Journey that we agreed to join in 1977.

Our engaging guest had convinced me that it is not the finished object but the act of creating a work of art that is important, the exercise of the imagination that precedes it, the love of work for the sake of doing things well that is inherent in it. A need of our times was urgently working inside many of the artists we would meet on the journey, Richard said. The artistic process was a way of life for those who, instinctively recoiling from the false glories of an artificial environment, live in harmony with the natural world. I began to understand how artists who delight in the observation of the natural world, in its ever changing patterns of growth and decay, come close to the discovery of universal laws upon which all of creation depends. In recognizing the forces that give form to natural things, the artist can create new forms that add to what is already "given." The new ideas I was grasping, in listening to Richard talk into the small hours, were already beginning to expand my mental horizons, stirring enthusiasm in me for the adventure of the journey ahead. New ideas signal new beginnings. Every turning point in life, I find, introduces a new way of looking at the world that arises either before or after the event itself. I prepared for the journey with growing anticipation and dusted off my poetic repertoire since Demarco assured me that the journey would afford many opportunities for me to share my recitations and songs.

Richard initiated the Arts Journey, a literal pilgrimage, in 1972 as part of an international summer school for artists interested in exploring Scotland's Celtic roots. Gradually broadening in concept, these journeys took the form of annual pilgrimages or rites of summer. By 1976, the journey had expanded into an odyssey of 7,500 miles, a sixty-three day expedition in which Richard led participants over land and water, to explore hills and rivers and underground caverns associated with legend and folklore from Malta to Sardinia, Italy and Yugoslavia, and back through Italy to France, England, Wales, Ireland, and Scotland.

As it approximated the expression of his purpose, the Arts Journey became more difficult, more of a financial and physical impossibility, causing Demarco to become all the more eager for it to continue. The act of daring inherent in luring a disparate group of artists, professors, housewives and joiners to parts unknown by the power of suggestion, having given them only scant knowledge as to where they were going or whom they would meet, while defying all the common rubrics of travel, could not be advertised in a tourist magazine and was not for the faint-hearted. Juxtaposed with the discovery of little-known artistic wonders in out of the way places, Bob and I discovered, were days of feast or famine, aborted schedules, missed connections, quarrels, reconciliations, and the whole spectrum of human interactions. I can remember one vivid scene of a ravenous few vying for a solitary sandwich on a remote train platform somewhere in Italy! While there was a main track to be followed and although a sum of money had changed hands to begin with, it was less than sufficient for the exigencies that unexpectedly arose when routes were altered without warning to accommodate last-minute participants and other variables.

The first step of our 1977 journey was a visit Richard, Bob and I made with Louis le Brocquy, an Irish painter living in southern France, and Sorel Etrog to the special unit of Her Majesty's Prison in Barlinnie, a forlorn world of its own near the city of Glasgow, where the spirit of rehabilitation prevailed against all odds. Demarco had arranged for me to sing and recite there for a truly captive audience of the six "most dangerous men in Scotland," who were on that occasion surrounded by fourteen guards. I told them that ancient Irish society honoured poets, harpers, judges, in that order of merit, having discovered in talking to the men that all six were musicians and/or poets.

I remember one in particular, a quiet young man who was dressed in his best, sporting a fine moustache, his thick waves of auburn hair brushed back from his freckled forehead. He shared a poignant verse about loss, his face continuing to haunt me after I learned he had taken his own life a few weeks later.

I am surrounded by members of my "captive" audience after a performance in the Special Unit of Her Majesty's Prison in Barlinnie, Scotland. Jimmy Boyle, fit and cheerful, stands at my side. Bob is on the far right.

Jimmy Boyle (later released), who had established himself as a sculptor while serving a life sentence, was the obvious leader of the group, an articulate and healthy-looking man with an infectious zest for life. He owed a lot to Richard, who had sent an art therapist to visit the unit some years before. She threw a lump of clay on the floor and challenged the men to make what they could of it. When Jimmy Boyle picked it up, he had the sensation of knowing the feel of it already and was intrigued by the shape that began to form in his hands. Before long, Demarco was on the scene to let him know that he was arranging an exhibition for him, which, to confound all naysayers, Richard planned to display in a church! While serving a life sentence in the special unit, Boyle produced many sculptures and wrote his autobiography, *A Sense of Freedom*, published the year we visited him. Since his release from prison he has worked with young offenders, published more books, and become a businessman. Jimmy, once rated Scotland's most violent man, is now regarded as its most famous reformed prisoner.

This unit was an experiment and it gave the inmates scope to explore their creativity. They created colourful Mexican-type murals and decorated cells. Beauty had restored itself to the hearts of these men as the only real antidote for violence.

When play begins to disappear or is absent, beauty makes its departure little by little, as the distortions of life become more and more pervasive. This is the hidden reality behind the many lives that are turned to crime. To re-form is to restore the human being to his rightful connection with beauty, truth and goodness. The practical problem to be solved by everyone is, as Emerson so keenly noted, "how to spend a day nobly." I observed how much this effort was being addressed in the unit and I longed for the day when all prisons would be centres of rehabilitation. Since then, however, the emphasis on law and order has grown more urgent in the world, even in Canada, where there has been a decrease in crime over the past twenty years. While the impulse toward rehabilitation has seemed to weaken in the political arena, it has become more obvious that people do not improve by being punished but by being given joy and purpose in living. We discussed these matters after the gates of Barlinnie prison closed behind our little group, more than ever thankful now for our individual freedom and, in the weeks that followed, not inclined to complain about anything!

Louis le Brocquy was a peaceful presence in our midst, a man who listens and looks into the innerness of things.

Once remarking that his brain was in his hands, he revealed the faces of Yeats, Joyce and Beckett to people anew, in a series of studies. Looking from within the quiet of his mind, he allowed his hands to guide the paintbrush into shifting images, uncovering in each ghostly likeness the fleeting expressions of lively intelligence characteristic of both subject and painter. Born in 1916, he is Ireland's eminent and most internationally renowned artist. He never attended art school, preferring to learn by direct contact with the great works of the past, as he travelled through Europe as a young man. He was there for the beginning of the journey and we met him again in the Demarco gallery on our return to Edinburgh in August of that year, where his exhibition of the heads of W.B. Yeats was being mounted. His mother, Sybil, had been a friend of Yeats and he encountered the poet often as a boy. I performed my one-woman show, directed by James Flannery in Toronto, against the setting of these works, with le Brocquy, Flannery, Etrog and other fellow travellers in the audience. Their enthusiastic applause must have been noted by the reporter whose favourable review appeared in *The Scotsman* next day.

The "myriad mindedness" of Yeats, captured in le Brocquy's painterly "themes and variations," reflects the living, intuitive thinking that enlivened Yeats's poetic vision in bringing forth "Sailing to Byzantium," "The Second Coming," "Easter 1916," "Ribh Considers Christian Love Insufficient," "The Wild Swans at Coole"—some of the poems I delighted in reciting that evening. His daughter, Anne, when she saw the paintings for the first time in Dublin, found it a "haunting and unforgettable experience," to be confronted by so many familiar images of her late father that filled her with "an astonishing feeling of vigour and intellectual aliveness. I could almost see my father," she said, "about to sit forward on the edge of his chair, talking with animation and waving, as he did so, a hand in emphasis." Louis generously presented me with one of these charcoal drawings after my performance. It hangs on the wall next to my desk, a continuing source of inspiration and memory.

The sculptor Sorel Etrog first entered our lives in 1970 when his patrons, Samuel and Ayela Zachs, sponsored a Toronto run for The Oxford Playhouse production of the plays of Francis Warner and Beckett, in which I played a part as already mentioned. Bob later commissioned him to design the Celtic Arts production of Yeats's Cuchulainn cycle of plays. Sorel was a frequent visitor to our home and decided to join us on the journey when he would make the acquaintance of Louis le Brocquy. Sorel's portrait of Beckett, starkly different to the one painted by Le Brocquy, is another prized possession, given by the artist to mark the birth of our son, Declan, in 1974. Executed with the dynamic intensity characteristic of Etrog's style, it captures the enduring penetration of Beckett's unflinching gaze. Where le Brocquy's metamorphosis seemed to emanate from the paint itself, Etrog, accustomed to producing sculptures of monumental scale, presented a fixed portrait that suggests the single mindedness of Beckett's genius. Sorel's sculptures are familiar and well loved landmarks in Toronto. He uses massive bolts and hinges of heavy machinery, steel plating and sheet metal, bending and shaping the material of industrialism with Goliath-like intent as if in defiance of it, while shaping it into the dynamic structures that now grace gardens, industrial buildings and cities around the world. The works of Etrog and le Brocquy represented a balance of opposites in my mind, making me realize that it was no accident that such a combination of elements should have joined forces in the special unit as if to assist in the urge towards freedom, reconciliation and creativity to which we had been privy.

Bob referred to the Edinburgh Arts Journey as "a deli-
cately wrought web held together by friendship and faith."
I regarded the expedition as a moving mystery school,
its wisdom derived from the juxtaposition of height-
ened experience and mundane events of the journey as
we made our way in tandem, participant observers in an
unfolding drama. According to some Irish lore imparted
to me by Seán Ó Riada, we are attended in our journey
through life by three magical elements—*ceo* meaning mist,
ceol or music, and *seoltóireacht* or sailing, a combination
of poetry, song, and story, ingredients essential to me in
every performance I gave. I had regaled my Demarco Gal-
lery audience with the following story:

*It happened that Fionn Mac Cumhail and his heroic band were
once resting after a battle when a debate arose between them as to
what could be considered the finest music in the world—was it the
clash of shields on the battle field, the first sound of the cuckoo in
spring, the laughter of a young girl? The possibilities were all but
exhausted when one of them turned to Fionn.*
    "Tell us, chief," he ventured, "what do you think?"
    *"The music of what happens," answered the great Fionn defini-
tively. "That is the finest music in the world!"*

The journey of life gives entry into "the music of what
happens" by way of presence, poetry and pilgrimage,
three elements of the Celtic way which may be adapted
to any time or place, at home or abroad. Demarco's jour-
ney was a pilgrimage that awakened poetic consciousness,
poetry being the secret life of all the arts, the mysterious
movement of the soul between self and things, revealed
in whatever medium it works through, be it literature,
architecture, drama, music or dance. The visual arts had
been a closed book to me, a book that was now opening
up though direct contact with the makers of the works

themselves. "This moment, the grace of this one rapturous moment, is the place of pilgrimage to which I am a pilgrim," was a line by Paul Murray that I often recited inwardly as the days progressed, in a rich palimpsest of impressions. Juxtaposition of elements arose in serendipity as if we were guided by some inner need to find the connecting links between things. When I saw the Nuraghe towers in Sardinia they called to mind the round towers that dot our Irish landscape. The experience of winding my way by a damp earthen spiral pathway to the top, then rounding down again in pitch darkness to emerge into the light with a great sense of relief, remains vivid still in memory. Like the bee-hive huts in County Kerry, and the Irish burial chambers I was familiar with, these towers gave evidence of human ingenuity and ritual that would endure for thousands of years. I was eager to visit the museum in Cagliari where artifacts from the Nuraghes were on display, ancient carvings of stone, narrow bone-like figures, and household implements made of clay.

Our next port of call was Nice and the Meaght Foundation exhibition in which, to my great surprise, I could identify an unmistakable similarity between the austere sculptures of Alberto Giacometti on display and the artifacts I had just seen in Sardinia that now seemed like maquettes for these larger works. The journey was teaching me about the spirit that connects places and people. This relates to the phenomenon of presence. Richard explained it this way: "The human presence upon the earth is a blessed presence. What we have been trying to do is not fall in love with any product of human activity, but with the human presence itself, or to be more precise, the divinity of the human presence as it reveals itself through the enduring work of human hands... It is our duty to go beyond the work, to defend the mystery of the presence of the artist in a particular time and place and his relationship with every image, concept and stone, he or she used to make the work, directing our attention to the meaning and beauty of these creations."

A ferry ride from Nice landed us in Corsica, a mountain island in the Mediterranean that is an island like no other. Our Toronto friends Bill and Cathy Graham had urged Bob and me to visit them there during their annual summer sojourn but Richard was reluctant to part with us and insisted on our going en masse. Firmly hugging the wheel of a rented car we had all piled into, he navigated a jagged mountain slope in what became the most nerve racking car ride of my life, the striking features of the landscape were a welcome source of distraction from the thought of imminent death. Freely roaming and grazing sheep were numerous and much of the mountainous terrain was covered in maquis—a scrub of broom, gorse, juniper, laurel, and myrtle mingled with heather, lavender, thyme, and sage, the combined aroma of which ever permeates the Corsican air. I now understood why Napoleon's fabled yearning for his native island during his years of power was rooted in this distinctive scent.

We had warned Bill and Cathy in advance of our arrival, and the magical feast spread out for us in the restful shade of their colourful garden was gratefully acknowledged by a much larger company of hungry and road weary guests than our hosts had originally bargained for. Thus fortified, our fellow travellers parted company with us, Richard assuring us that they would all return before long. It was a joy to spend a few days with Bill and Cathy in their home away from home, the stately simplicity of their white-walled villa somehow reflective of its owners lack of pretension and purity of purpose. It is said that Corsica is rich beyond wealth and that human rather than material values are the measure of its people. Bill and Cathy, being also of this character, are regarded as kindred by the people of the place. Like their home in Toronto, this Corsican location had become an equally cherished centre of hospitality for family and friends from near and far where we too were extended the full measure of Graham generosity, good cooking, fine wine, conversation and *joie de vivre* in an idyllic setting. Only the lure of the Edinburgh Arts Journey could interrupt this idyll, Richard and company soon enticed us to rejoin their ranks, Paris bound now for further adventure.

For our second journey in 1979, Demarco had managed to procure, skilful crew and all, a three-masted sailing ship, *The Marques*. When formerly rigged as a barque, this ship was called the HMS *Beagle*, known to a multitude of viewers throughout the British Isles when it featured in a popular BBC television series on the voyage of Darwin. Demarco's was a voyage of self-discovery, an exercise in consciousness and imagination that tested the stamina of each participant. From unfurling sails to caulking the decks, keeping watch, cooking, cleaning, and attending seminars with participating teachers on a wide range of topics, the activities the voyagers engaged in on the journey served to increase sensory awareness and the powers of attention in all travellers. I cannot give much personal account of the sea voyage however, having boarded the ship only once while it was docked in Dublin, when the gentle, almost imperceptible rocking of the sturdy vessel in a seemingly still Dun Laoghaire harbour made me violently seasick!

Richard Demarco took to the high seas with his Edinburgh Arts Journey in 1979. The three-masted sailing ship, The Marques, *was rigged as a barque and known as* The Beagle *when it featured in a popular television series on the voyage of Charles Darwin.*

Richard at the helm of The Marques, *leading an exercise in consciousness, imagination, and self-discovery that was also a sea voyage that tested the physical stamina of every participant.*

Bob's mother had flown from Newfoundland to look after our children when we travelled in 1977. My sisters Anne and Frances, both of whom had children of their own, took charge of our little ones when I resumed my bardic function on the journey once again, joining the overland route through France and Italy. The token performing bear, I had agreed to being trotted out in caves or in palaces as the occasion demanded.

One such location was the enormous palace-cum-cave that was the villa of Count Panza di Biumo in Varese. Collecting was a mission that Count Panza had vigorously pursued since the mid-fifties. He eventually stopped buying for a while, choosing to divest himself of a surfeit of priceless paintings and sculptures, lending them—or giving them away in his huge bequest to New York's Guggenheim Museum. He was, needless to say, one of Richard's friends, and we were all invited to view the ancient service wing of the villa, which had been converted into a row of grotto-like cells of colour and light, monastic in ambience, much of it the permanent installation of innovative American light artists such as James Turell and Robert Irwin. Seeing them, I was left with the vivid impression of a series of magic wardrobes, each one leading to the further surprise of the next. Every cubicle of darkness was illumined by a narrow shaft of light or dancing rainbow of colour penetrating through tailored openings and fissures in wall or ceiling. I remembered what Goethe said about the struggle between forces of light and darkness giving rise to colour, remarking that "colours are the deeds and sufferings of light." Personality likewise arises out of the struggle between Self and soul in every human being, feeling being a kind of light in the soul that can disperse into a colourful display of personality. Dwelling in the meditative silence of these installations, I noticed how I became aware of the light only in contrast to the surrounding darkness when every material thing, even my own body, is nothing but spent light. A "flash" of inspiration can also appear as a light that dissipates the muddle of confusion it illuminates and my experience of the journey was beginning to give rise to many such moments.

We moved on from Varese to nearby Milan, where a retrospective exhibition of the work of Italian sculptor Fausto Melotti, who was turning eighty at the time, attracted large numbers of people. We arrived too late and found the gallery had closed for the day. We were just about to drown our disappointment in ice creams when John Hale, a sculptor whose studio we were to visit next day, serendipitously crossed our path. "Melotti is a good friend of mine!" he cried. "Let me take you to meet him. It will be far more instructive and enjoyable to talk to him in his studio than to look at his work in a gallery!" Leading us down a side street, we reached Melotti's studio within minutes and were warmly welcomed by the celebrated artist, who spoke to us in mellifluous Italian that was simultaneously translated by his assistant into English. She explained how much his work was influenced by a background in mathematics and physics, although he had graduated from university with degrees in music and engineering. I looked around at the diminutive, finely wrought, curved, flat and linear shapes, delicately perched upon metal rods, all barely asserting their identity as material objects. Elusive, fragile and refined, their musical phrasing, modulation and rhythm was almost audible to the ear as if resonant with something beyond the range of the senses.

Melotti cheerfully led us from the main floor of his studio down to the three other floors below, all full of a mesmerizing range of artworks, not one of which resembled another. The temperature dropped dramatically as we descended, until we were standing in what seemed to me a catacomb of old. It was then that Demarco, who always chose his moment well, invited me to sing for Melotti. "Ūna Bhān" (or "Fair Una") was the song that came immediately to mind, an eighteenth-century lament by a poet whose beloved had died. As I sang the last verse, my eye fell on a splendid sculpture of a boat, finely fashioned from scraps and nuggets of brass, the paper-thin sails appearing to float in mid-air. I sensed a mythic connotation and thought too of *The Marques* that remained always vivid in the minds of many of the group. When

I had finished there was a hush, and then Melotti said, "That reminds me of Tristan and Isolde ... what is the song about?" Translating the Irish verse into my own words, I recited:

> *I would lie with you on a boat in full sail*
> *Beside your virgin body that no man has assailed.*
> *If I am never to rest with you in my life,*
> *Death must take me too, to lie with you,*
> *unconsummated wife.*

How precious such moments appear now in memory and how grateful I am for the Celtic continuum of song that seeks its expression in the most unexpected of circumstances!

Bob wrote a comprehensive account in *The Celtic Consciousness* of his conversations with fellow travellers on *The Marques*, of the heightened awareness that came with approaching sites by sea. They encompassed the Celtic world, tracing the route of Tristan and Isolde to the Scilly Islands and Brittany and in a final dramatic moment, discovering Carnac by moonlight. He noticed that Demarco's approach to pilgrimage was similar to that of the early monastic voyagers, who were of a mystical persuasion and more concerned with mysteries of the human spirit than with any possible association with actual or imagined historical events. What was important was that something should happen here and now in one's mind and will.

One dialogue that Bob recounts is his conversation with Norman Mommens, a remarkable Belgian born sculptor/philosopher who carved in marble. Norman lived with his wife, the writer Patience Grey, in the Apuglia region of southern Italy on a farm devoid of electricity or other modern conveniences. They were perfectly content, she remarking that, "People are only now beginning to realize how much they do not need." Norman told Bob that he had long been expecting to meet such a group, which he identified as "a vortex of renewal moving across Europe." His parting comment to Bob was: "Never, it would seem, has there been a greater need for the traditional journey or sacred pilgrimage. Only through it can some people know their own soul and their own sacred plot of earth, as if for the first time." I reminded Bob that T.S. Eliot conveyed a similar message—that the purpose of all our exploring would be realized when we returned to where we started from, discovering it as though for the very first time. "We might then realize that we did not have to go anywhere, we just have to come back to ourselves and know that every journey is a process of discovering ourselves." Bob nodded his agreement with my words.

The journey awakened a true appreciation for the beauty of landscape in me, for the joy of human companionship and the music of what happens. I also discovered the importance of location in relation to art. The work of an artist, seen in the context of his studio and chosen landscape appeared as a totally natural expression of his being. This was eminently true in the case of John Hale, a sculptor we visited in the Lake Como area, whose work reflects the rolling hills and ancient mounds that surrounded his home. He remarked when we arrived at his studio, "You have the look of people who have come by sea. Destiny happens to the aware!"

The importance of Demarco's work has come to be recognized. In 2007 he was awarded Poland's Gloria Artis medal for his cultural activities in that country; in the same year, he was appointed a Commander of the British Empire at home. The year also marked an enormous retrospective exhibi-

tion entitled Demarco's Festival at the Scottish National
Portrait Gallery, celebrating Richard's sixty years of serv-
ice to the Festival as artist, teacher, theatrical impresario,
patron and creative visionary. For many French, Italian,
Polish and Russian people the name Demarco is synony-
mous with Edinburgh. Hailing a taxi at the airport, one
only needs to sound his name to be whisked to his door.

Seizing each moment as though it were his last, he is
as finely attuned to the Spirit of the Times as he is to the
creative potential of the people he meets. Whoever enters
his orbit for the first time is sure of an urgent awakening
to a richer, fuller appreciation of life, to the greater flow-
ering of his or her talents and to the prospect of happy
encounters with kindred others. I was not surprised to
notice that many of the photographs in his extensive per-
sonal archive are his recordings of first meetings between
people "in settings and situations in which creative energy
is discernible." This absorption with the meeting points
in human life is also evident in his distinctive drawings of
stairways, hillscapes, squares and laneways, all the thresh-
olds that life presents to his artistic eye, settings where
meetings can happen, are happening or have happened.
The Edinburgh Arts Journey exists within the wider con-
text of his own life's journey, his metaphorical "Road
to Meikle Seggie," on which I first ventured with him in
1977. This road exists in reality as a winding, undulating
seven-mile stretch linking a network of Scottish land-
marks near Edinburgh. "The road once taken," Richard
states, "it teaches those who travel on it, preferably on
foot, to discover its extensions all over Europe," as if to
suggest that, in being imbued with the spiritual riches of
my own culture, I will find a common bond with other
cultures.

"To draw something well is to touch its resistance,"
remarked artist John Berger. Richard Demarco under-

stands this well, since he is exemplary of the modern hero, a fully conscious individual whose every gesture serves to counter negative forces of apathy, cynicism and the fear that cause societies to falter. A controversial and charismatic public figure and darling of the press for over five decades, Demarco is a man who believes that anything worthwhile can only be achieved through dialogue. To this end he summoned a host of friends, of which I was one, to Edinburgh in August 2007 to take part in a conversation that ran for almost a month at the Scottish National Portrait Gallery. His own portrait is prominent in the main hallway of the building, the only representation of a living person gracing the walls of the gallery. I believe that the reason for this is that Richard has an extraordinary facility in bringing the painted images of other dead heroes to life again in people's hearts. His creative participation in the sixty festivals to date was duly celebrated with a lavish collection of archives that provided continuity and context for the many roads that meet in Demarco. It was he who founded the Traverse Theatre and he who brought Kantor, Gratowski, Beuys, and many other major artists to town. He was on hand each day to bear eloquent witness to the dizzying display assembled, to the obvious delight of admirers clustered, as ever, around him.

I sat in for three mornings in a row on the more formal dialogue that was taking place in the John Ruskin Room above. An international roster of specialists in fields of theatre, visual arts, education, arts administration, architecture, Scottish history and writing held forth with Richard on the topic of the day. When my own turn came, I addressed the theme of Celtic Consciousness and had a lively debate with Richard about the relevance of that consciousness today, adding a song and poem or two in illustration of my argument. As he had so often in the past, Richard provided me once more with a vital context in which to advance my artistic calling in a contemporaneous and meaningful way.

Notwithstanding his more than seventy years towards heaven, my impression is of the childlike quality that endures in Richard Demarco. This reminds me of what poet Rilke once wrote: "art is a way of life faithful to the natural instincts and therefore faithful to childhood; not any self-control or self-limitation for the sake of specific ends, but rather a careful letting go of oneself." My children still remember the excitement that surrounded his visits to our home and the interest in the visual arts that was sparked by his presence. My son Robert instantly offered himself for adoption when he learned that Richard had no children of his own! Talking all the time of people he had known, people he admired, people he hoped to work with—a catalyst extraordinaire—Demarco once declared, "My part is in scouting, discovering people and places everywhere I go that are vital and inspiring, and then making connections." Ever since meeting Richard, I have been inspired to do likewise and I continue to count myself as one of his vast and faithful army of explorers.

9

Flames of the Eternal

…I am a part of all I have met;
Yet all experience is an arch wherethrough
Gleams that untraveled world…
…Come, my friends,
'Tis not too late to seek a newer world…
TENNYSON

These words of Tennyson seem particularly relevant to my travels with Demarco and to the poetic journey of life in general. I am "a part of all I have met" to the degree that I engage with and reflect upon the life I encounter, since thinking provides my essential link with the world around me. "If you wish to recognize your Self, look into the mirror of the world and its beings. What lies within your soul will speak far more clearly to you from the eyes of your fellow being than when you grow hard within yourself and sink into your own soul," cautioned Rudolf Steiner in a lecture he gave in Berlin in October 1906. My life with Bob brought me into contact with a wide variety of individuals and every relationship had something to teach me regarding my own strengths and foibles. My gathering impressions convinced me that I lived in a world that is full of meaning and that to do the good is a fundamental human impulse.

Gleams of that "untraveled world" to which Tennyson refers are also reflected in the stars above, leading me to the people with whom I am already inwardly connected. According to Plotinus, the stars are like letters that inscribe themselves at every moment in the sky. They signify that everything on earth, the disposition of human nature and all interactions between people, are significant, synchronistic with the whole, and existing in an interconnecting relationship with everything else. I do not believe that we are moved around like puppets at the behest of forces beyond ourselves, random, metaphysical or divine. I believe that the intuitive faculty is our point of entry into a creative, cosmic world process that is pictured in the stars above and reflected in the human psyche as the essence of free individuality.

This intuitive "I" or higher Self in me and in you, attracts to itself everything we need for the realization of our goals, resulting in occurrences that facilitate their manifestation. The inspiration, or "hunch," that prompts me to register for a course or attend a conference can be seen in retrospect as the effect of causes that could be said to lie in the future. Unbeknownst to ourselves, we are often, in the actions or decisions we take, preparing for some future event. If you look backwards from the event, you may be struck by the fact that something like a plan was leading you towards it in an earlier period of your life. For instance, my marriage to a professor of Irish Studies was the future cause that attracted me to the course of schooling provided me in childhood. Likewise, my meet-

ing with anthroposophy was predated by several signifi-
cant encounters that all prepared the necessary receptivity
in me.

Just as clocks tell time but do not create time, unfold-
ing patterns can be traced in the heavenly bodies but do
not originate with them. The causes lie in our own karmic
predisposition and freedom of choice. The encounters,
deeds and sufferings of previous incarnations prepare a
predisposition in us for making amends and reaping the
harvests we have planted. Each has his or her own col-
lective of individuals to reconnect with in each lifetime
in ever appropriate relationships and collaborations. We
may accept the prevailing configuration of the heavens,
just as we would accept the architectural plan for a house
as given, while at the same time choosing to live in it
according to our own lights and therefore, freely.

I have already described my resonance with the wis-
dom, writings and practical lives of visionaries who lived
at the turn of the twentieth century. Their thinking, espe-
cially in its poetic form, nourished my soul and gave me
confidence in my own spiritual and national identity. It
also introduced me to a stream of esoteric teachings and
writings; the more hidden the truths, the more worthy of
investigation, I thought. I sensed that it was important to
align with a worldview that would facilitate the emergence
of the "newer world" that poets had foretold. I became
more and more conscious in this endeavour, ever alert to
signs that could point me in the right direction. I found
it significant, for instance, that a descendant of Ralph
Waldo Emerson had crossed my path in a theosophical
context (as already described) because Yeats and AE had
been influenced by the American transcendentalist move-
ment and by Emerson in particular, in formulating their
ideals for a Celtic literary revival.

Theosophy is an oriental teaching, introduced to West-

ern devotees by Madame Blavatsky, and purporting to rep-
resent the "secret doctrine" behind Buddhism and other
world religions. In his study of Ireland's literary renais-
sance, E. Boyd claimed that the founding of the Theo-
sophical Society's Dublin Lodge had been as important to
the movement as the publication of Standish O'Grady's
seminal *History of Ireland*, "...the two events being compli-
mentary to any complete understanding of the literature
of the Revival." While the movement aimed to avert the
incursion of materialism into Ireland, Yeats and AE were
wary of the danger of its dissolving into passive "Celtic
Twilight" whimsy. Yeats was a member of Blavatsky's Lon-
don group for almost two years but he proved too talka-
tive and distracting for her, and was eventually expelled.
He was eager not for union with some mystical nirvana
but for truths that he could test in action, in becoming
more engaged in shaping the life of his nation, in working
for change in the world and in challenging his fellow man.
AE, on the other hand, had no need for such schooling.
Having realized his own "unity of being," he gave himself
selflessly in service to the arts as well as the practical cause
of agricultural renewal in rural Ireland.

Yeats eventually found what he was looking for in his ini-
tiation into the Rosicrucian tradition, which he described
as "a movement downwards upon life not upwards out
of life." The study of such occult teachings was a pursuit
Yeats claimed was "second only to poetry itself," and its
most enriching source. His detractors have failed to recog-
nize that his esoteric spiritual practices demanded a strict
discipline, and underscored his keen grasp on the political
and social issues of his time. His poems reflect an inner
spiritual resonance with all that was happening around
him. They also chart his life as a journey of self-renewal
and of laborious endeavour, based in what he called, "the
fascination of what's difficult." Seamus Heaney, writing

in the Guardian argues that "Yeats's work survives as a purely motivated, greatly active power for good."

My involvement with Yeats's work since marrying Bob aroused my interest in Rosicrucian literature, although at that time I could only know "about" things in an abstract academic way. However, I had no idea that the Rosicrucian tradition, ever adaptable to the changing conditions of life, had found its way into our contemporary world in a significant social movement called anthroposophy, or that George, the wife of W.B. Yeats, had been familiar with Steiner's writings and may have informed her husband of them. Anne Yeats revealed this to me much later at her home in Dublin, when she told me about her own keen interest in anthroposophy.

Inner readiness had to coincide with practical need in me before I made my discovery of this body of work. I had returned in 1981 from the eventful year in Dublin that saw the release of my first album of songs, my visit to Pamela Travers that coincided with poetry performances I gave in London, the restoration of AE's grave and other experiences beyond those recorded in an earlier chapter of this book. I missed my Irish parents and siblings and found it hard to adjust to the rhythm of Canadian life. The erratic patterns of my husband's illness that continued to escalate against a background of child rearing and guests seemed more challenging than ever. I was beginning to despair when a serendipitous meeting led me to the wisdom of Rudolf Steiner and the larger worldview I had been seeking. It came about as follows.

The death of hunger striker Bobby Sands in a Belfast prison in 1982 brought the Toronto Irish, some eight hundred strong, together to commemorate this landmark event in Irish history. I was called upon to sing the Seán Ó Riada Mass in the Irish language at this ritual gathering in a large auditorium. The Irish poet John Montague sat beside me and publicly recited a poem that he had extemporaneously penned during the ceremony. As we left the building on that bright May evening, a friend issued an invitation to dine with her at her Toronto Island home the following evening. During the crossing on the ferry next day, an intense dark-haired man of striking looks, close to me in age, approached us.

"Hi, I'm Alexander Blair-Ewart and I have a feeling we are all going to Jaffa's dinner party."

He spoke in a British accent and smiled when he learned I was Irish. When I named my place of birth, he exclaimed in delight: "Tuam, County Galway!!—I know it well! After my father died in the war, my mother married a farmer from your area and left Glasgow with her five children to live with him there. I was only seven miles away from you between the ages of seven and fourteen!"

He later astounded me by his vivid recall of every hill and tree, the names and characteristics of the neighbours he remembered and especially by his recitation of a whole page of an Irish language textbook we had both studied in primary school.

Our hostess had prepared a wonderful meal for us, laying a perfectly cooked Atlantic salmon in the centre of the table as soon as we had taken our seats. "It is the salmon of wisdom!" I declared to Alexander who was sitting next to me. "Perhaps one of us will receive the wisdom of Fionn tonight!" he said, picking up on my reference to a popular Irish legend about the young Fionn Mac Cumhail, who acquired the gift of "second sight" when he tasted what became known as "the salmon of wisdom."

As we savoured the delicious fish, Alexander and John began to talk about Rudolf Steiner. Upon hearing this name for the first time, I experienced what I can only describe as a shaft of light entering my heart, an extraordinary sensation that I can never forget. I became very attentive to the conversation, intrigued by its terms of reference: such allusions as "etheric" and "astral" were entirely new to me, as was the term "anthroposophy", a subject seemingly of profound interest to them both. John and Alexander explained that in addition to being a path of spiritual science—a way of knowing the nature of spirit—anthroposophy also consisted of a body of exact knowledge in practically every realm of human culture. It was of vital necessity, Rudolf Steiner believed, for people to avail themselves of this knowledge in order to curb the rising tide of materialism and embrace the full potential of their humanity.

Alexander was a gifted teacher and became a frequent visitor to our house, painstakingly drawing on his own independent research to elucidate the profound riddles of human life; our spiritual nature, our relationship with the dead and the many guidelines for social renewal that Steiner's lectures addressed. My new friend was familiar with all the books Steiner had written and with a substantial number of the some 6000 lectures he delivered in the course of his travels to many European cities at the turn of the twentieth century.

Conversations with Alexander informed me on spiritual matters in a way that books, to that point, had not. I loved to listen to him talk and he gave undivided attention to all my questions. Alex, as he preferred to be called, was born in Scotland and often reflected on our common Celtic ancestry, remarking that the current Celtic revival that Bob was spearheading demands that we know, in modern terms, what a Celt is.

"How would you define a Celt?" I asked him.

"If people are to be defined by the best that is embodied in them, I would say that that the definition of a Celt today would be—an esoteric Christian."

"How would I recognize an esoteric Christian?" I asked.

"The esoteric Christian experiences the life of Christ and the mystery of His passion and death not as a teaching to be studied and promulgated but as a spiritual power of renewal streaming over the earth, as something to be directly engaged moment-to-moment. The Grail legend, Rosicrucian teachings and the Gospel of John are all expressions of this mystery."

I mentioned my interest in the part played by Rosicrucian and theosophical teachings in the Celtic literary revival that took place in Ireland at the turn of the twentieth century.

"The awakening of esoteric knowledge always addresses the real spiritual needs of contemporary culture," Alex responded. "The mystical and occult outpouring you mention was largely a replay of all the occult traditions of the world—possible in Europe because Europe had embraced Christianity. It was also a resurgence of the spirit which animated Celtic druidism before the coming of Christ."

Because the druids had received a lot of bad press, and were often characterized as intractable pagans inimical to St. Patrick's Christianizing impulse, I wondered about the purpose of their schools.

"As spiritual leaders of the people, druids," Alex told me, "became the first to embrace Christianity because they had prepared themselves for it. They knew that the original "sun-power" had united with the earth during the Resurrection. The nature-spirituality of the druids was then absorbed into Celtic Christianity which spread rapidly because it was well attuned to the norms and needs of rural and tribal society."

I had often told the story of Lugh in my presentations, the Celtic sun god who prefigured the Christ, wielding a sword of light and scattering the forces of darkness like chaff before wind! Christ is referred to as "Lord of the elements" in the Irish language—an immanence of fire, air, earth, and water reminiscent of druidic lore, that permeates the lush green landscape of Ireland.

"How did 'the knowledge of the oak,' attributed to the druids, differ from the knowledge we have today?" I wondered.

"Our way of knowing now is more conceptual," Alex replied. "We are inclined to think we have understood something when we have gathered information about it. Druidic "knowing" was different—although having far less data than we have at our disposal today, they understood a thing by merging their consciousness with it, by forming imaginations, visual or aural impressions that could reveal the inner properties of herbs, roots and other natural forms, for instance. They could observe the activity of the sun and recognize how it pours into flowers, plants and animals. Their waking life was a continuation of their dream life, not at all like ours today."

"That reminds me of the first Irish poem we know of, called 'Song of Amhairgin,'" I said. "In it, the poet declares himself 'an estuary into the sea, a wave of the ocean, the sound of the sea, a powerful ox, a hawk on a cliff, a dewdrop in the sun, a plant of beauty.' He was proclaiming his unity with every natural form! John Keats must have been of the same lineage—maybe all poets are—saying of a sparrow, briefly perching on his windowsill, 'I take part in its existence.'"

"Needless to say, the druid priests were poets—and physicians too!" Alex continued. "Rudolf Steiner described them as 'great comforters,' who could appeal to people's hearts, healing and consoling many. An intense devotion to the living presence of Christ was cultivated in the souls of pupils in mystery centres of the time created for that purpose. Monastic communities, which included women as well as men, served a similar purpose later on, inspiring the peregrinations of Irish missionaries who would revitalize the religious life of Europe. Their faith was based in a philosophy that linked heaven and earth in mutual interdependence and a 'learning through love' that enlivened their teaching."

"We have a saying in Irish, *tá mo chroí istigh ionat*, meaning 'my heart is inside you.' It is another way of saying 'I love you.' When we put our hearts inside things, giving undivided attention to nature, poetry, architecture, painting, music, sculpture or people, we come to an intimate knowledge of life. Perhaps this is how the knowledge of the oak lives on in us," I mused.

Alex responded: "The Hibernian Mysteries [*Hibernia* is the old, Latin name for Ireland] were deemed 'the greatest of all mysteries.' Their purpose lay in awakening the life of the senses so that human beings could feel consciously connected with their environment. What evolved in human nature in those ancient times lives on as a source of insight and imagination in us. The poetry, language and music of Ireland are the expression of that mystical stream that never fails to warm the human heart. Celtic missionaries recognized no social or cultural barriers in their efforts to uplift the spiritual life of early Europe! They adapted to the social and cultural mores of other nations, realizing that Christianity must always address itself to the total spectrum of life. And it may yet be given to Celtic culture to once more exemplify a living Christianity based in divine presence, imagination, wholeness and simplicity."

Alex gave me the first book of my extensive Steiner collection. Entitled *Christianity as Mystical Fact*, the book sits before me on the shelf, a reminder of a deeply significant friendship. When Alex took it from his pocket to give to me during our first long talk he explained:

"This book is the first of a series of spiritual teachings

which mirror the path followed by our mystical Celtic ancestors, presented in a way which is intelligible to a modern reader. The purpose of a true esotericism, I might add, is never the mere preservation of arcane traditions and ritual forms but the constant rebirth of humanity's spiritual heart."

The book, which I avidly read, described how the way was paved for Christianity in occult mystery schools of ancient times. Rudolf Steiner reveals how he arrived at his profound insight into the cosmic nature of the Christ and how He may be accepted into our souls as the spirit of freedom. Steiner writes about his preparatory years of long and arduous schooling in natural science, philosophy and—most importantly—in the development of his own cognitive and moral capacities. He once remarked: "The Gods have placed self-control before the highest bliss of knowledge—and they demand it!" Steiner developed his unique capacity in penetrating human consciousness, past, present and future, through the exercise of pure thinking alone. It requires a gathering and strengthening of all the powers and depths of the soul and the intensification of attention and concentration. He once observed that "thinking itself becomes a body which draws the spirit of the universe into itself as its soul."

Steiner gave no ready-made answers for the problems of life but addressed the actual quality of the consciousness brought to bear on them. The clarity of Steiner's thought was compelling in itself and addressed fundamental questions such as, "Who am I as human being? Where have I come from? Where am I going? Is there life after death? What is the purpose of illness? What does it mean to be free?" Such questions were the subtext of the many volumes I read, in which the results of Steiner's spiritual research were presented without any hint of moralizing or persuasion, turning my mind and heart to a deeper source of truth and love than I had ever before encountered. Steiner himself said "The primary form by which anthroposophy comes to people is—ideas. The first door it knocks at is insight."

I can offer only a brief synthesis of a few of the many themes touched on in the comprehensive sweep of these writings and lectures:

We are beings of body, soul and spirit; the combination of animal, human and divine elements with which we meet the world. Our instinctual physical nature is a given, while an individuated, autonomous self or "I" connects us to one another at a spiritual level. Thus we inhabit two worlds simultaneously. The soul, our seat of feeling, mediates between both poles. The conscious balancing of sympathy/antipathy in the soul clears the way for a living intuitive thinking that engenders a cognitive feeling capacity, not to be confused with emotion. For instance cognitive feeling helps me to recognize whether or not a plant is poisonous while I at the same time delight in its beauty. Everyday interactions provide ample opportunity for Rudolf Steiner's recommended exercise of soul-hygiene. "Know thou thyself," is an injunction relevant in every age and place, for in coming to know oneself one comes to know the entire cosmos as reflected in every human being.

Our physical self is but a picture of the larger reality of spirit that animates it. This spirit has its existence in a spiritual world, which it enters every night when it leaves the sleeping body, returning to quicken and renew it upon awakening. Our bodies are sustained by a complex weaving of spiritual forces, the description of which corresponds in my mind with the movements of a Beethoven symphony. Beethoven described it well in declaring that there was "no loftier mission than to approach the spiritual world in the silence of the night or early morning,

Rudolf Steiner (1861–1925) became a respected and well-published scientific, literary, and philosophical scholar, particularly known for his work on Goethe's scientific writings. His multifaceted genius has led to innovative and holistic approaches in medicine, philosophy, religion, education (Waldorf Schools), special education (the Camphill movement), economics, biodynamic agriculture, science, architecture, and the arts (speech, drama, eurythmy, painting). In 1924 he founded the General Anthroposophical Society, which has branches throughout the world.

stirred into being by moods which the poet could translate into words, but which I could put into sounds." Our true being or "I" has its existence in a spiritual world where the dead also abide, those with whom we are eternally connected through an elaborate karmic interweaving of repeated earth lives.

Steiner traces the evolution of human consciousness through epochs of history and through the phases of self-development that the soul undergoes between birth and death in the balance of joy and sorrow. The necessary, creative improvisation that the evolution of consciousness demands and which can only be realized on the plane of earth is expressed in cycles of repeated earth lives. That the spiritualization of the earth also depends on the evolution of human consciousness was recognized by Steiner as well as by a contemporary of his, poet Rainer Maria Rilke, who wrote movingly about this in the *Ninth Duino Elegy*:

> ... *Earth, is not this what you want:*
> *invisibly to rise within us?* —
> *Is it not your dream to be one day invisible?* ...
> *Earth: invisible!*
> *What is your urgent command,*
> *if not transformation?*
> *Earth, dear Earth, I will* ...

The soul leaves the body after death, gradually dissolving until it ceases to exist as a separate entity. The spirit of the human being that passes into the spiritual world after the soul has dissolved, is indestructible and undergoes profound planetary experiences for an indeterminable period. When the time comes for it to incarnate again, new sheaths are formed for its entry into a physical body. Constant readjustments are needed throughout life in bringing body, soul and spirit into proper alignment with life purpose. Illness represents the annihilation of a pre-disposition or imbalance in the soul that may hinder the spiritual development of the person if it is not brought to light. We speak of being "blessed by illness," which is often a means of accelerated spiritual growth because of the stamina gained in coping with such an initiatory experience and the responsibility for self-development incumbent on the patient in recovery. Illness, according to Steiner, is not a hostile or arbitrary event but has a pro-found meaning in the context of a person's biography, of his or her community and of the age.

What is most striking about anthroposophical litera-ture is the fact that its tenets and principles are commu-nicated out of a fundamental spirit of love that awakens a reverence for life, rather in the way that good poetry does. Rudolf Steiner recommended specific exercises for the student in cultivating a disposition of reverence, patience, equanimity and perseverance, along with strict control of thoughts and actions. To make a step forward in knowledge, he said, would require three steps in moral development. He cautioned against spending more than a number of minutes on these exercises each day, their primary purpose being to strengthen soul capacities with which to meet the demands of daily life.

As I read more of Steiner's teachings, I found that his basic texts are best studied in the company of others who bring their own insights to bear on mine, reading no more than the group can reasonably digest in one sitting. I delved into lecture cycles on topics that would span a wide range of interests—education, medicine, inner develop-ment, the gospels, philosophy, speech, drama, agriculture. I eventually took several excellent courses on a number of these themes at the Toronto Rudolf Steiner Centre, where I forged lasting bonds of friendship with kindred others, such as Wendy Brown whose life task as guiding force and devoted co-worker has brought anthroposophical wisdom to wide public attention in Ontario over the past twenty five years.

Of all his books, *Intuitive Thinking as a Spiritual Path* (originally titled *A Philosophy of Freedom*) was the one Dr. Steiner believed was of utmost importance. He declared that in the meditative absorption of the contents of this book you will understand your creative participation in world evolution and the real meaning of ethical responsibility. It asserts that the human ability to think intuitively must be fostered as the appropriate cognitive and redemptive aspiration of our time. It is through intuitive thinking that the "I" is strengthened and called into free spiritual activity, Steiner contends. The book is a phenomenological exploration of freedom as a creative force that, once accessed, awakens a disposition for independent and moral action. Christ was synonymous with the spirit of freedom for Rudolf Steiner. In a lecture cycle on the Gospel of St. John he declared: "Thus for Anthroposophy the central figure in the whole tableau of reincarnation, of the nature of man, of the survey of the cosmos, is the Being whom we call the Christ ... it is a picture with one central figure on which everything else depends."

Profoundly moved by these many texts, I sometimes could not read more than a page before my heart overflowed with a sense of the nobility and mystery of human life revealed to me in every line. Rudolf Steiner's thinking had an organic quality to which I could readily respond, one thought arising from another with inner necessity and grace. My thoughts became more ordered in the simple exercise of following his train of thought and I could begin to realize what it is to be formed and led by the truth. The answer to every genuine question that took shape in my mind soon resonated in serendipitous ways, in chance encounters, conversations, and sometimes in a letter, newspaper or book. I soon discovered the joy of working with Steiner's "Calendar of the Soul"—designed to express all that echoes in the soul when it unites itself with the seasons of the year.

All my life I had been concentrating on what to think and now I was finally learning how to think. I began to realize that no concept, however useful, is ever finished and that to be fully alive was to be always open to new experiences. Better to proceed, I realized, with an attitude of not knowing which would be constantly informed by experience and my corresponding response in thought, feeling and action. I could place my trust in a spiritual world that Steiner declared was "full of wisdom," profoundly moved by his descriptions of the spiritual beings that surround us: "The created world is nothing but the outer garment, the outer glory of creating hierarchies. Actual reality is only attained with knowledge of the spiritual beings at work in the various heavenly bodies…They are the true reality. Nothing else is real, neither space, nor time, nor matter." I was no longer bound by limited definitions of what the purpose of life might be and I had found a means of bringing rhythm into the chaos of my day in the practice of certain exercises. I learned the value of an early morning meditation such as the following:

More radiant than the sun
Purer than the snow
Finer than the ether
Is the Self
The spirit in my heart
That Self is I
I am that Self.

Excited by all I was learning, I eagerly sought to incorpo-
rate these new ways of being in my own life and in the life
of my family. Bob was as enthusiastic as I was, to begin
with, and we often studied together but as my interest
deepened he unfortunately grew to resent the new direc-
tion of my thinking. Cocktail parties and idle chat lost all
their appeal for me as I became more conscious in matters
of health and food, becoming quite intolerant of exces-
sive drinking and swearing off alcohol myself.

Seeking to extend the benefit of Steiner's insights to my
children, I enrolled them in the Toronto Waldorf School,
where I became an active member of the school commu-
nity. Rudolf Steiner founded the first Waldorf School
in Stuttgart, Germany, in 1919, believing that education
and teaching must become an art and be based upon true
knowledge of the human being. When he visited a Wal-
dorf school, Steiner's first question to the students was,
"Do you love your teacher?" He would ask the teachers,
"Do you love your students?" This spirit of love spilled
over into home life where the names of their teachers
were invoked in reverential tones by our children and I
can nostalgically recall the way my son Robert's face lit up
when he came in sight of Mrs. Haller and Emer's joy in
running up the hill from the school bus to take her place
in Mr. Belenson's classroom every morning.

All teachers came inwardly prepared to impart the
knowledge they had lovingly absorbed and could artis-
tically convey, without reference to text books or audio
visuals in the classroom, but by means of storytelling,
colourful blackboard illustrations and practical exercises,
the curriculum being based in phenomenological under-
standing of the developing child. They could acknowl-
edge how from birth to age six or seven, children absorb
the world through their senses and learn through imita-
tion; how their charges become more centred in feeling

and imagination in the primary school years and how the capacity for rational, abstract thinking usually begins to emerge in the middle school years. These teachers place a strong emphasis on the arts, on manual dexterity, co-ordinated physical movement, learning through the body while the development of an aesthetic sense permeates all school activities. It was no wonder to me, as a parent and former teacher, that Waldorf was becoming the fastest growing educational movement in the world since it provides the truly holistic, child-centred, loving, artistic, practical and wonder-filled education that parents know their loved ones deserve.

I still welcome every opportunity to visit the Toronto Waldorf School. Located on the outskirts of the city, the novel architectural design of its main building is set like a jewel within a wooded, lovingly cultivated landscape. TWS Christmas Fairs, concerts, plays and conferences continue to invite my eager participation and I have found the school community to be a very receptive audience for poetry having performed there as well as in several of the Waldorf schools that now number 900 worldwide. My children naturally flourished in this environment, developing into independent-thinking, imaginative, socially engaged and well-rounded individuals like their fellow graduates with whom they maintain strong bonds of friendship. The main goal of education, apart from the acquisition of knowledge and skills, Steiner believed, lay in fostering the ability to learn from life in all its dimensions. "The student must have the possibility at school to acquire an inner strength—which can only grow during this time—so that it cannot be broken again in later life."

Besides formulating a path of inner development and inspiring social renewal, Rudolf Steiner worked with and influenced some of the best known and most influential figures of the twentieth century, among then Albert Sch-

weitzer who said of him: "We both felt the same obli-
gation to lead man once again to a true inner culture. I
have rejoiced at the achievements his great personality
and his profound humanity have brought about in the
world." Owen Barfield called Steiner's work "the best
kept secret of the twentieth century," comparing him to
the paradigm-creating figures of Aristotle and Acquinas.
I can say of the people I know who share my interest in
the ideas of Steiner—"my glory was I had such friends!"
Foremost amongst them is Christopher Bamford who,
as editor-in-chief, writer and publisher, works almost as
tirelessly as Steiner himself did in bringing the fruits of
anthroposophy to popular consciousness, acknowledging
of Steiner that "there is no field of knowledge that he did
not plough and reform."

The roots of anthroposophy lie in Rudolf Steiner's
understanding of and empathy with his own period.
His approach to spiritual development was threefold: to
include the inner meditative life of thinking; to foster the
cultivation and appreciation of the arts; and to enable com-
munity building through a great variety of social endeav-
ours. Seeds sown by Steiner in his books, lectures and in
countless private consultations often conducted through
the night (he only slept for two or so hours) germinated
widely and continue to take root in hearts and minds
today. A new culture is emerging in thousands of projects
coming to flower around the world that are imbued with
love for humanity. *Lilipoh*, a quarterly magazine I love to
read, celebrates the flowering of such projects in North
America.

This spiritual path is appropriate for practical life,
artistic activity and social renewal as I would discover in
becoming active in one such project that had an interna-
tional dimension. There was certainly an element of seren-
dipity at work in the meetings that led to my involvement

with the IDRIART movement, as it was called, sweeping across Europe and America in the eighties and nineties and providing me with an ideal artistic context for the further exploration of a new framework for thinking and personal enrichment.

The Mission of the Arts

"To become a human being is an art."
NOVALIS

Christopher Bamford, whom I had known since 1978 when he contributed to Bob's book *The Celtic Consciousness*, was now the publisher of Lindisfarne Press. He called me in October of 1984 to ask if I would help raise funds for the publication of a book by a Hungarian musician/chemist named Georg Kühlewind. The book was being translated from the German and would be entitled *Becoming Aware of the Logos*. I succeeded in raising these funds and as a result I received one of the first published copies. I remember spending the Christmas period of that year reflecting on this inspired meditation on the prologue to the Gospel of St. John. It was a book to be read deeply and completely in a slow but rewarding exercise of "right reading," which implies taking in only as much as I can satisfactorily digest in one sitting. I refer to this text as my "desert island book," since the many layers of meaning to be uncovered within its pages seem inexhaustible.

Georg Kühlewind, Hungarian scientist, musician, and author, was a devoted student of Anthroposophy who undertook to make the work of Rudolf Steiner a living experience of his own. He developed a large student body in the course of his travels between Europe and North America, tirelessly explaining his unique approach to meditative work and laying great emphasis on the Gospel of St. John as a meditative text.

The fruit of many years of study and meditation for Kühlewind, this book teaches the way of grace and truth in a radical, original manner. The author communicates the essence of such central themes as the logos as speech and relationship; the logos in the beginning; the light in the darkness; the speaker; life; spirit. The book appeared to me the fulfilment of core exercises and indications given by Rudolf Steiner, out of which Kühlewind's original research was bred as an essential and timely renewal of the essence of anthroposophy.

Kühlewind recognized that the purpose of anthroposo-

*Besides being a publisher, Christopher Bamford is the author, trans-
lator, and editor of numerous books, including* The Voice of the
Eagle: Celtic Christianity *and* Homage to Pythagoras: Redis-
covering Sacred Science. *I know him as an engaging public
speaker, generous host, great cook, and cherished friend, and have
enjoyed visits to the gracious home he shares with his beloved wife,
Betsy, in Massachussets. I was happy to have them visit my house
in Barrie in 2005 when Christopher presented a memorable work-
shop on the theme "One Community, One World: Human Beings
on Both Sides of the Threshold."*

phy lies in the development of soul capacities with which
to meet the challenges of our times. If the intuitive faculty
for forming new concepts is lacking in the reader, what
Rudolf Steiner feared most could happen, namely that
the contents of his books could be applied like articles
of faith. I would later discover that the methodical, phe-
nomenological self-observation advocated and demon-
strated by Kühlewind in his many books and workshops

Miha Pogačnik has travelled the world in the service of IDRIART, an artistic movement he founded that joins countries and people in a series of festivals that trancend national, religious and linguistic boundaries and enliven social encounter, awakening human hearts to the meaning and form inherent in music.

engenders a schooling of consciousness that is based in a freedom of attention. This was the central tenet of his teaching life. I had the honour of meeting Georg Kühlewind a year after I first heard of him and could express my admiration for this work. He confessed to having been "overshadowed by the spirit of John" while writing the book and of feeling bereft in its aftermath. When he presented me with another of his books the following day, entitled *Stages of Consciousness*, the inscription read, "In memory of our first meeting of a very long friendship."

Georg Kühlewind provided an important link with a movement that would influence my life greatly over the next few years. It was in March of 1985 that I received a call from pianist Graham Jackson, asking if he could introduce me to a Yugoslavian violinist who was visiting Toronto. Within half an hour I was opening my door to Miha Pogačnik and to a new chapter in my life. No sooner was he seated in my living room than he came straight to the point: "I wanted to meet you because I sensed as soon as I heard your name that you were the person who should represent IDRIART in Toronto."

"What," I asked, "is IDRIART?"

"IDRIART," he replied, "is that which is not yet."

I liked him instantly because I knew he spoke my language! What he had to say sounded strangely familiar although he was bringing me news of a revolutionary movement in the arts that had been officially named Institut pour le Development des Relations Interculturelles par l'ART. He told me that he became director of the Chartres Summer Festival in 1981, when the famous cathedral was used for the first time in recent history for the performance of music. By 1983, the annual festival was attracting up to two thousand people from thirty-five countries. Out of this event a vital concept in the performance and appreciation of the arts arose. People inspired by the Chartres experience carried on the initiative and chapters soon sprang up in over twenty countries where Miha inaugurated arts festivals prepared by volunteers. Pogačnik believed in breaking through cocoons of money and elitism, realizing that a well-dressed, affluent audience is not necessarily God's gift to the artist. From a young age, Miha was determined to devote his time to educating audiences so that the experience of the listener might more closely match his own informed, focused attention as a player. I reminded him of a statement of Gogol that seemed relevant to his aspirations: "If art does not accomplish the miracle of transforming the soul of the spectator it is not fulfilling its mission in the world."

Miha responded in his heavily accented way: "I am in total agreement with that! We have set ourselves the goal to work in such a way that everybody participates inwardly so that new vistas may open for many and not just for the players. When artists and participants take on the responsible role of performer the festival itself becomes a work of art ... lectures, artistic courses of various kinds, introductions to more active ways of participating in the arts, music, drama, and eurythmy (an art of movement) are offered. Exhibitions are set up, possibilities arranged for meetings and discussions and we try to apply musical principles to all this work."

I became aware of his deep sense of mission, when he said in an urgent tone, "Today the whole world is in a very dangerous and explosive state with one main problem being the isolation among peoples. Artists are called upon to take a more active social role. To use mythological language: we together with our Muses are called to serve the zeitgeist who does not want to know any national boundaries. What is unique about IDRIART festivals is that our audiences move along with us to different countries. We try to organize short but strong events at specially chosen places worldwide, always ready to change, to rethink, to improvise."

His remarks reminded me of ideas I had while reading *Becoming Aware of the Logos*. But as he had not mentioned any connection with Hungary, I tentatively asked: "Does the name Georg Kühlewind mean anything to you? I have recently read a book of his that somehow has prepared me for what you are telling me…"

Miha gave a cry of delight. "Georg is my mentor! He and Jurgen Schrieffer are the godfathers of our movement! You will meet him at our festival in Sacramento, California if you will join us there next year."

And thus the meeting with Kühlewind came about.

My life was greatly enhanced during the seven years I spent as an active co-worker for this exciting movement. Inspired to bring people together at a time of tremendous change in the world, Pogačnik's visits to Canada brought us news of distant places where the need for social renewal was urgent. As the calls from our brothers and sisters in Central and Eastern Europe, in Russia, South America and Tibet, reached our chapters, IDRIART began to be acknowledged as the Red Cross of art. Miha's letters to me were always punctuated with exhortations, urging us to travel with him. In a letter to co-workers in 1991 he wrote: "It is incredible what is wanted and needed in the USSR and Central Europe…The greatest need of people everywhere is to meet you, to talk to you, to know you and to work together with you. Please do come. Your active participation is the core of IDRIART."

I organized a memorable concert for Miha at the Toronto Waldorf School and maintained a spirited connection with him for several years before moving to British Columbia. Classical violinist Victor Costanzi and his harpist wife, Rita, were Miha's representatives in Western Canada. As distinguished and popular musicians, they played a vital role in the artistic life of Vancouver. They invited me to visit them and interrupted their own busy concert schedule to organize a concert for me on January 19, 1990, a few weeks after I left Bob. The warmth of their welcome, the ambience of the city, the fact that my younger children, Declan and Emer—now teenagers, could be enrolled at the Waldorf High School near their home, all contributed to my decision to move to North Vancouver the following summer and live close to my new friends. My fruitful collaboration with the Costanzis over the next six years, paved the way for more Canadian visits by Miha and his associates. Accomplished harpist, Rita Costanzi, and I presented annual winter solstice concerts together—in the IDRIART spirit—to capacity audiences at Vancouver's Christ Church Cathedral and forged our bond of friendship.

The tenth anniversary of the founding of IDRIART occurred in 1991. A major festival was held in Chartres cathedral that I attended along with other Canadians. Participants were drawn from the many countries in which the movement was by then established. I was happy to be amongst them.

Chartres stands as the most complete, architecturally and iconographically, of all the great Gothic cathedrals of the world. It is a monument to human striving, love and devotion; it is also a place of great spiritual resonance, its site Celtic in origin, constituting geometry in

Victor and Rita Costanzi, my IDRIART co-workers in Vancouver, accomplished professional musicians and dear friends who now reside in New York city.

space and musical in all its aspects. Chartres has become, in the words of August Rodin "a hymn of praise for eternity…When faced with a marvel…the sublime summary of centuries…one is hushed by an admiration that surpasses words."

It was this hush which set the tone for E. Peppings's *St. Matthews Passion*, a choral work of unearthly purity and one of the most remarkable of the twentieth century, performed on this occasion by a choir schooled in Werbeck singing and conducted by their teacher, Jurgen Schrieffer. This method of singing involves the cultivation of inner hearing and releases therapeutic forces, which were powerfully experienced by the listeners that night. Participants in the choir were drawn from many walks of life, as indeed were the builders of Chartres Cathedral, amongst them the hundreds who chanted as they hauled huge stones from quarries some five kilometres away.

Georg Kühlewind's arresting talk at Chartres arose out of the spirit of the moment and I took some notes at the time. "Attention is the natural prayer which we perform towards the truth that is living in us, to bring it to show itself. Our power of attentiveness is our sacred power force but it is threatened from many sides. It has the possibility of growing more and more autonomous. If attention is concentrated on a theme of a man-made object or a line of sacred text, it has the power of changing from grasping to opening. If attentiveness is empty, then something can fill it from above."

Kühlewind would expand on this theme at every opportunity and continued to do so in the course of our collaboration in his several workshops that I hosted and the "long friendship" which lasted until his death on January 15, 2006. His book *From Normal to Healthy*, an outline of his spiritual psychology that provides a rich source of insights for the healing of anxiety, depression and other mental illnesses, would have been of invaluable help to me in coping with my husband's syndrome. However, it had not appeared in English translation before I left Bob but I have since come to appreciate the practicality of its contents.

Instead of focusing on a patient's behavioural symptoms, Kühlewind's method, now embraced by many professional therapists, relies on a self-conscious re-experiencing of the true self, of presence and of connectedness with the whole, in the patient. He advocates the development of faculties of receptive attention and cognitive feeling through meditation and other specific exercises tailored to the patient, many of them artistic. For Kühlewind, the activity of thinking is raised to the level of art because the free faculty of attention is our source of creativity and love and the activity of a spirit in us that is never "sick."

My most abiding memory of the festival was of a rather unusual outing, which had a peculiar druidic fitness to it. An excursion was planned whereby hundreds of people set out in the dead of night from Chartres, in a convoy of buses and cars, led pied-piper-like by Miha Pogačnik, the strains of whose violin lured us on. In the gathering dawn, I could barely discern a large Celtic dolman upon which Miha admonished me to stand. With feet firmly placed on this stony altar of time, I felt empowered to speak and sing sounds appropriate to the occasion, while hundreds stood with their backs to me, our faces now raised in homage to the rising sun. I recited "Remembrance" by Robert Masterson, a Vancouver poet whom I had come to know.

The waves return,
Glittering with remembered sun,
Ancient songs seizing our tongues,
The broken pillars standing anew,
The temple rising, rising, rising,
The circle shining true …

Gongs began to sound, their diminishing tones drawing us with them into meditative silence. It was a beautiful Sunday morning; with open hearts and happy faces, we formed a circle and quietly ate the abundance of good croissants and hot coffee, which seemed to appear out of nowhere. Then Miha played again. I sang all the way back to the car, field after field of glorious sunflowers lighting our way. I remembered more words of Pogačnik's: "Every landscape on this earth carries within itself a memory and its own story that seeks to reveal itself, and in that way to contribute to the diversity of human society."

As well as affording me the opportunity to meet with Kühlewind and providing me with the chance to perform in many different settings and contexts, my involvement with IDRIART brought me into contact with the Camphill movement, which carried the artistic impulse forward in several countries. This association began for me when I was planning the Dublin IDRIART Festival of 1987 in collaboration with members of a community for young adults with developmental disabilities, located in Dunshane, County Kildare. With the help of Camphill co-workers I mounted a very successful event and introduced Pogačnik, Schrieffer and other IDRIART stars (amongst them the late Derek Bell of The Chieftains) to Irish audiences which now included many of Miha's European fans.

Camphill was founded in Scotland in 1940 by an Austrian doctor of Jewish background, Karl König, and some colleagues of his who were determined to take "a morsel of the true European destiny and make it into a seed so that some of its real task might be preserved." As political refugees, they formed a symbiotic relationship with handicapped children, who seemed to them the social refugees of their time and place. König pioneered a movement for curative education in a residential setting with a view to helping these children—adults were also embraced by the movement in later years. Camphill emphasizes community in a social and spiritual sense, its methods and goals primarily based on the ideas of Rudolf Steiner and his "fundamental social law" which states: "The well-being of a community of human beings working together is greater the less an individual claims for himself and the more his requirements are met out of the work of others." Hospitality is one of the hallmarks of a Camphill community, the well-appointed and environmentally friendly facilities allow for a healthy flourishing of artistic activity and meaningful social exchange. The existence of Camphill communities and Waldorf schools guaranteed the success of every festival, I noticed, providing setting, grace and ground for planning and preparatory events.

When I returned to Ontario in 2001, led by serendipity once again, I settled in downtown Barrie, where an urban Camphill development was in the process of forming. Diane Kyd, who, with her husband, Chuck, had led the Camphill initiative in the area for many years, invited me to put the principles of IDRIART into practice in a community outreach that came to be known as "The Novalis Project." We adopted the slogan of "arts inspiring social renewal" and were guided by the many epigrammatic sayings of Novalis, around which I would form our seasonal programmes.

Novalis, a term that signifies "a clearing of ground for

new things," was the name assumed by a poet-philoso-pher-scientist who was born in Germany in 1772 and lived for only twenty-nine years. The ideals embedded in his writings seem pertinent to our twenty-first century. By observing the movement of his own inner life of thought, feeling and will, he gained a deep understanding of human nature. His seeking into depths of wisdom filled him with purpose and joy. He said, "The world must become more romantic—to make romantic is nothing but a qualitative raising of our experience to a higher power." I interpret this as a call for the awakening of imaginative capacities that slumber in human souls, and Novalis Project work-shops involve participants in a schooling of conscious-ness.

Led at first by the late Georg Kühlewind, the work-shops are now directed by visiting authors Michael Lip-son, Christopher Bamford, and others. Donald Hall, an art master from Bolzano, Italy, conducts our annual water-colour painting courses and his way of teaching points the way to a healthy, intensified quality of sensing. A mood of contentment always prevails during Donald's discourses on the history, meaning, and purpose of art, delivered between painting sessions when participants cluster in rapt attention around him. World-renowned spiritual psychologists Robert Sardello and Cheryl Sand-ers have been significant mentors and cherished friends of mine since they attended my concert at the Toronto Waldorf School in 1995—they presented one of our first courses at Novalis Hall on the theme of "Living More Fully from the Heart." Soon to follow was their colleague, musician/singer/composer/educator, Therese Schroeder-Sheker, who held a capacity audience in thrall in her evening concert in which she reflected on thirty years of experience in working with the dying. It preceded her "soul retreat for care givers" in which she focused on issues central to her pioneering work in the Chalice of Repose Project. I had once given the keynote address for her graduating students and she had featured me as a soloist in two of their annual concerts in Missoula, Montana. I came to know her well when we were both presenters at five of the Sardello School of Spiritual Psychology conferences, when I developed a deep admiration for her vision and accomplishments.

On the home front, Canadian author, lawyer, parliamentarian, professor, and publisher, Patrick Boyer, endeared himself to audiences for three years in a row, applying a rare flair for intuitive, living thinking—an art form in itself—to his informed and original presentations of vital political and social issues.

The visit of John and Carrie Schuchardt, from the House of Peace in Massachusetts, advanced our neighbourhood in the practice of a "hospitality that heals" since this remarkable and inspiring couple had welcomed over 400 refugees from approximately thirty countries to their home over the previous sixteen years. They provide healing refuge from the despair of war and enable each refugee to realize a fundamental and sacred right to peace, living as they do in therapeutic community with working adults who have disabilities.

Harpist Rita Costanzi, actor Glen Williamson, pianist Luiz Carlos de Moura Castro, singer Claudette Leblanc, Cuban musician Hilario Duran, Ballet Creole, the Esmeralda Enrique Flamenco Dance Company, Symphony in the Barn and the Scott Marshall Jazz Trio, harpist Mary Anderson, are several among the virtuoso artists who grace our stage at Novalis Hall—an architectural and acoustic gem located in a rural Camphill Village setting— all are imbued with a reverence for the meaning, form and poetry inherent in music and dance.

Each Camphill residence in our burgeoning neighbourhood appears to me an oasis of peace where time seems to stand still. The hustle and bustle of the usual household seems absent in the quiet order that prevails and I always feel the better for a visit. The Camphill co-workers with whom I collaborate, Diane and Chuck Kyd, and Ute Weinmann, have an innate reverence for the mystery of disability and the special way of life it engenders, a life rhythmically ordered around common everyday chores and the celebration of seasonal festivals. A daily experiment in relationship and self-development for co-workers, qualities of patience, equanimity and compassion are demanded of them by the people in their care—whose peculiar ways require special understanding. In this daring demonstration of curative education, I have seen "normal" abilities unfold in "companions" over time because of the loving attention and steadfast vocation of their caregivers.

I recently listened to Jean Vanier in a CBC radio interview speak about the l'Arche movement, that bears many similarities to Camphill, and the transformation he experienced in himself in working with developmentally disabled people. He was responding to questions he believed they were asking such as: "Do you love me? Do you see in me someone of value?" He described these questions as "often the cry of God," a God who does not intervene directly but demonstrates a deep respect for the freedom of each individual. He talked about the mystery of Christ's love and said to live with vulnerable people was to realize this mystery—"changing me, transforming me." It is a mystery the handicapped person lives, who has the courage to be weak. "People with disabilities can lead us into a new world," he said. "This leading through weakness is a manifestation of God." He talked about ways in which God "uses us" and that we should try to understand

His message to the world today. "It will reveal," he said, "the story of the presence of God in weak people." He suggested that humanity is being directed to form new relationships, listening especially to people who are different and that there is an urgent need to establish "places of freedom" where they can be enfolded.

Apart from the curative education which is its primary focus, the Camphill movement is noted for innovative architectural structures, bio-dynamic farming, and a range of home industries such as weaving, candle-making, book binding, baking, knitwear, and woodwork. As a model social organism, it addresses leading questions such as, "What is brokenness? What is the meaning of suffering and pain? Am I important?" Holding these questions in a conscious way is central to the mission of Camphill. It requires a real sense of the value and meaning of community as being more than the sum of its individual parts, and the heartfelt commitment of each individual to the mission itself. The implications of the Camphill experiment are far-reaching for social life today. In my next chapter, I will describe my own difficulties in coping with the "peculiar" behaviour of my mentally ill husband, in the absence of a closed social surrounding such as I now enjoy in the small and unpretentious lakeside city of Barrie. It would have been helpful, in years gone by, to belong to a therapeutic, supportive community that could also have served as a training ground for me, faltering caregiver that I was then in the more limited context of a nuclear family unit. My experience of living in a Camphill neighbourhood, leads me to conclude that only a dedicated enactment of such ideals as underpin this movement can bring about the quality of care required by a growing number of people like my late husband, for whom present day institutions offer only temporary solutions for the res-

toration of human dignity, creativity and engagement for
which so many cry out.

> *But suddenly the great*
> *Heartbeat enters into us invisibly*
> *And we cry out ...*
> *And then we are being, change and countenance.*
>   RILKE

11

Into the Deep Heart's Core

*...We had the experience but missed the meaning,
And approach to the meaning restores the experience
In a different form, beyond any meaning
We can assign to happiness...*
T.S. ELIOT, *Four Quartets*

*My life changed dramatically in 1969 when a near-fatal car acci-*dent occurred in which I escaped injury by involuntarily folding into a foetal position under the dashboard, as the vehicle Bob was driving careened over a wall. He had attempted to avoid a head-on collision with a car that unexpectedly turned out of a side road in our direction. Darkness had fallen as we headed towards Tuam on a balmy September evening. Bob was less fortunate than me. Hurled through the driver's window, he sustained multiple injuries to his spine that led to a long hospitalization in the care of the Bon Secour sisters—in the nursing home where our children had been born. He recovered from the injuries to his back and pelvis in the following months, but the damage to his nervous system was more

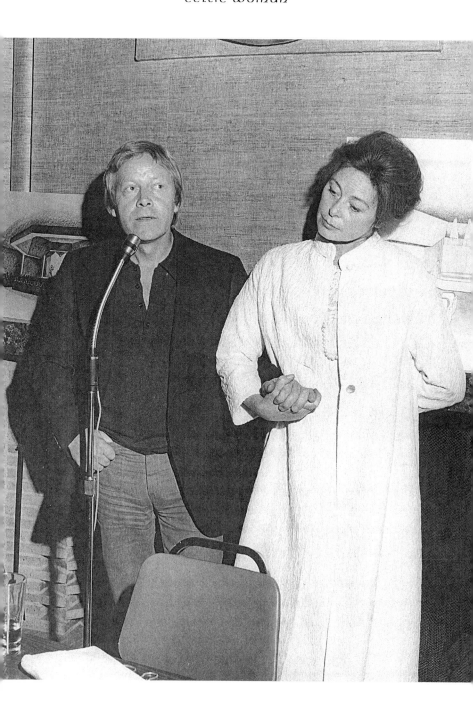

subtle, precipitating the manic depressive disorder that began to assail him two years later.

Notwithstanding recurring back pain after the accident, he maintained a heavy workload, travelling back to Toronto to lay the foundation for his Irish Arts Theatre production of *Juno and the Paycock* that would star Irish actors Siobhán McKenna, Jackie McGowran and Niall Tóibín, directed by the equally famous Seán Kenny. We spent a week in Hollywood in the spring of 1972, staying with the lead actors at the Chateau Marmont hotel where plans for the show were advanced. Seán Kenny was staying in the home of his close friend and colleague, dancer Gene Kelly, and we spent a memorable night there when Seán regaled us for hours with his account of crossing the Atlantic in a forty-foot boat, a story that had hit the international headlines some twenty years before. As a poor architectural student then, it was his means of realizing a dream, sailing from Ireland to America as cheaply as possible to sit at the feet of Frank Lloyd Wright. He duly served his apprenticeship to Wright for several years before garnering accolades as the designer of two London hits of the day, *Blitz* and *Oliver*. People had come away from both these shows, Jackie McGowran remarked, "humming the sets."

With such doyens of the theatre world in place, it was

Siobhán McKenna and Seán Kenny mark the inauguration of the Irish Arts Theatre at a reception held in St. Michael's College in 1971. Siobhán's introductory remarks remain vivid in memory: "I come from my country, the well of my soul, to bring you the great Irish writers..." The event was followed by copious drinking and revelry which caused them to miss their flight home. I made room for them in our house and had a lot of fun in the company of Siobhán who "brought the house down" wherever she was.

necessary for Bob to raise a great deal of money before the opening of *Juno* in early 1973, besides overseeing every other aspect of the production. Already in a state of exhaustion, he went on to Newfoundland from Toronto and there learned of a tragic incident involving two of his brothers, that had broken his mother's heart. He was at the end of his rope when he reached Dublin. Deeply concerned about his mother's distress, he could not bring himself to talk about the troubling incident. I suspected that he had also been drinking heavily while he was away. He sometimes broke into tears and became quite withdrawn from me and the children. I attributed these symptoms to his workload and anxiety about money, and did everything I could to cheer him up. We were on an extended sabbatical leave, living near the sea in an elegant Dun Laoghaire apartment. Briain and Robert had settled into a little Montessori school across the road where I was teaching Irish. We enjoyed the rhythm of daily life and the proximity of my sisters and their children. I expected the shadow cast over Bob's usually optimistic disposition to pass, hoping that we would soon resume our normal family life. Instead his agitation increased when December approached and we started to prepare for our return to Canada.

I shall never forget my first visit to Michael and Gráinne Yeats's Dublin home. Bob had been on tenterhooks since the invitation to lunch with them on December 23 was issued, and I was often reminded of the important event that lay ahead of us. I went to bed early the night before,

A happy moment captured here between father and sons Briain and Robert who liked to roam the Dun Laoghaire waterfront with Bob. His first breakdown occurred six months after this picture was taken.

not waiting up for Bob, who was dining with Lorna Reynolds, his collaborator on a *Yeats Studies Journal* they were editing at the time. The evening marked the onset of a paranoid episode—his first of many. I was not aware, as I slept soundly upstairs, that he made his entry into our house by breaking through a basement window, sustaining, in Houdini fashion, only a few small cuts. This was his means of evading the enemies he imagined were pursuing him.

Bob's behaviour appeared very odd the next morning and he would not hear of my cancelling the lunch. With growing apprehension I boarded the bus for Dalkey with him. When we arrived we found the entire Yeats family—Michael, Gráinne, their four children, and Anne—seated at a round, highly polished mahogany dining room table. We were late and the family was about to start without us. Bob took his chair without a word, glaring morosely at everyone. He maintained a sullen silence while bowls of dark brown soup were set before us. As I put a spoonful to my mouth he hissed, "Treasa, don't drink the soup!"

With a nervous laugh I improvised, "Oh, that's right Bob, I'm allergic to oxtails!"

I am sure Michael was wondering if this was the same professor who had badgered him with letters over the years, a person who had not appeared to be short of words. I made self-conscious attempts at small talk until a large chocolate mousse was placed in the centre of the table. Nobody could have known that on that day anything brown signified enemy action for Bob. With a decisive leap he bounded across to my side of the table, pulling me swiftly to my feet and out the door, declaring in tones of outrage, "Well that's it! My wife and I have had quite enough, thank you all very much!"

I looked back upon bewildered Yeats's faces as I gestured soundless apologies. There was more drama to fol-

low that evening, before men in white coats came at a
doctor's urgent bidding to carry Bob, now heavily sedated,
off in an ambulance. I was beside him as we were driven
from one hospital to another, until a bed could be found
at St. Patrick's hospital, where he remained for several
weeks until the mania receded. His dearest friend, Lorna
Reynolds, referred to this episode as "a brain storm," a
phrase I often repeated to others in my effort to make
light of what had been a very traumatic experience for
both me and the boys (then aged five and three), held hos-
tage for hours by a totally crazed Bob who insisted that
we would all "die together" in the room he had cordoned
off from the rest of the house. His doctors, when I sought
for answers, were always circumspect about the nature or
cause of the episode, seeming to rely entirely on drugs in
a "fix-it" attitude that I came to associate with every other
hospital which gave him refuge over time.

I could not but admire Bob's stoicism in meeting dead-
lines and work commitments while enduring the con-
tracting bout of depression that followed—which strong
medication did not entirely mask. The children and I could
enfold him in love and cheer him up as best we could, in
this more approachable phase of the illness. His iron rule,
however, was that there should be no mention of the epi-
sode at home or abroad, that it should remain a secret
between us that was a closed book. I encountered great
hostility if I ever crossed that boundary or attempted to
restrict his dietary or drinking habits, although sensing
that only a radical change in lifestyle would mitigate his
condition. The frenzy that had possessed him and led
to his hospitalization had given the term "frightened to
death" real meaning for me. I knew that I was as unpre-
pared as he was for what might happen if the terror that
had seized him on that fateful December day, took hold
of him again.

Ross Laing in his usual colourful garb. Before she met Ross, Emer had declared: "Everyone makes such a fuss about that doctor that anyone would think he had rainbows coming out of his suspenders! When Ross removed his sweater during his first family counselling session in our home, we all burst out laughing because he was actually wearing rainbow-coloured suspenders!

The years that lay ahead would prove severely testing for the "happily ever after" vision of marriage that I harboured. My identity was bound up in the tradition of wife and mother. Bob played the role of the "God" of my imagination and it seemed natural to me that life would order itself around him. It was his daily moods that made the "weather": he was the decisive element that determined the climate of every project to which I devoted myself. Priding in being his ideal helpmeet, I was deeply interested in his scholarly field and eager to assist in his Irish mission in every way I could.

Bob's manic episodes did recur, occurring annually and then bi-annually for a period of seven years. In the months between, however, we enjoyed a good rapport and I, a renewed sense of hope. I felt justified in keeping up appearances, throwing a mantle of protection over the children and covering tracks when things unexpectedly veered off the rails. It was in the latter years of our life together that I experienced a sense of helplessness in coping with a paranoia that became fixed in him and which precluded my reaching him at all. During that period, he was assailed by a melancholic and obsessive preoccupation with the past, and his eyes were full of a sadness that lasted until the upswing came, erupting in exuberant expectations of the future, which often came to pass in the exciting conferences and theatrical productions he brought to completion. I enjoyed them wholeheartedly, although my appreciation of these events coincided with the knowledge that I would also be simultaneously dealing with the inevitable fallout that paradoxically unfolded behind the scenes, another reminder that the opposite is also true.

My duties as hostess to many itinerant scholars and artists and the exigencies of now rearing four children, (Declan and Emer having arrived in due course) ensured that I had little leisure time during those years. I acquired a unique education outside the classroom, gathering gems of knowledge in the course of everyday life. Interesting and hectic as this way of life proved, it played against the backdrop of dramatic and disturbing scenes, some of which involved the intervention of police officers, as the bipolar pattern became entrenched. Highly sensitive people are most susceptible to fear, a pronounced element of our collective soul-life, although we can learn to find the depths of love within ourselves that cast out fear. I was often frightened by the changes in Bob's personality and frustrated by my helplessness in coping with this unpredictable malaise.

The measure of Bob's courage is nevertheless evidenced in his twenty years of indefatigable effort in opening up the consciousness of North America to a Celtic continuum. This revival was effected in a series of lively and memorable festivals of art and scholarship that came to popular public attention and laid the ground for his political manoeuvres in relevant corridors of power both in Ireland and in Canada. The first major festival, held in Toronto in 1978, gave the movement for Celtic renewal an international dimension with one of the two thousand participants coming from as far away as Persia. *The Celtic Consciousness*, a book that I refer to elsewhere in these pages, emerged as Bob's record of this cornerstone event for Celtic Studies. Ever inclusive, he employed a diversity of scholarly approaches in a comprehensive exploration of the myth, music, history, literature, folklore, art, and archaeology of the Celtic world and its relevance to the culture of our time.

I however, had to find a doctor on the eve of the festival to provide a quick-acting medication that would ensure Bob's participation in the elaborate programme he had devised. A breakdown was thereby averted and he would draw on reserves of willpower in functioning as master of ceremonies throughout the week, all the while on the verge of collapse.

I had my own slot on the programme to bear in mind, a concert to be performed at Convocation Hall mid-week with the French-Canadian group Barde; there were practical arrangements for babysitters, guests and household matters to deal with also in the midst of the rescue mission. I was fortunate in having youth on my side and an optimistic disposition in maintaining the balancing act that resulted.

Bob's clairvoyance became more pronounced with the advance of his illness—he had astonished me during our courting days in his accurate descriptions of people we were about to meet for the first time, and I always listened carefully to his seemingly irrational ramblings in which predictions of coming events were often encoded. For example, we spent our sabbatical year in the Dun Laoghaire home of Dr. Lydon. Then in her eighties, she had been Ireland's first female psychiatrist. Bob made his fateful plunge through her basement window in the dead of night during the first of his paranoid episodes. When she came to his assistance in her bathrobe, his insistent question to her was, "Have you made your will? Who is the main beneficiary?" She confessed to me after he had been hospitalized that his words had stirred her conscience and that she had reflected on his demand and now felt a moral obligation to substantially alter her will. I immediately helped her to bring this about and she died suddenly a few months later. While I cannot reveal the confidential details of how essential this bequest proved in the destiny of the beneficiary, I became aware that a tragedy was averted through Bob's overtly impertinent but now apparently justified "manic" intervention.

Someone described his condition to me as "a cancer of the brain," the unmitigated growth of cancer cells that is synonymous with bodily decay being likened to rampant mania that juxtaposed with debilitating depression in him. The seventh card of the Tarot's major arcana, featuring a charioteer holding the reins of two galloping horses, became a salutary reminder of the mastery that the individual "I" forces must maintain in balancing extremes of sympathy and antipathy that run riot in the soul if left to themselves. I was witness to the havoc wrought in Bob's psyche and surroundings and it was obvious to me that a force of resistance had been weakened in him, possibly through damage to internal organs during the accident or in childhood. The accident had precipitated the onset of a syndrome which could only take root if he already had a predisposition to it that might have had a hereditary or organic basis. I learned more about this after I had separated from Bob and I continue to have a keen interest in the subject.

Rudolf Steiner, in developing the scientific foundation for an anthroposophical approach to medicine, frequently used the word subtle in describing the organic disorders connected with mental illness. Many distortions result from developmental disorders in early life that later manifest as emotional imbalance. Some phase of growth, often emotional, may have been disrupted or bypassed thus creating a disposition towards mental illness in a person. Addiction to alcohol (or other artificial substances) will hinder the individual in his attempts to withstand such affliction. Steiner characterized alcoholic addiction as the attempt made by the "I" to build a wall on one side while simultaneously knocking it down on the other. Bob's addiction unfortunately increased as his illness progressed while his reliance on pharmaceutical drugs induced further complications eventually leading to his fatal heart attack at age fifty-seven. I recently shared a conference podium with Dr. James Dyson, a leading practitioner of anthroposophical medicine, remarking later to him on the difficulty I had in forgiving Bob for his bizarre and sometimes cruel behaviour. Hearing me out in profound silence he gently said, "We feel betrayed when the person we love no longer sees us."

Our children struggled valiantly in adapting to their

father's condition and to my preoccupation with it. This experience has taken its toll on the adult life of one of them in particular. All four continue to process its effects although I can also attest to depths of compassion that awakened in them at an early age as a result of this challenge. I remained a relentless "rescuer" until I could slowly acknowledge that I was not being met half-way by the "victim," who had abandoned himself to chance, to bullying rage or to thwarting any attempts at therapeutic intervention—invariably choosing to absent himself from family therapy sessions held in our home or elsewhere, determined, it seemed, to go his own way against all odds.

I remained enslaved to this dynamic until I realized that I was powerless to change anyone but myself. I eventually gave up on the conditions described but I did not give up on myself, striving from that time onwards to acquire necessary capacities of soul that would bring me into healthy relationship with the people around me. Whatever existed as my own unique purpose in life, I knew was hidden in all I had lived through to date. But I had to recognize that I had reached a crisis before I could move on. It was the fall of 1988 and I had returned from Ireland with Declan and Emer (who had persistently lobbied for a speedy return to Toronto), after a one-year trial separation from Bob. Once again I received the assistance I needed through the kindness of a friend, poet Penn Kemp, who suggested I talk to our mutual friend, Dr. Dermot Grove-White. He invited me to attend the opening of the Toronto Institute for Self Healing with which his medical practice was affiliated. Intrigued as to the nature of this institute, I agreed to meet him there.

I arrived at the Queen Street address mid-morning on the opening day, expecting to find a coffee party in progress. When I entered the large, light filled, carpeted room, I found a very different scene in place. There were bodies of every shape and size, colour, and race positioned on the floor, either lying or sitting, while others gathered in clusters or knelt on colourful cushions to give comfort and encouragement and dispense paper tissues to those supine and tearful. Dermot was soon at my side, exuding the kindness and compassion I had always recognized in him through years of encounter in the Irish social circle to which both belonged. I often relied on him for assistance during Bob's episodes. "What on earth is going on here?" I asked him. "Am I in the wrong room?" Gesturing towards a spot on the floor that had just been vacated he invited me to stretch out. Positioned behind my head and gently touching my shoulders, his familiar presence was comforting amidst sounds of sighing, crying and groaning. Then he asked me how I was coping at home. This was enough to open a floodgate of tears that must have welled up in the pent up tension of years, so consistent was the flow. It was the beginning of a therapeutic washing away of care and trouble that would continue over many months.

My friend explained that this room would provide the setting for a new style of encounter that Dr. Ross Laing, whose apprentice Dermot was, would introduce to patients like me who were seeking to improve the quality of their lives and relationships. I was not destined to meet Ross Laing for another few weeks so Dermot filled me in, saying that Ross (with whom everyone at the Institute was on first name terms) described himself as "a metaphysician in the Socratic mode and a radical psychiatrist in the Claude Steiner mode of transactional analysis." Dr Laing would conduct group sessions and private consultations here, assisted by Dermot and a few other therapists-in-training. A member of Ross's core group from 1988 to 1990, I was privileged to engage in the first wave of his experiment in which self-healing is defined as "becoming the true self." This approach implied that it was the manner in which I thought, felt, and acted that brought about my actual state of mind and circumstances and that I could alter my outer circumstances by becoming a witness to my ways of avoiding relationship.

I had been struck, in the course of my early readings, by a statement Rudolf Steiner had made: "The estrangement of individuals from one another will happen of its own accord but what is to flow from the human heart must be consciously sought. Motivation for a new way of working in the world must be wrung consciously from the heart's blood." I hoped to discover this "new way of working" in the context of Ross's experiment. Many of those attracted to this work as I was, existed in circumstances more challenging than mine, some among them were homeless, dysfunctional or terminally ill. Every level of society, every national background, age and profession found representation in the stream of hopefuls that beat a path to this oasis of compassion. Would that every metropolis could provide citizens with such sanctuary in good times and bad, I often thought.

Ross Laing pledged himself to "comforting the afflicted and afflicting the comfortable." He invited me to observe how remote my habitual behaviour was from what I wishfully imagined it to be, how far removed I was in the actual living of my life from the ideals I espoused. Aldous Huxley, Ross believed, was on the right track when he wrote: "If only I knew who in fact I am, I should cease to behave as what I think I am. If I stopped behaving as what I think I am, I should know who I am." In the safety of this haven I became a willing witness to my denials and compromises of a lifetime. I became aware of the paradigm shift in behaviour and attitude that was required of me if I wanted to live a truly healthy life.

While the spiritual researches of Rudolf Steiner had

unravelled many riddles of existence, I was nevertheless still a creature of habit and social conditioning. I wanted to put freedom of thought and social understanding to the test and to embody the truths I had gleaned. Ross provided me with his own demonstration of how to "walk the talk." Acquiring a set of concepts from the New Age smorgasbord will not of itself guarantee a fundamental change in direction, however. The urge for renewal is widespread although the recovery of the true self can pose a very arduous task to the seeker. Anne Stockton, a close friend, once remarked to me, "Ideas do a stimulating dance in the middle of our minds. But do they travel horizontally in one ear and out the other? What trickles down into the heart? How much drips down into the will?"

The symptoms of distress in evidence today are the mark of a culture we all help to shape. Its antidote must also emerge out of a social context, I believe. The one-on-one relationship between therapist and client is only a single feature of a more comprehensive group process that provides a necessary social setting in which to put new resolve to the test. I discovered at the Institute that any dysfunctional aspects I would identify in my interactions with others could be safely addressed and resolved in this environment. Those seeking the services of Ross Laing and his colleague-in-training at the time, Dermot Grove-White, were suffering from contraction in the soul-life, in flight from circumstances that brought hidden fears to the surface of consciousness; fear of failure, fear of success, fear of violence, fear of intimacy, fear of life. The variations on the theme were endless although we might not have been able to identify their common source.

Ross, through rigorous discipline and witnessing, had already found the depths of love within himself to lead us into an open-eyed encounter with the autonomous force of fear itself. This experience was a pivotal, inescapable entry for me into what Yeats had termed "the foul rag and bone shop of the heart." Another respected friend, Robert Sardello, had also made brave entry into the fray with the publication of his book *Freeing the Soul from Fear*. He said of fear in his introduction: "Besides showing up as individual psychological difficulties, we now have to contend with this destructive force as a cultural phenomenon that touches us all more deeply and significantly than we might ever imagine. The soul-life of humanity is in danger."

Ross Laing would confront this danger by holding steady to his goal of thirty years. Because he had witnessed his beloved brother die at the age of twenty from Hodgkin's disease, he had resolved to devote himself to finding the cause of, and antidote to, the cancerous condition. When he became a doctor, his keen observation of patients convinced him that the way we breathe is crucial to the health of the physical organism, since every cell of the body relies on oxygen for survival. He made me aware of how shallow my normal breathing could be. He could also prove that the images I carry of myself, positive or negative, directly influence my state of bodily health and quality of life. He had once been a shy, awkward and relatively anti-social person himself. "Nobody could empty a room faster than I could!" he joked. I could hardly believe this to be true of someone of such peaceful, loving and magnetic presence. "The more you visualize the qualities you aim towards, the more likely it is that form will follow. There are contrary influences, dependencies, but they do not determine the outcome!" Dr. Laing declared.

Four basic exercises were developed at the Institute that I readily incorporated into my daily routine. Their benefits soon became obvious to me:

Deep Diaphragmatic Breathing: To breathe in such a way that the waist expands to its maximum with every breath for twenty minutes twice a day.

Affirmation: As we began each conscious breathing session Dr. Laing encouraged us to repeat the following words: "I am willing to experience and express the fullness of my feelings and thoughts in ways that uplift me and all creation."

Stroking: We were frequently reminded to express self-appreciation, self-acknowledgment and unconditionally loving compassion, to foster a spirit of gratitude and celebration in daily life, to engage in physical stroking that would create a sensation of warmth in the heart

Responsibility: We had to present a willingness to explore the concept of taking full responsibility for creating the quality of our own experience.

Oxygen is the nutrient most essential to the human organism. Every cell of the body relies on a constant flow of breath and every kind of chronic illness is associated with a disturbance in tissue oxygenation. As I learned to pay attention to my breathing I noticed that it reflected different states of tension or relaxation in me. I had become accustomed to a "fight or flight" modality in day-to-day life and the shallowness of breath that resulted was quite inadequate to my physical needs. Ross recommended that I observe how a baby breathes and do likewise. The practice of belly breathing morning and evening and whenever I was under stress became over time habitual and is now my abiding source of relaxation and energy. Rather than dwell on the content of troubling thoughts, I was advised to watch my breathing instead and in this way bring about a change in my actual state of being. This enabled me to leave the "victim" mentality I had previously fostered behind and to realize that I could choose the quality of my own thoughts by slowing down my breathing and observing the contents of my thinking. My new life began as soon as I made this fundamental shift in my inner experience.

The greater the difficulties the greater the potential for good contained in them. I sought refuge at the Institute when I could no longer cope with the daily circumstances of my life.

Besides causing frequent upheaval in our family life, my husband's illness led to his periodic suspension from university teaching, although the quality of his teaching and popularity with students was never in question during his months of reprieve from the illness. It was touching to read the many letters of support written by students when his responsibilities to them came into question, each one gave testimony of the love for literature that Bob had awakened in him or her. I however, was confounded often in my attempts to maintain household order when Bob assumed the role of enfant terrible, torn between a need to protect the children from the general upheaval and my fears concerning Bob. He could function at fever pitch, going without sleep for several days when a manic phase held sway; such periods were followed, however, by deep depression that was painful to even witness. Being now relegated to the position of "enemy" in his bizarre order of things, I had to accept that there was little hope for further intimacy with the man who had once shared everything with me. Yet I hesitated to take the step of leaving with the children, afraid of the battle that could ensue.

I remember Ross's first question to me in a private consultation: "Why are you here?"

"I am here because I can no longer cope with my husband's paranoia."

"You cannot cope with your paranoia," he responded.

"You misunderstand me, Dr. Laing. I am speaking about my husband's paranoia."

"Your husband is your mirror," he gently replied.

I shrieked in horror at such a suggestion. I was unaware as yet that the numbness I experienced in my physical body was due to the grip that fear had on me at a cellular level. The emotional disturbance that now daily claimed my attention was an outward manifestation of my deep-seated fears. I learned about my own subconscious conditioning by watching and assisting other group members in their processing of similar material and through Ross's intuitive interventions. All my life I had been excessively tolerant of unwelcome behaviour, hungry for approval. I had avoided confronting disturbing issues and was often willing to compromise my own interests.

The only curriculum offered at this academy was life itself, and our homework entailed a willingness to deal with issues that arose on the home front and report on them to the group. I had to overcome my initial aversion and shame in airing intimate details of my dramatic home life before any gathering. I soon noticed, however, that I overcame this reluctance when I could speak freely without fear of reprisal or judgment. Only in acknowledging my frustration and fear and in letting the unshed tears of years to freely flow could I eventually find the courage to leave Bob for my own sake. Ross noticed that I could hardly utter a sentence without mentioning the name of my husband. He asked me to count the number of these references in the course of the day. I had to continue to report on this in nightly phone calls to him until I had entirely broken the habit.

Habits do not evaporate of themselves but we can outwit them if we adopt the right strategy. The energy that is thereby released can be channelled into more positive action. After two years of attendance at the Institute, I succeeded in breaking free of my preoccupation with Bob's behaviour, which had remained unaltered. I alone had changed, and could now begin to remove myself from the situation. Laing's definition of the guilt that had dogged me, "The impulse to change being turned back against oneself," had helped to free me of it. I had a new and practical goal to live up to—the ability to maintain an open heart regardless of circumstances. I also realized that I could no longer devote myself to helping anybody who had not specifically asked for that help.

The emphasis in our group work was not so much on what we would talk about, but rather on how we spoke to one another. Laing operated on the premise that 94 percent of the unspoken in our communication can be gleaned from the tone of our voices. When we really listen, we become aware that most people speak out of a tone of desperation, he said, and this is due to the fact that we were never truly loved for our own sakes. I was often stopped in mid-sentence: "Are you aware of your tone?" In listening to others, we were encouraged to hear what was going on behind the words and to respond accordingly, thus establishing more of a feeling connection with the other.

We learned to question one another without resorting to accusations, never starting with "You should…" or "You always…" or "You did not…" Laing also expressed the wish to "clear the world of gossip." This impressed me particularly, as one of a people about whom G.K. Chesterton said, "The Irish are a fair people. They never speak well of one another!" We agreed to be very direct with our silent judgments during group sessions but to speak in a positive vein about one another in absence. I read out a passage from Rudolf Steiner to the group one day: "In future time we will become aware that in our communication with others all sorts of unconscious opinions, habits, sympathies and antipathies, aversions, undigested aggressions and so on play a role. We not only perceive very little about other people, we colour what we do perceive, transforming it in accordance with our own preferences and prejudices…and it is with this inaccurate image of the other person that we enter into a dialogue with him or her." I was grateful for this opportunity to devote a period of my life to consciously observing such attitudes as these in myself that might otherwise have gone unnoticed in what I think and say.

When criticism was levelled in its proper context and resolved there and then, it curbed our tendency towards backbiting, I noticed. A decision not to speak about anything that transpired in the circle increased our collective momentum and ensured the integrity of our enterprise. I resorted often to poetry in the course of our sessions and spontaneously recited at moments when we were all at a loss for words. One of my favourites was from R.D. Laing's insightful book of poems entitled *Knots*. A mentor for Ross Laing, the maverick Scottish psychiatrist (their shared surname means "angel of mercy") had based his work on the observation that although we can experience each other's behaviour we fail to experience each other's experience.

What happened at the Institute constituted the only show in town for me during those years. I could observe and participate there in the unfolding, wholly absorbing drama of my hugely extended "family" life. I witnessed scenes of apparent conflict and saw them move towards resolution as a colourful cast of characters from every walk of life played their extemporaneous roles. I noticed the habit of creating scapegoats, a symptom of hidden guilt and fear in any tight knit group, was laid to rest as family units within the group were restored to the harmonious vibration of love that bound them together in the first place. My children and those of other group members entered into the therapeutic process since nobody's problem exists in a vacuum. Bob ventured to join in a few times but eventually felt too threatened by the process. Family members of other regular attendees flew in from far-flung places when a moment of reconciliation was at hand. Such joyful reunions confirmed my belief in the power of love. I often lay on the carpet and listened to Laing interact with new arrivals. One day, a young couple presented their story. They were in love and had decided to live together, except there was a snag—the young man already had a wife. What should they do? Ross's first question was addressed to the girl.

"Have you spoken to your sister?"

"I don't have a sister," came her reply.

He repeated the question until she realized that the sister he alluded to was the woman whose husband she loved. Ross then suggested that this "sister" attend their next session since she was also implicated in the drama. In listening to such an exchange, I was more than ever mindful of the divine Presence that makes entry where two or three are gathered in the enterprise of self healing.

Many statements, uttered by Ross Laing in passing, are forever etched in memory:

> Healing is perfectly natural. The only reason we don't know about this is that we work against it twenty-four hours of the day. You don't have to do anything except breathe with the diaphragm and be willing to experience the fullness of feeling.
>
> You must demonstrate your ability to keep your word no matter what . . .
>
> Unconditional love is the practice of unconditionally living on the creative edge.

Everyone attending the core group on a regular basis was encouraged to introduce the self-healing modality that had worked for themselves to others. I once asked Laing in the course of my apprenticeship with him how I would know when I was ready to introduce his technique to others since he offered no formal curriculum or final exam. His answer was that I would know I was qualified when ninety percent of the people I came into contact with would realize, by my example, what it was to become a "true self," his definition of self-healing. "Unless information is embodied it has no chance of generation," were his actual words.

I continue to practise the principles he taught me always with his elusive goal in mind and in the joy of sharing the benefits to which I can personally attest. I am still, however, learning to overcome my tendency to repress unwanted or uncomfortable feelings. This involves shifting my focus from a diverting train of thought to a feeling or mood which might have arisen out of the blue and giving it due attention without unduly indulging it. Feelings are forces that engender qualities of soul and an openness of heart. Only out of the hard and bitter agony of experience can the feeling life be transformed and the way cleared for meaningful action. "Free will" implies the ability to do what one knows one must do—a "freedom for" as well as a "freedom from" the impediments that thwart our will to action. These can often be traced to a suppression of feeling.

As a result of the lessons I learned at the Institute, I was fortuitously "ahead of all parting" when I left the family home with my youngest child Emer, our few suitcases bursting at the seams. A generous friend who encouraged the move had given me his assurance of financial support in the coming months. Another friend offered us rental accommodation in her home until we made our intended departure for Vancouver, where I had been invited to perform in a festival of Celtic music. Prior to leaving the house, I had scrubbed it clean, polished the floors, shampooed the rugs, pressed all my husband's suits and laundered everything in sight. Bob was away at the time and I knew he would be devastated when he returned to find I had gone. I still regret the pain I caused him and I realize that the temporary solutions I sought out and optimistically provided for him fell far short of the actual needs of everyone in question. I also know that the one who takes the physical action of leaving a marriage is often doing so in response to the other's having already departed the relationship by another door, so to speak.

We had made our last foray as a couple in July 1989, travelling to India on the insistent recommendation of a recent acquaintance, where Bob was convinced he could dissuade me from my intention of leaving him. I was then still naively in search of a miracle that would restore equilibrium to our lives and was easily persuaded to spend a month in the exotic environs of the Poona ashram of Osho Rajneesh, a guru previously unknown to either of us. A distinguished professor of philosophy, Rajneesh, (previously known as Bagwan), whose student body was so huge that it could not be contained within any lecture hall, had found it necessary to give his talks in the open air. This bursting out of established structure had been Bob's invisible model for his own endeavours, so Osho's style struck a chord with him. The guru was a great storyteller and I laughed heartily during the daily videotaped showings of his talks. Sannyasins, or disciples, were always collecting jokes for him, many of them quite off-colour. A sheaf of the latest ones would be handed to him before a talk. Taking them in at a glance, he would then weave the most hilarious philosophical discourse around these yarns. It made me realize how much the philosopher and born comic have in common. We were invited to view the ashram's vast library that included a copy of Bob's

The Celtic Consciousness. A staff member relayed Osho's request for me to add my presentation of poetry and song to the many fine musical offerings from all over the world, heard nightly in the magnificent white marble-floored Buddha Hall.

Unfortunately, the nervous exhaustion and confinement endured on the long plane ride home brought on a severe manic episode in Bob, leading to explosive airport scenes and to what had by now become the inevitable hospitalization. Five months after our return from India, I secured a legal separation, making the break with the support of the friends I mentioned. Bob's preoccupation with conspiracy theory was total by then. Fixed obsession was an obvious side effect of psychiatric drugs, copiously administered over years of affliction. Assailed by fearful foreboding as coming events cast their shadow in him, he exerted a monumental effort of concentration and financial risk in producing his Armageddon series of books, with such arresting titles as *NATO and the Warsaw Pact are One*, *The New World Order*, *The Throne of the Anti-Christ* and *Corruption in Canada*. Most of his research was conducted in bars where he was more and more frequently at home after I left him. Many of the scenarios that robbed him of sleep are ironically coming to pass in our world today, and the limited editions of his Armageddon books are much sought after by conspiracy theorists and are now fetching high prices on the worldwide web. He fled from Canada in 1995, in fear of his life because of his personal associations with some wayward and ruthless individuals, and spent a few restless and tortuous months in Dublin, cared for by my sister Anne, until his heart gave out on February 29, 1996.

When someone enquired of me in Vancouver, shortly after his death, if I had once been married to "the O'Driscoll who wrote conspiracy books," I replied, "No,

I was once married to the Robert O'Driscoll who wrote
The Celtic Consciousness."

Despite his fall from public grace and the deprivation
and loneliness of his final tragic months in Ireland, Bob
accomplished the goals of his Irish mission and was a true
catalyst for change. In writing this chapter I could relive
the inner tensions that drove us apart while recognizing
that the spiritual purpose of our union had been realized
in the birth of our four children and in a spirited collabo-
ration that bore fruit on an academic and social level. If
we had not been so caught up in a whirlwind of activity
we might have had a more trusty "ship" of relation in
which to navigate rough waters. There is a larger than life,
mythic quality to the image of Bob I carry in my heart,
reflective of the spirit that animated his eternal striving
and that led him, willy-nilly, into the belly of the beast.
The selfless dedication of his life can be counted in many
gathered treasures of my life, moulded and influenced as
it was, by the pure formative force of his love. The mys-
tery of who Bob is in spirit continues to grow in my heart
as I contemplate the life we shared and hearken to the
thoughts expressed in lines by William Blake:

> Go, merciless man, enter
> into the infinite labyrinth of
> another's brain
> Ere thou measure the circle he
> shall run,
> Go, thou cold recluse into the
> Fires
> Of another's high flaming bosom
> And return uncondensed,
> and write laws
> If thou cans't not do this,
> doubt thy theories ...

12

The Way of Right Speech

To keep silent. Who has kept more
silent inwardly
touches the roots of speech.
Some day each sprung syllable
Will be for him a victory
Over what is not silent in silence…
RILKE

My *years at the Institute awakened my keen sense of the impor-*
tance of our communication with one another, be it
written, verbal or unspoken. Although I often failed in
my attempts to communicate with Bob, woefully lack-
ing in the restraint, diplomacy, and objectivity required,
I took heart in the lines by Rilke quoted above which I
came across in Georg Kühlewind's *Becoming Aware of the
Logos.*

In the course of our first meeting, Georg had handed
me the name and phone number of his translator, Michael
Lipson, recommending that I contact him in New York,
where he worked at the time as chief psychologist in the

Harlem Hospital for children dying of AIDS. It would be several years before I would serendipitously meet Dr. Lipson at a School of Spiritual Psychology conference in Massachusetts; he remains a dear friend and mentor ever since, and, like me, can recite many poems by heart. Our conversations are always peppered with quotations. "You can sometimes be with a person who is so intensely present that there is nothing that could be spoken between you that would be equal to the impact of that presence," he once remarked.

"I had many experiences like that at the Institute of Self-Healing," I told him, "in one-on-one conversations with Ross Laing. Sometimes a compelling silence left everyone in the circle at a loss for words. I could sense in those instances that I was tuning in to where language, or the Word, originates."

"If I knew where the great songs come from I would go there more often!" Michael said, quoting Leonard Cohen.

"A native elder similarly remarked after sitting through a silent Quaker meeting, "It was good to spend some time in the place where words come from …" I rejoined.

"If your focus of attention is intense enough, it calls the heavens into resonance and connects you with the stars." Michael reminded me.

I had just attended Michael's workshop, "Right Speech: The Art of Shared Humanity." The practice of this central feature of the Buddha's eightfold path, Michael argues, will restore us to a world full of meaning. It implies learning to pause before and sometimes deliberately refrain from speaking or to only mentioning what is significant and relevant to a given topic. I told my friend that such an approach to speaking was employed by Dr. Laing, whose invariable question was: "What is your purpose in saying that?" I had gradually learned to form a clearer intention

Michael Lipson is a clinical psychologist in private practice in Great Barrington, Massachussets. He previously served as chief psychologist at the Harlem Hospital for children dying of AIDS. He has translated books by Kühlewind and has developed a meditative practice inspired by his esteemed mentor Georg. I look forward to Michael's bi-annual visits to my home in Barrie when he presents his popular meditation workshops at Novalis Hall for a growing number of students.

before starting to speak and found that the words then flowed of their own accord.

My daughter seemed to have an innate sense of this since early childhood. When she entered Waldorf kindergarten the teacher noticed that she was not very talkative. When I asked her about this, she quickly replied: "I only speak when I have something to say. Other people chatter!" Out of the mouths of babes and sucklings...

"When we speak truly, we are in line with the whole universe in its truth so that it is the world-as-meaning, the world of meaning that speaks through us," Michael replied.

"So much of what we hear and read today is meaningless, even distorted, for the sake of political correctness or to further some hidden agenda." I said.

"Faust, in one of the early scenes from Goethe's play, was translating the prologue to the Gospel of St. John and distorted the first line to read 'In the beginning was the deed ...' At that very moment a black poodle running around his study transformed itself into Mephistopheles. Goethe was suggesting here that when non-meaning prevails demonic entities are unleashed," Michael informed me.

"Meaning strikes home by surprise when a flash of inspiration comes in the form of a witty remark. Cliché, on the other hand, because it implies repeating catch phrases, as in TV ads, inures us to non-meaning; such slogans as "Guinness is good for you!," and "because you're worth it!" lodge mantra-like in the mind as half-truths, leading us down a blind alley, unless we consciously reject them. Cliché represents a kind of weed in the garden of language. James Joyce set about coining a new language that was reflective of the actual flow of human consciousness when it is not parcelled into old thought-forms but is allowed to form itself into whatever pattern of words best conveys an intuitive, inherently spiritual, always new, activity of thinking," I said.

"Novalis, living at the turn of the eighteenth century, contended that speaking should flourish for its own sake as a revelation of the inner nature and purpose of language. He urged us to become masters of an endless play—he himself loved to improvise and banter to counter the serious and ponderous style of other speakers of his day," Michael replied.

"Great poets continuously bring language back to the freshness of original meaning. Rilke, who lived a hundred years after Novalis, urged us to speak out, to bear witness, to praise and celebrate ordinary things. He advocated a reverence for language, describing whatever came to his attention "with an intensity the things themselves never dreamed they'd express." The quality of our listening also comes into play in conversation when we need to strike a balance between a give and take that can sometimes be one-sided," I remarked.

"When two people arrive at this balance between speaking and listening they might well say to one another what the poet Holderlin once said: 'We are a conversation that can eventually become a song'" Michael concluded.

It was easy to arrive at such a satisfactory rhythm of speaking and listening when I was talking to Michael. I am fortunate in having other friends who, like him, are also truly conscious in what they say and do. They practise meditation as Michael does, a few of them having taken up Rudolf Steiner's thought exercises. These entail a focusing of one's thoughts on a simple man-made object such as a pencil, pin or paper clip, for five minutes at a given time each day. To become absorbed thus is a means of consciously "holding the reins" over the thoughts that normally whirl around of their own accord. I have gradually become more skilled in this with time and it seems to

advance the art of conversation, giving scope for improv-
isation and in going off at tangents, without losing the
thread of the dialogue. A good jazz ensemble such as my
favourite Scott Marshall Trio, can illustrate this technique
very well and it is one of the reasons I enjoy and promote
this kind of music.

On the other hand, if I have an emotional charge with
somebody I am close to, I find it very difficult to think
clearly, becoming defensive, argumentative or incoherent.
I sometimes find it better to go away and practise diaphrag-
matic breathing and then return to the thorny, emotion-
ally charged topic, by which time my companion will also
hopefully have calmed down. I can then acknowledge my
difficulty and we can agree on some ground rules, such
as allowing a pause to occur after each one has spoken.
To articulate what the issue is and how it can be resolved
requires a preparing of common ground. I have tended to
avoid confrontation all my life, and value the techniques I
learned at the Institute, which have to be called into serv-
ice again and again.

Somebody had once asked Michael in a workshop:
"How do we recognize one another after death?" Michael
responded that Rudolf Steiner spoke about the way in
which discarnate souls are always entering and opening
to one another in a process of "wording" that reveals and
distinguishes the essential nature of each one, a direct
expression of spiritual substance and kinship. I believe
that we are engaged in a similar recognition of essence in
one another when we practise the art of conversation.

Michael had pointed out in the workshop I attended,
that the sign and meaning side of words are not necessar-
ily synonymous. He gave an example from Shakespeare.
Hamlet, having decided to kill Claudius, came upon him
praying and postponed the deed, lest he send his wicked
uncle to heaven. But Claudius was only appearing to pray

and could realize that ... "words without thoughts never to heaven go." Reciting prayers by rote was something I did when I was young, with my thoughts roaming like will-o'-the-wisps all the while. In meditating on the lines of particular poem, such as those quoted at the top of the chapter, I learned to bring my thoughts and feelings into unity with their actual source of meaning. This process prepares me for what I identify as meditative prayer, which depends on working with a text I classify as sacred. The Gospel of John serves this purpose well and no poem, however spiritual its content, can provide such a force of regeneration in the soul.

Take for example the loving recommendation that appears in this gospel: "Let not your hearts be troubled." These words have immediate and vital appeal, going directly to the heart, because they are imbued with the power of the Christ. In the Gospel of John, Jesus speaks as the incarnated Logos, the embodied principle through which everything in creation comes into being. In meditating on the sayings of Christ as revealed in this text, I have found that they are not merely to be understood but have spiritual force in themselves, transformative in essence. The Gospel of John leads to an experience of divine love. It restores the troubled heart to a natural state of acceptance and receptivity and the sense of having found a true home in Him.

A story from the Gospel of St. Luke demonstrates how the speech of Christ Jesus could penetrate the hearts of his listeners. Two disciples were walking the road to Emmaus on the day referred to thereafter as Easter Sunday. They were talking together earnestly about the extraordinary events that had recently taken place in Palestine. Jesus appeared and joined them but they did not recognize Him. He asked, "What are you discussing?"

They told him about the teaching mission of the man

they knew as Jesus, his travels, condemnation, and cruci-
fixion, remarking in surprise. "Are you the only one who
does not know?" They could relate how some women of
their acquaintance had gone to the tomb that morning and
had seen a vision of angels where the body of Jesus had
lain. The stranger, who was the Risen Christ, explained
to them why it was necessary for events to unfold as they
did, interpreting the scriptures to indicate that all had
been fulfilled as was written. He accompanied them to
the resting place when they stopped for the night. It was
only when He broke bread at the table with them that they
recognized Him.

They said afterwards: "Did not our hearts burn within
us when He talked to us on the road, while he was opening
up the scriptures to us!" Enfolded in divine presence, they
had entered the matrix where all understanding originates
and their hearts burned in the consuming fire of truth.

All truths wait in all things
They neither hasten their own
Delivery nor resist it ...
— WALT WHITMAN

The separation from Bob after my years at the Institute
brought my involvement with university affairs to an end.
I was no longer privy to detailed reports on the progress
of Celtic Studies, no longer regaled by the latest scholar-
ship in the field. What I had learned would not be forgot-
ten and would be adapted to the now more compelling
context of a conscious spiritual life. A newly published
book fell serendipitously into my hands to provide a
bridge between this instructive period of my life and the
experiences that lay ahead of me. In this groundbreaking
work, *Speech of the Grail*, author Linda Sussman, a friend
and fellow bard, masterfully guides the reader in a creative

re-enactment of Parzival's journey of self-discovery. Her book is a profound meditation on "right speech" as the guiding principle of a contemporary path. She demonstrates how this undertaking can lead the initiate into the spiritual activity of intuitive thinking, openness of heart and a capacity for moral action. The engrossing story of the Grail legend, identified as "the founding myth of Western civilization" by Joseph Campbell, provides Sussman with the structure for a dynamic exploration of vivid, archetypal characters and images. Her inspired interpretation presents the reader with a timeless metaphor that turns dramatically on an act of speech.

The hero's adventure begins with an innocent childhood query addressed to his mother, "What is God?" It reaches its fulfilment in another question, posed to his sick uncle when he makes his second visit to the Grail castle many years later. Although he had found the castle relatively easily the first time, he had failed to articulate the required specific question because he had not yet learned to listen to what was living in the hearts of others. Only when years of hardship and deprivation had tempered his soul, and with the guidance of a few key individuals, could he make his renewal of faith and be given a second chance to enter the castle. Speaking finally out of compassion, he could give voice to a genuine interest and depth of feeling when he addressed Anfortas, the ailing Grail King thus: "Uncle, what ails thee?"

This simple question effected the simultaneous healing of his uncle and the entire surrounding land, which had been laid waste. The "wasteland" was a motif no less relevant in medieval times than in the early twentieth century when T.S. Eliot, inspired by his reading of this legend, gave the world his celebrated poem. Wolfram von Eschenbach was moved to write the story in the thirteenth century because he had observed the spirituality of the people of his day being undermined by a system of values at odds with the natural order of life. Eliot could also recognize the "wasteland" of inauthentic lives dutifully, obediently or grudgingly lived in the sacrifice of spontaneity, love and moral tact. The Institute became my antidote to a later version of this malaise that must be countered by every individual in his or her own way.

The active Grail substance of spiritual love permeates and nurtures people in accordance with their needs and capacities, and nourishes an invisible web of human relationships. The receptive imagination of poets and artists finds sustenance and inspiration there too. In like manner, the listening field of an audience is nourishing for me as a performer. In fact, it is essential to the success of each presentation I give. Experience has taught me that I unconsciously anticipate the expectations of certain individuals in a prospective audience in my choice of material in the weeks leading up to a performance. Somebody's favourite poem will mysteriously bring itself to my attention or I will find myself changing course in mid-stream on the night when an after-show encounter with a member of the audience will provide me with the reason. Sometimes an audience will have such collective intensity of attentiveness that I have to hold a strong focus in my delivery or run the risk of losing my thread completely.

The longer I live, the more convinced I am of the truth of what Joseph Campbell wrote, in reference to the Grail legend: "There is no fixed law, no established knowledge of God set up by prophets or priests that can stand against the revelation of a life lived with integrity in the spirit of its own brave truth."

This mediaeval epic is Celtic in origin and I can find resonance with its hero, who is described as, "a brave man slowly wise." The story begins with a striking image of a magpie, whose plumage is black and white, the colours of heaven and hell that mingle in every human soul. Every aspect of human life included in my own journey is explored in this tale, often with a humorous twist. We read about birth and childhood; portentous meetings and partings; the woman's experiences of joy and sorrow, death and grief; courtly, sensual and spiritual love, friendship, the cultivation of Christian and communal values, right speech, ritual gatherings and the power of magic. Above all, it charts an archetypal journey in which the consciousness of the hero evolves and transforms through a process of trial and error. In striking out on his own, he learns to forge a path of freedom and to gradually advance beyond self-interest to devotion to the common good. Readers may trace a similar pattern of development in their own lives, as I do in mine at a time when skeletons are being released from their closets in droves, affairs having surely become "soul size" now. We make the world larger in scope when we are united in the journey of self-discovery and "exploration into God" for which Christopher Fry makes ardent plea, in these lines extracted from his poem "Sleep of Prisoners," which I often recite:

> ... Affairs are now soul size
> The enterprise is exploration into God.
> Where are you making for?
> It takes so many thousand years to wake
> But, will you wake, for pity's sake!

13

Entering the Overlap Zone

Two monks called Kevin and Kieran, have the
following exchange as they peel potatoes:
Kevin: Being spiritual is thinking about spiritual things
while peeling potatoes!
Kieran: Being spiritual is thinking about peeling potatoes
while peeling potatoes!

While writing this, I usually rewarded myself at the end of each chapter with a visit to my parents' home in Tuam, a little over an hour's drive from Killaloe. Arriving there on a balmy evening in early June, I was just in time for the popular *Late Late Show* that had the whole country glued to the TV on Friday nights, since it left no stone of Irish life unturned. I was thrilled to recognize a few of the monks I knew well in the studio audience and was therefore not surprised when the abbot of Glenstal Abbey—a monastery I often visited in nearby County Limerick—appeared as host Gay Byrne's principal guest of the evening.

Mathew Arnold recalls in "The Scholar Gypsy" that ours is an age when "each half lives a hundred different lives" and this particular talk show proved the point. For, sitting to the right of the abbot in his modest thread bare habit, was actress Joan Collins, in glamorous attire and bouffant wig. Her one-time husband of three weeks standing, Merv Griffin—he of previous talk show fame—was on the abbot's left. Joan Collins spoke about her search, on arriving in Dublin, for "something to wear" for the show; Griffin held forth on the marvels of his 162-foot yacht, which was currently docked lakeside his own Irish hotel in County Galway. The abbot then voiced his sincere hope of raising $2000 for fellow Benedictines who desperately needed a water pump for their monastery in Africa. Joan Collins contrasted her own "love of artifice" with the simplicity of the monk's robe and admitted to being much married, while pausing to admire the abbot's profile. Looking past her dazzle, he confessed that he himself would be hopeless at marriage and said how greatly he admired anyone courageous enough to attempt it. This exchange was memorable, a meeting of opposites, bridged by the abbot's guilelessness and warmth of heart that highlighted the paradox inherent in the encounter.

Two days later, I was opening the door of the gate lodge to two of the Glenstal monks I had spotted in the TV audience. They had come to discuss our plans for a forthcoming conference I was helping to organize, to be held at the monastery in August of that year.

"Welcome!" I said, "Talk about six degrees of separation! I have never been this close to Hollywood stars before!"

In the exchange quoted at the top of this chapter, the approach of a monk called Kieran, is to "put all that you are into the least you do," even if it is the most simple of tasks. The word monk, I have recently discovered, actually meant virgin—a virgin being anyone who is at one with his or her essential self. The monastic life implies a meditative means of operating in two dimensions simultaneously, in passing human time that can be measured by the clock as well as in the immeasurable dimensions of timelessness. Eternal time floods through human time when attention is focused in the present moment, introducing transcendent elements such as synchronicity and coincidence. I enter eternal time whenever I come into contact with a significant other. Then, "time is away and somewhere else," and I become highly receptive to every nuance of a loved one's voice and gestures, I experience greater acuity in all my senses and my attention is fully engaged in the moment.

The whole purpose of meditation is the development of this capacity of attention through which we become more vitally connected with everyone and everything. My attention is nothing other than the measure of my spiritual identity in any given instance. How much sensory data impinges on me, what insights arise and what depth of meaning I can apprehend are all contingent on this quality of attention. Attention is the activity of spirit that I can know in myself and learn to exercise as the spiritual muscle that it is. I have often thought that the whole purpose of education lies in a schooling of attention in students. The person who has mastered the movement of his or her own attention can overcome distraction when it arises, applying him or herself with equal success to a variety of tasks and interests.

The most successful people I know have a highly developed power of attention that appears like a force of nature in one friend of mine. This man is whole in each thing. Master of his own destiny, he appears stronger, more centred, quieter, happier than anyone else I know. There is purpose in his every move, form following function with graceful ease in every task to which he turns his heart or hands. Work is play for him—he knows that intelligence grows and bears fruit in joy and can sustain an unusually challenging workload. Every company is grist to his mill and his genuine interest in others brings out the best in the people around him.

Attention and mindfulness pave the way for poetry. To be a poet is to pay attention and to warmly affirm your own experience. Poets seem to have one thing in common—a highly developed sense of the extremely subtle and paradoxical nature of life. They are capable of apprehending, in the words of Coleridge, "when the wings of the air-sylph are forming within the skin of the caterpillar." When a poem captures my heart, a desire to memorize the words usually follows. This exercises my attention to good and pleasurable effect and, I like to think, unites me in soul with the poet. It takes a bigger effort to concentrate on texts that are of less interest to me—such as instruction manuals for household gadgets—but this effort is never wasted. Attentiveness is honed through the awakened interest I take in whatever I meet, the daily activities of life presenting my surest means to an embodied spirituality.

I also notice that the force of my desire or need for a particular result always affects its outcome. (I refer the reader to the simple example of the German ballpoint pens cited earlier in this book.) An Inuit story attributes the origin of light to the longing for it: "In the eternal darkness, the crow, unable to find any food, longed for light, and the earth was illumined." Desire is of itself sacred and includes the Latin root for God. Desire implies a heightening of attention. A spiritual path popular in the East, involving the application of a deep penetrative awareness to our desires, became known as Tantra, the

pursuit of which facilitates an understanding of the dif-
ference between satisfaction and fulfilment in the seeker.

When I visited India, I heard master storyteller Osho
relate how Tantra, which he characterized as "a highly
developed form of love as play," arose as a path. Central
to the tale was Saraha, the son of a learned Brahmin. A
Buddhist monk devoted to traditional meditation prac-
tices, he had a vision of a woman who would become his
teacher and subsequently found her in the marketplace.
She was an arrowsmith woman of low caste but radiant
with life, and she had remarkable ease of concentration.
He recognized her originality and purity of intent and
watched carefully as she assumed the posture of the archer.
She seemed to possess the epitome of balance, grace and
beauty, to which Saraha surrendered, entering into a soul
love affair of disciple and master with her and becoming a
tantrika under her guidance. Now, concluded Osho, "He
no longer meditates. He sings of course, and dances too.
Now singing was his meditation. Now celebration was his
whole lifestyle. Play entered into his being and through
play, true religion was born."

Little did I know, when I first heard this story that I
would, a few years later, meet somebody who would affect
me in a similar way. While exercises in concentration and
contemplation over the years had schooled my attention
to some degree, I had to fall in love with a teacher who
would demonstrate in the most simple and practical ways
what it means to be in heaven and on earth at the same
time.

I had lived in Vancouver for almost two years before
I met Claude. On a wet Sunday afternoon in April, I
ventured across town on the hunch that I was to meet
someone. I drove resolutely in the direction of Banyen
Books, the city's most popular bookstore and a favourite

Since he first undertook the milking of goats as a boy, Claude has been nicknamed "golden hands."

haunt of mine. As I entered the store, I saw that the window bench, from which I often wormed my way through a stack of volumes, was empty. Ignoring the tempting display of new releases for once, I sat expectantly in my usual spot. Within minutes I was catching a flash of the sunniest smile I had ever seen. It illumined the clear-eyed, bearded face of an elegantly clad and handsome man in his late forties. Of slight but noble stature, he appeared to acknowledge me energetically as he rounded a nearby bookcase. "The heart went crossways in me," as we used to say when I was growing up in County Galway. I had to exercise great restraint in not running after him to breathlessly ask: Who are you? Do I know you? Have we met before? How do you come to be so fine, so graceful and noble, so light on your feet, to have such an air of *savoir faire* and *savoir vivre*, of wisdom, of happiness?

Instead, I remained rooted to the spot. Then I noticed he had spirited himself to the position of sitting next to me on the bench, and seemed to be quietly observing me without looking. Taking me in as it were. Silence reigned in which I could hear my heart beating. I self-consciously rose and began to leaf through a book, absentmindedly plucked from a bookshelf. Then I became aware of a presence behind me. In a quiet voice and rather seductive accent he said, "I must speak to you. Will you join me for a coffee?"

A world of possibility hovered around our corner of the cafe as we became acquainted. It was much later that I realized how appropriate his surname was. Bellin—from belle, but also connoting bell; clear and sound as a bell, having the ring of truth. He told me he had come from Nice to visit his brother. He had lived in Vancouver for many years, but he had returned to settle in the south of France where he was born. I noted that his English was as fluent as my own, his diction and vocabulary distinctive and expressive. We agreed to meet later that evening and continued to rendezvous until the day of his departure, a week later.

There were no "facts" about him to cling to; nothing that was familiar. His background was a mystery, although we did, oddly, have one acquaintance in common. A singer friend-of-a-friend in Toronto had once mentioned in passing that she had lived with a Frenchman named Claude in

Vancouver. There was another coincidence I should mention. A melody composed by Seán Ó Riada was playing on Claude's answering machine when I first called him in Nice. Entitled "Women of Ireland," the tune was very special to me because whenever Seán played it during the last six months of his life he made a point of letting me know that he had played it for me. Claude, who had no connection with Irish culture, had chosen this piece for his message months before our first encounter, a jazz version he discovered on the *Bob James 3* album, although there was no mention of the composer on the sleeve…

I was bound to Claude from the start by intangibles—his sense of life, an ease of manner, a quality of centred calmness, a lack of pretence, clarity of mind, my happiness in his presence. Whatever the attraction was, I missed him when he left after the first of several tearful airport scenes. I would always cherish him as we met and parted in one country or another, indefinitely.

For some time, I thought I could not live without him, but gradually discovered I could be happy whether he was there or not. As we crossed the threshold of the usual man/woman resistance to surrender, it became clear to each of us that a conventional mating was not in the divine plan for us. The dialogue we have with one another continues, the unpredictable quality of life itself dictates that there be no last word between us. The wonder of love is that it maintains a vibrant current of exchange that includes an interest in everything that would unfold for the good of the loved one. I once wrote the following to Claude:

Love's ordained priest
You bade me drink
Deeply of the cup of life,
Nectar of the here and now
Source of the seamless

Ordering of time and space
The fitness of things
Coming moment to moment
To light, in thought and word and deed
Love expands the way before us
Her enterprise ours as we meet and part and meet again
Living the mystery. Namaste!

I abandoned other interests to spend an intense period
of time living with Claude in Vancouver. Working for a
few hours a day in exchange for rent, we were installed
as caretakers in a large Vancouver mansion while Claude
recovered from a minor operation. A part of every day
was spent walking in one of the lush forests in or around
Vancouver. Claude moved in and out of the overlap zone.
The more I grew to love and trust him, the more my appre-
ciation for what he referred to as "real time" increased.
My induction was a slow process and largely due to his
patient guidance and constant reminders to "be here now!"
whenever I drifted into past or future preoccupation. I
learned by his example how to enter into the rhythm of
"nature's time" as he called it, as he drew my attention to
all the small wonders. As we ducked under branches and
rooted out trails, he urged me to move with open atten-
tion, seeing and hearing with greater sensitivity, looking
and listening in a more relaxed way.

A favourite poem, "Lost," by David Wagoner, became
a truly meaningful metaphor for life.

Claude explained that he first entered into the continu-
ity of real time when he was twenty-nine, becoming aware
of the closeness of the spiritual world to our sphere of
activity, a parallel world in contact with ours all the time.
He approached the subject, so dear to his heart, from sev-
eral angles.

"I know deep down that nothing else but real time

Claude set up his camera in the course of a conversation at his kitchen table, to take this picture of us both when I visited Nice in 1999.

exists. You have to accept this universal unfolding and realize once and for all that the past is a dead thing—only as good as a slide that you would project on the wall of your mind. And the future, as beautiful as you can envisage it, is also a diversion from the living experience that is always in the making. We know that in these difficult times reality is a hard thing for people to accept. But once the reality is tamed, it is accepted and seen to be beautiful. You have no more need for fairy tales. I find that life is truly magical when lived in the moment. I am asking you to be less caught up in your own agendas, associations; just concentrate always on what you are doing. I am not asking you to discard anything. I am inviting you to pay much more attention to the seconds that are passing you by. To be here now is to be conscious."

"How do I make a shift into real time?" I asked.

"You have to shift from your importance to the importance of life itself."

"Isn't our presence part of the life force?"

"No," he countered. "It is the life force. That is what is demanded of us."

"We think if we are sitting in a chair, we are present," I said.

Claude smiled. "Sometimes the lights are on but there is nobody home."

"Children are always present," I said.

"When we are present we are childlike," he responded.

Claude always had something to do; the concept of boredom was entirely alien to him as he busied himself with household tasks. His hands, small and strong, had their history of a life in which everything is present and alive to the touch. Since he first undertook the milking of goats as a very young boy, he had been nicknamed "golden hands." These hands retained their youthful readiness and inner vitality of gesture and touch. Inspiration always flowed into his hands, especially when beating out complex Cuban rhythms on the bongo. He would cheerfully spring into action when a task presented itself, making no distinction of interest between intellectual or artistic pursuits and mundane household chores. All were important in the rhythmic flow of the day. He was total in action and always brought what he started to satisfactory completion without too much fuss or strain. Because he set such value on himself he gave value to all he did. An unhurried calmness showed him the way in every act of repairing, cleaning, cooking, woodcarving, drumming, painting or gardening. I thought as I watched him: "Here is the truth of right doing," fervently wishing that I could do likewise. Because I have so internalized the memory of his speech and gestures, snippets of conversation come back to me. I hear him say:

"The more you are centred in what you do and how you are doing it, the more before and after become uninteresting. Because love is at work."

"Love?" I queried.

"Yes. If you are so involved of your own volition, it is because your heart is in it and love is in everything you do."

"People are an invisible element of a place made visible," a poet once said. Provence became visible for me through Claude before I ever set foot in that earthly paradise. It was the perfect setting for the jewel of such splendour that my friend represented for me. Claude's hometown, Nice, playground to the rich and famous presents a commercial face to the tourist. Although his love of finery and well-made things has been fostered there, Claude has not followed the lure of riches.

A drive into the hills, beyond Nice, presents another reality. Taking a detour one day in the course of my first visit, he drove along a winding path and stopped at a little river, the stream from which he had drawn water daily as a boy. He showed me the ruin of a modest house, remote by an hour's walk from the nearest neighbour, in the attic of which he had bedded on a straw mattress for the first nine years of his life. His parents worked in menial jobs in the city, and although Claude's two older brothers lived with them, Claude had been reared in the country as a solitary child in the care of elderly relatives, being considered a delicate child. Like a small animal himself, he passed the days in the company of cats and dogs and goats and chickens, communing with birds from the branches of gnarled olive trees. He laughed when I remarked: "You were as wild here as you later became as a city dweller, abandoning yourself to fast cars, dance halls and the arms of women, as you had earlier to wind and earth and branch!"

Never setting eye on pen or paper when other children were swotting over books, Claude was instructed by volatile winds, rocks and flowers and subtle seasonal change. No wonder he said when I asked him once how he would define freedom: "To be on holiday when others are at work!" Here he absorbed into his own being the patience and calmness and innate kindness of nature herself; it was a book that would always remain open to him. Being oneself, being natural is all that is needed, he would remind me.

From early childhood, he knew what it was to be independent and yet function as part of the whole. "People lose faith when they have lost their link with the world around them. I once had the feeling as a small child that I might get lost on my wanderings in this region. But I was told, 'only follow the river and you will find your way home.' In this way, I learned to find my bearings wherever I went."

He had been busy from morning until night in this secluded domain, collecting pine cones to start a morning fire, watering the vegetables that were their staple diet, carrying water in which to boil the homemade pasta. "They told me—if you want your dinner you must chop wood!"

Everything was useful and everything had meaning; his intolerance of waste and remarkable resourcefulness was seeded here. He had a special relationship with trees and told me, "If I had a choice, I would become a cork tree. It does not yield any fruit but gives of itself continuously." From brick red to dusty ochre, he learned the merits of every soil, the qualities of wood that would inform his skills as carver and carpenter.

"When my two older brothers came to visit from the city, we would make boats from the bark of a tree, bows with new branches of the chestnut tree, arrows from the stems of ferns. My only toys were the ones I invented myself.

"I saw how different plants grew according to season. I welcomed the appearance of new mushrooms, wild asparagus and lettuce. I was always asking 'What new thing can we find to eat?' Whenever a need arose I could find a solution."

"You learned the value of animals too," I said.

"Up to this day I have a hard time understanding why people have animals for decoration —all the animals had a purpose for us: the cats for mice and insects, the dogs for sheep. I vividly remember seeing little chicks playing on the cat's back! I walked for five miles to the village exchanging goat's milk, cheese and rabbits for oil and flour."

Claude swore that he has never eaten as well as he did when he lived here, and I noticed that his excitement in the marketplace had all the fervour of childhood. Surveying the abundant provision of colourful produce, ripened in the golden glow of direct Mediterranean sunlight, I could understand his frustration with the insipid look and smell of vegetables in other places. The Provencal dishes he had so painstakingly prepared for us in Vancouver paled beside the home grown gastronomic marvels he set before me now.

The glistening fish, lightly cooked, pan-roasted duck or corn-fed chickens, baby courgettes, mouth watering blette, flour-drenched fresh pasta, vine-ripe tomatoes, an endless variety of cheeses, scented orange-fleshed melons and other juicy fruits were just some of the fare that found a place at our table. The aroma of rosemary, thyme, sage and lavender that lingered over the surrounding hills made a subtle transition from nostril to palate through the magic of Claude's hands. He showed me how to pick out the best of those cornerstones of Provencal cuisine, olive oil, garlic and thyme, and how to add their flavours so that no one taste stands out above another. *"Faites simple"* was his motto and each culinary achievement was punctuated with *"Voila!"*

We often drove by narrow twisting roads along hills topped by mediaeval villages. I remember flashes of the cornucopia of markets, patisseries, fromageries, boulangeries, baroque churches, almond trees and fig orchards. We saw elderly men playing petanque, a kind of bowling, in dusty village squares, others sampling a little pastis—the quintessential Provencal aperitif—in the outdoor cafes that dotted cobbled streets. Ochre and red-washed walls reflected the surrounding soil, their red-tiled roofs offset by the expanse of azure sky. Ancient limestone buildings rose organically from rocky pinnacles that often loomed ahead. There was always an olive grove where we could stop to picnic. Everything I experienced served to explain the great leap my heart took when I first set eyes on Claude. Here indeed was life abundantly overflowing its limitations; my definition for peace. No wonder the olive branch was adopted as its symbol. It had originally been borne on the wings of a dove to Noah as proof of the existence of dry land, synonymous for him at the time I suppose with his particular vision of Paradise.

Claude does not espouse any particular religion; he was baptized a Catholic, but was never taken to church as a child. He once was given a vision of the Light, and holds a strong Christian identity. His keen ability to interpret the tarot symbols gives him hermetic lineage. He would make no claim beyond the development of his own conscious awareness. The only prayerful request he remembers making in his youth was for the gift of wisdom, the gift of recognizing Heaven's hiddenness within this world. Like Fionn Mac Cumhail, he would go anywhere and forsake anything for wisdom. Words attributed to Philo of Alexandria seem relevant to my description of Claude: "If someone has experienced the wisdom that can only be heard from oneself, learned from oneself, and created from oneself, he does not merely participate in laughter, he becomes laughter."

Whether in Canada, in Ireland or in France, my favourite time of day with Claude began immediately after breakfast when he would hold forth with astonishing clarity on some topic that was seeking to come forth between us, of personal and universal significance. "Thoughts are something active, living, the working forces of the world. We simply draw them out of the world."

There was no gap for him between thought and word. His thoughts issued forth with complete originality, born of the moment and clothed in the most appropriate and incisive language, a perfect example of what the poet Novalis demanded of the faculty of speech. I asked him how we could tell if a statement was really true. "If it is truth," he expostulated, "it is alive! When you apprehend this truth, this energy, it is something cosmic, divine–you've been allowed to enter a realm of reality, piercing through the veil of illusion. The truth will set you free means it will give you life. Becoming conversant with the world consciousness involves continuous conversation. You come up with new questions all the time. You can start anywhere!"

I remember a conversation we had when I last spent a few weeks with him in Nice. Like all the conversations we have shared in the sixteen years of our association, it had neither beginning nor end and was plucked from the ether as usual, highlighting some aspect of life-wisdom. It gave me entry once more into the overlap zone. We were talking about the way in which thoughts were subconsciously transmitted from one person to another and how becoming conscious of what we say could help us bring order into our thinking. He had this to offer:

"Words cannot do total justice to the fine thoughts we have. They are often a pale reflection of our ongoing reality. You must first have a grasp of what you are saying. Be completely honest. Describe the situation in real terms clearly and accurately without adding or subtracting. Concern yourself with your description of reality without judging or belittling, with a maximum of restraint. In practising this, little by little, you will notice that your thoughts have been disorderly. The more you give order to the words you speak, the more you are training your thoughts. Your subconscious is recording everything accurately, becoming now a reservoir of orderly thinking patterns. Your surroundings in turn, will begin to reflect this reality.

"So," he continued animatedly, "one of my approaches on the spiritual path is to be vigilant about my speaking."

I encouraged him to elaborate.

"It entails really searching for the word that is clearest and most true and usually the simplest, saying 'no' when you mean 'no' and 'yes' when you mean 'yes.'"

"Saying exactly what you mean and meaning what you say," I interjected.

"Yes," he continued, "in this way I become a more responsible person, able to stand behind my words. Instead of my thoughts giving form to my speech in a haphazard way, my speech now begins to influence my subconscious and one of the functions of the subconscious is to release information. If I am attentive and vigilant in what I say, my thoughts will have no choice but to sift themselves and what will remain of that purifying process is the essence of what I feel and now succinctly convey."

"But does that make you more readily understood by others?" I asked.

His answer surprised me.

"It is not important to be understood. It is not important whether or not people agree with me. It is important that I am convinced about my point of view. If I am not convinced, I will always be on shaky ground. I will drift from one approach to another. Before I start to speak I must have a point of view—a position."

"How would you advocate arriving at a position?" I queried.

"You arrive at it through many channels: education, knowledge, the love of parents, equanimity, integrity, character—by whatever means the truth can be in motion in your heart."

"Is experience important?" I asked.

"Fundamental truth bypasses experience. It is connected with faith and it is based on something more solid than anything I have learned from books or seen on television, or read in the newspaper. All of that only forms opinions. A point of view, on the other hand, is based on reasoning and a concept of truth that I would term intuition, a concept of light that I would call imagination and a concept of love functioning as compassion. When these three facets are in place for some time, lets say for a cycle of nine years, I will then have learned a great deal about limits, about access (in terms of being able to receive images), about excess (in terms of being overly emotional), and limits (in terms of what may or may not be spoken). Now my point of view becomes truly referential. Now I am convinced that I can add something of substance to a situation and I have left opinion behind on the sidewalk!"

Claude once made the point that humanity made its start when it learned to generate fire. The current force analogous to fire, with which humanity is now charged to generate, is that of Love.

"Love changes everything. It inevitably changes the nature of what is happening, for the good. Our task is to be able to see love everywhere. We must become receptive enough to be able to facilitate the coming of such a force."

He constitutes such a force in my life.

14

Embracing the Dream

We are only just now beginning to consider the relation of one individual to a second individual objectively and without prejudice, and our attempts to live such relationships have no model before them. And yet in the changes brought about by time there are already many things that can help our timid novitiate…
RAINER MARIA RILKE

An elderly Irish bachelor confessed his regret at never having married.

I asked him, "Why not?"

He said, "Well it was not for want of trying. I have known women throughout the length and breadth of the country."

"You mean you have been looking around?"

"Yes—I met a woman once in Limerick. She was beautiful, she was wealthy, but she was not religious, so I dropped her after a while."

"Where did you go then?" I asked.

"I ventured on to Cork and there I met the finest, most

religious girl. But although she was beautiful she had no money."

"I suppose you moved on from her too?"

"After that I met someone I liked in Galway, but she was not much to look at."

"But still you persisted?"

"Yes indeed. I worked for a while in Dublin where there is a surplus of women. Sure enough I walked out with one who had a good income, who was lovely to look at and spiritual into the bargain."

"It's a wonder you didn't marry her," I remarked.

"The unfortunate thing with her was, and it is the reason I gave up the chase—she was looking for the perfect man!"

His story reminded me of a popular song that states that, "The greatest thing you'll ever learn is just to love and be loved in return."

One of the first love stories to catch my schoolgirl fancy was the mythological account of the meeting and mating of the heroic Cuchulainn with Emer, the only noblewoman in Ireland worthy of his attentions. She in turn recognized him instantly as the man of her dreams. An old book gave account of their first meeting: "May the Lord make straight the paths before you," were her words of greeting when she lifted her lovely face to gaze into his eyes for the first time.

"And you—may you be safe from every harm," he replied.

The spontaneous concern of each was for the other's well-being. This is a sign of true love. The love that is protected from every base instinct is the love for one another that is for the other's own sake.

They struck instant rapport, Cuchulainn remarking during their first meeting, "Never before this day, among all women with whom I have at times conversed, have I found one but thee to speak the mystic language of the bards which we are talking now, for secrecy one with the other."

"I think the hero in our generation is not the individual but the pair—two people who together add up to more than they are apart," Theodore Zeldin noted in a commentary on BBC radio. Zeldin is a writer who promotes a contemporary model of male/female relationship based on the art of conversation. He declares that "whenever words dance with each other, opinions caress, imaginations undress, topics open."

When I was young it was not unusual for couples to be engaged for fourteen years, before conditions favourable to marriage could be adapted to their circumstances. We used to joke about farmers in our area, leaning over their shovels, squinting after the young girls on summer evenings, thinking to themselves, "Isn't it great to be sixty and to be old enough to go courting!" The delay was due to the fact that a farm could only withstand one mistress, and it was not until after the death of his mother that a son could contemplate bringing another woman into the house. The indispensable tradition of matchmaking, to which such hopefuls could then resort when the desire for a mate became urgent, is still a feature of life in County Clare. Lisdoonvarna, a town famous for its healing waters, is a popular meeting and matchmaking centre, which now attracts the unattached but available of both genders from every corner of the earth.

Clare, where I came to write my book, has featured in my life since early childhood, when I used to spend summer holidays there with relatives. But I did not appreciate the richness of its topography until Bob and I began to frequent the annual Merriman Summer School, in the late sixties and early seventies, when a gathering of scholars, artists and politicians could be wholeheartedly at home in the rural ambience of County Clare.

"Set dancing" sometimes began at ten in the morning, and it was a popular alternative to lectures. Background or foreground reels and jigs gave way when a singer was present. I shall always remember the energetic and soaring rendition of great Munster songs by one of Ireland's most popular historians, John A. Murphy. Another popular alternative to the lectures were the stimulating conversations in session in every corner of the pubs. It was at these affairs that I learned to perfect the art of hanging out.

The highlights of our days were the field trips we took with archaeologists, whose knowledge of all the treasures of the landscape was exhaustive, delivered on site to a thoroughly captivated audience. Remnants of monument and stone could more fully inhabit the locality again through the imaginative associations we gave them. These trips gave living testimony to Yeats's contention that in this country every strange stone and little coppice has its legend in written or unwritten tradition.

County Clare was also the inspiration for a book entitled The Antiquities in Clare, which includes a translation of the Gaelic poem "The Midnight Court," written by Brian Merriman in 1790. At that time, Merriman was a hedge-school master in the village of Feakle, some twenty minutes drive from my present writing place. It is this poem of some one thousand lines that drew us to County Clare every year. It has held sway with social historians, literary critics, censorship boards and the general reader for over two hundred years. Deploring repression, women's inequality and clerical celibacy, the poem advocates unrestrained heterosexual activity between consenting adults. For one critic this gives evidence that a primitive form of erotic life had held its vigour in rural Ireland. A young woman gives petulant voice to a litany of superstitious and magical rites that she employed to gain the attention of a man in the following lines of "The Midnight Court," translated by Frank O'Connor:

> … *Every night as I went to bed*
> *I'd a stocking of apples under my head,*
> *I fasted three canonical hours*
> *To try and come round the heavenly powers,*
> *I washed my shift where the stream ran deep,*
> *To hear my lover's voice in sleep;*
> *Often I swept the woodstack bare,*
> *Burned bits of my frock, my nails, my hair,*
> *Up the chimney stuck the flail,*
> *Slept with a spade without avail* …

Seamus Heaney, in a learned essay on "The Midnight Court," points out that the poem can be read as "a tremor of the future" and recognizes it as an original and unexpected achievement in world literature of the eighteenth century. In a parody of the "aisling" or "vision" poetic convention of that period, the poet exults in the scenic beauty of his native place in the lyrical opening verses. But he is not visited by the customary ethereal beauty, that usual personification of the Irish folk spirit; instead, he is rudely accosted by a grotesque female figure demanding that he appear at a special court to be convened at midnight near the village of Feakle. Presiding over this tribunal is Aoibheall (pronounced "Eevel") a formidable fairy queen who resides in Craglea. (Craglea is not far from Tinarana. It is a tall grey rock, jutting out of the mountain, that I see in the distance as I take my daily walk). Merriman is being held accountable for the failings of his sex, in chapter and verse passionately proclaimed by an array of female witnesses. He is denounced and condemned to torture by a pack of feminists-before-their-time, a nightmare he escapes by waking up.

I have had to look beyond the Irish psyche and the attitudes of my own conditioning, to discover an alternate approach to sexuality that might present a more optimistic "tremor" for humankind. I was led at first to Vladimir Solovyov, a mystical Russian prophet and Christian metaphysician who lived at the turn of the twentieth century. During his short lifetime, he advanced a powerful social message concerning the love between man and woman. The transformation of the world, he believed, depended upon this relationship and the evolutionary channel it represented.

His approach to the subject in his book *The Meaning of Love* is earnestly scientific, opening with a biological survey that refutes the age-old assumption that the fundamental purpose of sexual attraction is the propagation of the species. He proves that the higher we ascend in the hierarchy of organisms, the more this purpose wanes, but the more urgent the power of sexual attraction becomes. He calls for the exaltation of the sexual instinct, behind which spiritual powers operate, believing that love is important not only as feeling "but also as the transfer of all our interest in life from oneself to another, as the shifting of the very centre of our lives."

Both the poet Coleridge and Rudolf Steiner argued that love and egotism must interpenetrate, not in order to suppress one another but to bring about a union of opposites. All unity implies working through the resistance through which the ego perpetuates itself. For a couple to mutually surrender to the current of sexual love on a continuing basis implies an overcoming of the limiting definitions they hold of themselves and the recognition of their fundamental unity of being. To fall in love is to apprehend the spirit of another in a blinding flash; it is this reality that sustains romance and enlivens the sexual current, which clearly reflects the quality and purity of the love connection. Relationships are experiments in love to which we need not attach yardsticks of success or failure; love has a way of placing these means of inner growth in our path so that individuality, as opposed to egotism, can ripen in us for the sake of the world.

Lovers have the power to awaken a potential "third eye" in one another, termed *an ball seirce* in the Irish language, the Sufi term for it must be "the jewel of reality" because the Persian poet, Rumi, had this to say:

> *Nobody can wear the jewel of reality*
> *Except the one in whose fire it is born*
> *My friend wears it on his forehead*
> *Our foreheads touched tonight and mine burns …*

Solovyov believed that no external influences, however beneficial, could touch the roots of egotism in us that only the momentum of the sexual act, in a committed relationship, could undermine. In this form of love, penetrating as it does the whole of our being, we can recognize the truth of another, not merely in abstraction or in feeling, but in actual deed as the justification of our inborn capacity to love. Thus we are called to the conscious expression of love as a duty of our humanity and the goal of our evolution. Egotism does not disappear of its own accord, because our motives, habits, opinions and even attractions are coloured by it. Sex exists for me as a function of relationship—a means of conversation that includes the body and yet goes beyond it and beyond words. Male and female bodies are formed to express an inherent attraction of opposites although their potential for spiritual union transcends the reality of gender.

Relationship must be constantly tended and nurtured in a creative way. We may relate to one another's essential selves through the exercise of right speech, for instance. I remember Osho talking about throwing away the trap or the snare once you have caught the fish or the rabbit. He then added the following: "Words exist for meaning. Once you have found it, you can forget the words. The question is: "Where can I find the man without words so that I can have a word with him?" This expresses the essential quest for a significant "other" or "others" that underlies all social striving.

The physical act of love can be compared with meaning in relation to language. It does not consist in simply feeling, but in what may be accomplished through feeling, just as it is meaning that lends significance to the words we use. Sexual love can include three essential human elements: the animal, the social-communal bond, and the internal spiritual bond. Any one of these elements is incomplete if it is isolated from the rest. Sex for its own sake, the exclusive preoccupation with social or family life and spiritual love that denies the flesh, or that considers itself superior to the others—all such separation can lead to perversion. In fact, it was the separation of these intrinsic elements in the Ireland of his times that caused Brian Merriman to pick up his pen in order to restore to society what was lacking of a basic, healthy, animal instinct, free of conventional guilt.

The great poet and novelist D.H. Lawrence went further than any writer of his time in his exploration of human sexuality. It is no wonder his books caused such unquiet and were so summarily banned. He carried forward the spirit of the Romantics, who neglected the animal world and the sexual element in nature and tended to avoid the implications of animal instinct in humans. Including in his honest observation insects, fishes, birds, beasts, and flowers, he affirms the grandeur, mystery and substance of our common life.

Poetry arises for Lawrence out of the immediacy of nature and woman. Through making room for all that we are in the fullness of our natural lives we can access and embody a connectedness with the world around us and with one another. Bodies can only meet unselfconsciously when we rejoice in the conditions of our own mortality and move through them into a deeper communion with the love that continues to permeate our souls, aging bodies notwithstanding.

The impression I retained from my earliest sexual escapades, and some later ones as well, was that Irish people could only permit themselves such abandonment when under the influence of drink, and that the act was short-lived and much overrated, yielding little satisfaction. It was a long time before I discovered that sobriety and skill on the part of the man, and an absence of shame and wide-awake conscious attention on my part was my means of breaking the chain of repression to which I was heir. But liberation also brought responsibility, and childbirth made me aware of the sacredness of the sexual act. Restrictive taboos have now been lifted for most people and it is left to each individual to shine the light of consciousness on an area of our lives that is often obfuscated in thickets of emotion, avoidance or abuse. Only in bringing consciousness to bear on our own memories, actions and proclivities can we hope to align sexual conduct with the purpose intended for it by love.

I knew that one shouldn't hide the physical act of love any longer, because that game was repugnant. I knew we had to look at it differently, simply to look at it. I prefer our

*manner today, accepting more readily our risks than the
lies of the past, but love is in danger. I see clearly that it is
in danger.*

This passage appears in a remarkable book, *Conversation
Amoureuse*, by Jacques Lusseyran, who was born in Paris
in 1924. Blind from the age of eight, he developed unpar-
alleled capacities of insight which enabled him to experi-
ence images and colours in the soul that others observed
with physical eyes. Robert Sardello, in his introduction to
the book Lusseyran addressed to his wife, points out that
to move beyond his own subjective images, the author
had to free himself from all disruptive emotions such as
fear, anger, jealousy and impatience, and that he had to
live the reality of love in full consciousness. This intensi-
fied his acuity of touch, hearing and smell considerably
and allowed him to enter into meditation on the "inner-
ness" of sensory experience. A great sensitivity towards
the "other" matured in him and later deepened in the
experience of marriage.

Sardello, a pioneer of this phenomenological approach
himself, has focused his own singular light on the subject
in a book entitled *Love and the Soul*, and writes the follow-
ing about Lusseyran's approach: "A man dreams, not so
much of the perfect woman, but of the luminous femi-
nine, a dream that, for the most part, exists only partly
consciously. He desires the flesh and blood woman. And
a woman, does she not experience the same division in
counter fashion? Love has a hard time of it, however, as
long as dream and desire live a separate existence."

For a woman, this contrast exists in a dream of the
flesh and blood man which can be indefinitely sustained
and a desire for relationship pursued by her by every
available means of engagement with the man in question.
Relationships uniquely reflect the many combinations of

these variables and we evolve towards complementarity only gradually, arriving there by means of one partner or several.

Many illusions I harbour about myself and others fall away as I age and become more autonomously attuned to the lovability of another without distracting reference to my own personal needs. I can now make a distinction between love itself and the conditions with which it must be surrounded if it is to be socially sustained. I know that love is unconditional in itself, as the reality in which we live and move and have our being, whose existence does not depend on me or you. Relationship, on the other hand, is conditioned by the circumstances of life and bound by individual issues that must be consciously negotiated, experimented with, accepted and mutually reviewed over time. The one commitment I made to Claude was to keep the lines of communication always open between us and I have seen the conditions of our relationship change over many years while love, expressed as meaning and understanding, continues to connect us in a flow of new ideas mutually explored.

I am of the opinion that women suffer more consistently for love than men. The satisfaction of physical desire in a man can be swiftly accomplished in the act of love, but the more abstract desire for relationship inflicts a slow torture of wanting-but-not-getting on a woman whose rational mind becomes for the time being impaired! In love with love from a very early age myself, I later realized that this was a form of self-feeling, the anticipation of pleasure that the dream awakens in the body. It sometimes happens that when a man responds to these subtle mating signals he is rejected, because the reality of his ordinary flesh and blood nature, his lack of artifice and straightforward physical need, can shock a woman out of her reverie. This scenario occurred in my life a few times making me aware of the dramas I was capable of activating. When I look back on the more unconscious period of my life, I see how much I was enmeshed in the invisible entanglements of my own dream weaving.

Nuala O'Faolain's novel *My Dream Of You* brought this whole issue to point for me. A contemporary of my own and a frequent participant in the Merriman school, Nuala has so internalized the wanting-but-not-getting syndrome that afflicts so many women, taking readers to the bottom of desire and longing with such uncompromising candour, that her book is itself the antidote for the condition it laments. It is fortunate that love does not ultimately depend on our intervention in drawing together those who are kindred at levels of body, soul and spirit and the great adventure of life is in allowing ourselves to be surprised by the divine fitness of what unfolds as in the case of O'Faolain's heroine.

"One touches Heaven when one touches the human body," wrote Novalis. Lusseyran elaborates on this truth in the following passage: "The couple capable of listening to the least movement of these two bodies lent to them for love, this couple would break the chain and the souls would enter…But the condition is this yes given to the body, this all-inclusive yes." James Joyce conveyed a similar message through Molly Bloom's memorable soliloquy that he peppered with affirmatives. It is the part that most people remember of his novel *Ulysses* and the passage with which I have often ended my recitals.

We must be prepared to approach one another with the utmost purity of intent and be mindful of the need to care for and nourish the body. The man of my experience who was most profoundly and in an objective and subjective sense a lover was alert in every nuance of the sexual act as he was in every other area of life. He helped me to, in his words, "demystify the sexual act and overcome fantasy" while entering more fully into the authenticity of the moment. I began to understand that, when entered into with open eyes and a deep respect for the autonomy of the other, sexual expression was something complete in itself. I could release him from the dream without breaking a loving connection with him, able to love somebody at last for his own sake.

Man and woman can navigate these crossings between dream and desire by bringing conscious attention into their every gesture towards one another until the act takes on meditative rhythm. Hands must be allowed to function with the sensitivity of the artist. When we regard the nude figures sculpted by Rodin, for instance, we understand to what degree he had perfected a sense of touch. With earnest, solitary patience and with tireless hands this concentrated workman revealed mysteries of physical attraction. Rilke, who was, for a period, his secretary, remarks of Rodin's famous sculpture *The Kiss*, "we feel as if waves were passing from all the surface contact points into their bodies, the thrill of beauty, of invitation and of power..." I think there is more to be gained for the art of love-making in the study of such works than in the passive witnessing of the spectacles of copulation guaranteed today at the flick of a button, that ultimately numb sensory imagination.

Lusseyran was imbued with an ideal of the feminine since age sixteen, and when inwardly ready, he was inevitably "found" by the flesh and blood woman whose existence he had fathomed. "She was somebody whose presence moved me, questioned me...I could not have said where she was or when she would come. But I knew what she would demand from me...she was going to urge me on to live...She would finally draw out of me everything I contained."

The woman who would embody this vocation would

be self-actualized. She would not yield to the temptation to make his life more important than hers. Love insists that we do not mistake another's destiny for our own, it being above all a path towards authenticity and communion. If the dream can ultimately lead the woman to love in the flesh, the man can let desire lead him through the sexual act to the actual source of that eternal feminine that lures him on. They will discover that there is a part of each of them that is already the other sex, each having penetrated through intimacy, the experience of the other that goes beyond words. This brings the war between the sexes to its logical end and makes what Lusseyran terms "the new marriage" possible.

The continual adaptation of two people to one another can be mirrored in the sexual act. Such energetic exchange is a source of harmony, rhythm and trust in the life of a couple because every action we perform to its completion helps to free us from compulsion and dissatisfaction. By being totally engaged in an act of love, sex becomes demystified and we become free of the co-dependency that is often associated with so-called sexual needs. The most challenging task we are charged with as human beings may be that of fully loving a person for his or her own sake. Perhaps Rilke was right in pointing out that it is the task for which all other work is merely preparation. Blessed are the people who, in later life in the interests of sharing a common task, find or rediscover a kindred spirit with whom to pursue that elusive goal.

The restraint involved in conscious loving, the sensory awareness it demands, the mutual attention to timing, preferences and shifting moods required, is often enhanced by periods of celibacy, of natural withdrawal and regeneration. It is a path of discovery, for which each couple must chart the course, in shaping the love between the sexes into a more conscious relation of one human being to another. Today's men and women are responsible for the future of love, of lovemaking as process, because increasing the presence of love in the world involves imagination and creativity. Making room for bodies and souls to cohere in the same earthly dimension can only occur when we bring consciousness to bear in the exercise. This brings an inexorable flow of grace and harmony into our lives, and advances Rilke's vision of the love that consists in this: "that—two solitudes protect and border and greet each other."

15

A Sense of Renewal

The first step to a qualitative, further development of consciousness is a formation of a consciousness of the present, in which one no longer needs to rely on the contents of the past in order to stay awake, but can say, out of the experience of the present, I Am.
GEORG KÜHLEWIND

My time of retreat was drawing to a close having yielded me many days and nights of fruitful reflection in the glow of my Tinarana turf fire. Understanding the events I had lived through from the perspective of hindsight's longer view was a soul-enriching and self-actualizing exercise for me, a fructifying process that resulted in this book, almost now complete.

Georg Kühlewind's words, quoted above, did not impact my life overnight. In truth, it has taken me a lifetime of experience, study, inspiration, and above all, the example of others whom I deeply respect, including Georg himself, to arrive at a direct understanding of them. Marshall McLuhan had pointed in a similar direction many years before, noting how terrified people were of being present to what was actually happening. McLuhan knew that what we mistake for the present is really the past, since every thought we form is already a dead thing as is everything with which we surround ourselves. Only in the actual process of intuitive thinking can thoughts be said to be alive. Not until I succeeded in grasping Kühlewind's inspired approach to thinking and could put it into practice, did I realize the value of Marshall's epigrammatic pronunciations. I now know them to be spiritual truths, clothed in contemporary language. The kindness and generosity that I observed in Marshall was the "message" he imparted and, if I had been ready, I could have learned a great deal more from him. He had once remarked, "It's the person who is sent, not the message."

Dr. Ross Laing introduced me to what he referred to as "truthing," the process of bringing what is hidden to light, of attentiveness to the actual state of heart behind the words we utter. There is often an implicit agreement between people to support and harbour each other's denials. Ross frequently asked each member of our core group "What are you resisting?" and recommended that each one face whatever he or she was avoiding if we were committed to the process of "truthing." Making a change requires a shift in consciousness, a willingness to become more conscious in what one thinks and says and does. New beginnings arise when words carry weight between people.

My stint at the Institute prepared me for the encounter with Claude with whom I could put what I had learned into practice. The phenomenological approach of engaging with things spontaneously as they unfold was a marked feature of his day-to-day living. I found that when attention is engaged in what is actually happening as opposed to what did or might happen, fears, cravings and fixed positions fall away and the "ordinary" becomes of itself more compelling. In acknowledging my feelings, I believe I accessed a deeper sense of purpose. I knew that, like faith without good works, my ideals would be lamed by my failure to act upon them. Here I could take courage from the inspiring example of the mentors I have introduced in these pages.

Georg Kühlewind pointed out that the new love is not concerned with requital and is therefore not overtly concerned with sex. Decadent forms of sexuality are not free because they are not conscious, he believed. Without diminishing pleasure, sex can become a free, conscious act, a function of authentic relationship and a celebration of the sacred mystery of love as Vladimir Solovyov revealed. Although we are often overwhelmed by how great the rift between the sexes is, for some time now the conversation of love has been moving in a new direction. If rapport on a spiritual and soul level has not been established between partners before they embark on their physical mating, their communication skills may prove inadequate when romance begins to wane. Love for the other's own sake and love beyond desire is the actual, realizable goal of earthly love. To achieve this goal it is essential for couples to engage in a form of interaction with one another that keeps them on the creative edge, daring to question assumptions that together they take courage in exploding. It is the nitty gritty of soul-work, a coming into fullness of feeling and verbal expression, that brings about the transformation we seek.

What was remarkable about my experience with Ross Laing, was that this adventure in "truthing" was conducted in the presence of many other people who had allowed themselves to be exposed in their deepest vulnerability. This provided me with a new model for what community with others really entails. By the grace of truth, those gifts of *charis* and *aletheia*, bestowed by the Christ, something new can manifest in each moment, a cycle of love can be initiated which owes nothing to tradition, ritual or myth only to the very fact of being wholly present to one's environment.

The majority of people I saw turning up at the Toronto Institute of Self Healing were seeking to stimulate channels of communication that had dried up between partners. It seemed to me that men and women operate on different levels and it is useful to recognize this from the outset. A common story about a pair who had been dating for six months serves to illustrate these differences. The woman thought it was time they discussed their future plans. Driving home one night after an enjoyable dinner she decided to broach the topic:

"John, do you realize that we have been dating since last October and that we have seen each other three nights of every week?"

"Really darling," he responded. "Has it been that long? Ah yes, I remember now! I met you when I had just had my car repaired. The carburetor and alternator had given up on the very same day! Such inconvenience! You know I have never been fully satisfied with this car."

He continued his discourse on this favourite topic of his until it was time to drop her off at her address, and he wondered why she slammed the door. He went home slightly perplexed, but slept soundly, having successfully avoided any statement of commitment. She meanwhile burst into tears as soon as her roommate appeared and launched into a litany of complaint about the insensitivity of men. If Ross had been present he would have made it safe for both to speak their minds clearly and arrive at a compromise that was satisfactory to them both.

Now that men and women are becoming equal from the point of view of education and career, the old role-playing formulas can no longer be sustained. Both are breadwinners, both have interests outside the home, both travel, both have their own friends. A new order is called for in which relationships will not deteriorate into entanglements. Central to the work of Ross Laing, his wife, Andrea, and their co-directors at the Institute, Dermot and Fran Grove-White, is the creation of the effective model of relationship they themselves exemplify. I attended several of their couple groups in which partners were encouraged to really listen to one another and witness the contrasting modalities through which they function, coming to clearer perspective of each other's point of view. Participants were encouraged to approach one another with honesty, vulnerability and a willingness to accept responsibility for creating the relationship they had. The current of love and the movement towards autonomy generated in these sessions was awesome.

When, a few years later, Claude would initiate a conversation with the words: "Let's not just talk about what we know, but remain open to what we don't know," I could sense the approach of an eternal moment, a qualitative deepening of the love we shared, and was reminded of something Kühlewind had written: "The Logos connects human beings through the Word—all else is temptation or a temporary connection. To look for the connecting element elsewhere is to disregard the new commandment." Love bridges the separation between two individuals and it has to arise continuously anew out of the transformation of self-love. The Word or Logos arises always as new beginning, springing from a unifying source that is synonymous with Love itself.

Love reveals itself in this new millennium as a light in thinking, a torch the poets and others I have quoted throughout this book have always held aloft. It is a thinking that is the very essence of freedom and creativity, owing

nothing to the past; it is the thinking that Claude charac-
terized when he described thoughts as "something active,
living, the working forces of the world ... something cos-
mic, divine." Although he did not know it, his statement
echoes a definition given by Rudolf Steiner. Electricity,
Dr. Steiner contended, is comparable to human thought.
The relationship that ice has to water, physical atoms have
to the flow of electricity, and our formations of finished
thoughts have to the more fluid stream of living intuitive
thinking, an awesome human energy source.

As imprisoned light, each atom in the universe bears
within one of its minute parts a microcosmic likeness of
what will emerge in future creation. Spirit, which I under-
stand as light-filled consciousness, permeates all matter
and is continually slipping into the atom that is the basic
cell of materiality or substance that clothes the unfold-
ing reality of all possibility. In a similar way, ideas are
imprinted through the activity of imagination, inspira-
tion and intuition, appearing in the creative life of thought
to introduce new beginnings in the world. Our electric
currents of thought affect everything in our atmosphere
and have a direct bearing on what will unfold in our lives
in the future, most particularly in the condition of our
health and destiny. When creative dialogue, the fruit of
conscious exchange, is allowed to flourish between friends
and lovers, new impulses towards harmony and coopera-
tion enter the fray of life.

Each one of us is a living, changing organism in which
the whole of creation is reflected. The conductor of this
symphonic interplay of material and spiritual forces is
the unique "I" or Self that we, in acknowledging it in
ourselves, can learn to recognize in one another. People
sometimes take a limited view of themselves, succumb-
ing to the circumstances of the moment, but the view, "I
am hopeless," "I am awkward," "I am alcoholic," "I am

depressed," does not define the whole person. Inherent in the syntax of the Irish language is the concept of the passing nature of attributes and possessions. We say *tá sé agam*—it is at me, denoting the presence of something in my vicinity, but not my identity with it. The first instance of the practice of forgiveness in our lives surely arises in relation to oneself. I will stumble less through trial and error, find less to forgive of myself the more I gain perspective of the relationship I bear to the larger picture. Once, when I was going through a crisis, a wonderfully wise friend, social artist Paul Hogan, cycled across the city of Toronto with a colourful canvas he had just painted fastened to the back of his bike. The cheerful image had the desired effect. Equally uplifting was the postcard of the starry heavens that he had pinned to the top of his painting. An arrow pointed towards the tiny dot that represented our earth among a cluster of galaxies. The caption read: "You are HERE!"

While each one may be small in the large cosmic scheme of things, every individual presence counts immeasurably. I view each person I meet as a living culture, engaged in a vital exchange with his or her surrounding world. To be spiritually discerning is to realize a deep sense of purpose in life and give thanks for the awesome evolutionary means that lie at our disposal. Everything that emanates from me or which impinges on me from the outer world occurs by grace of the senses, my bridge from inner to outer reality. Rudolf Steiner called the senses "wellsprings of the soul."

He numbered them twelve, contrary to the popular consensus of five. When we refer to our sixth sense we often mean one or other of the seven additional senses Steiner identified. The first eight, designated lower and middle senses are the following: touch, life, movement, balance, smell, taste, sight and warmth; these relate to body and soul faculties. The other four, termed by Steiner the spiritual senses, can be juxtaposed with the four bodily senses of touch, life, movement and balance. The more effectively these latter four are developed in early childhood, the more likely we are to have the spiritual senses functioning well in us in later life, those of hearing, concept, language and "I" sense.

I experienced a deeper understanding of the "I" when I visited the Goetheanum, headquarters of the worldwide Anthroposophical Society in Switzerland. The majestic building, which towers above the town of Dornach, houses an enormous wooden sculpture that Rudolf Steiner carved to near completion during his final years on earth. It had survived the burning, by arson, of the first Goetheanum, housed as it was outside the main building. Entitled *The Representative of Man*, it features a lone figure standing against a background of opposing forces. Emanating nobility and poise, one hand raises upwards, the other points below, in the eurythmic gesture for the German "*Ich*" or "I". The eternal momentum of the Christ's redeeming presence in every human soul, the living reality of "Not I, but Christ in me," is brought to vivid expression in this sculpture, normally kept under lock and key and viewed by appointment. By grace of serendipity once again, I had arrived in the building at the precise moment when some viewers were expected by Virginia Sease, a leading and erudite member of the governing body of the Society, referred to in German as the Vorstand. When our eyes met, Virginia explained that she had just realized that the prospective visitors had actually reserved for the following day. "Perhaps it is you I have been waiting for!" she laughed. "Come with me…" Another long awaited hope of mine was being realized…

The size of this inspired work had not been reflected in the photograph of it that hung on my wall at home. I could not believe my good fortune in viewing the original for the first time in the company of a woman whose qualities of leadership I so admired, a brilliant scholar who had devoted her life to the anthroposophical movement. Climbing the wide stone staircase together, she unlocked the heavy door of a large high-ceilinged room. The towering woodcarving evoked an immediate feeling of reverence in me. Forever etched in memory are the moments that followed, when I joined in meditative silence with Virginia in the presence of Rudolf Steiner's faithfully executed representation of human purpose, balance and love.

*In the meeting between two people there is a kind of subtle non-*physical touching going on. I tend to scan for the impression of the essential being of the person I am meeting, which is a kind of "force form." Making contact with other people entails the proper functioning of my sense of language, concept and "I." The latter is perhaps the most elusive of all the senses but I believe it is the one most important to cultivate in the twenty-first century. The renewal of social life depends on it. Steiner did not mean by the "I" sense that you bolster your own ego but that you become aware of somebody else as an "I," looking past surface impressions to what is truly individual in the other. Through this sense, we pay attention to who is speaking as much as to what is said. In this way, we move from the experience of one another's behaviour to experiencing the essential being of the other. The need to cultivate this capacity lay also at the core of the work of the Institute and the writings of R.D. Laing from whom Ross drew inspiration.

The more authentic a person is, the more transparent the individuality. This is true for everyone. When a speaker stands behind his words, you know you can count on that person to follow through in action. Too often people fail us in this respect. Promises made in the heat of the moment often fail to engage the will of the speaker and are quickly forgotten. To build trust in oneself and in others, words must be binding, active agents of responsibility.

The "I" sense that is present in everyone is under attack whenever a person suffers from an addiction. This sense builds a bridge between people that can be undermined by drugs or alcohol. Addictions tend to grow in the soul if left untreated just as artistic forces can also expand to the benefit of the artist's life of soul. While under the influence of artificial substances, we become unreachable by others and we lose the ability to penetrate through to the "I" of another. This tragedy of isolation gives rise to the despair suffered by addicts. The manic-depressive syndrome also produces this distressing effect in both the sufferer and the caregiver, as I discovered. Artistic activity is one of the principle means at our disposal in countering the forces of adversity.

Rather than accepting limitation, we must redouble our efforts to reach those who seem most remote from us. This effort can be developed on the inner plane and always proves effective in the long run. When one of my sons was going through his period of teenage rebellion, he began to experiment with drugs, then readily available on the streets of Toronto. I was beside myself with worry, powerless I thought, in the face of the collective peer pressure to which he was subject. It was as if I had lost all connection with him. The late John Davy, long-time science editor of *The Observer* and at that time Master of Emerson College, was visiting at the time and he gave me the best advice I ever received as a parent.

"You have had a sense since birth, have you not," John said, "of your child's unique spiritual presence? Regardless of his behaviour at present, you must concentrate on always seeing this light in him and gradually you will call it forth into expression. His "I" forces are not yet strong because he is under twenty-one. You must help sustain them for him."

I have employed this technique of holding my children in the light of higher being in the face of all odds, and I recommend it to other challenged parents.

The most creative forms of dialogue arise for those who start out from a common set of assumptions they have freely reached. When not at odds about the fundamental nature and purpose of life, companions can enter into a mutual exploration of the truth. Lady Gregory's remark about John Millington Synge comes to mind. "I do not have to rearrange my mind to talk to him."

I once enjoyed fruitful dialogue with a young monk who holds a similar frame of reference to mine. I always departed from our brief but satisfying exchanges full of a sense of having seen and been seen in my essential self. This experience constitutes what we call in Irish *anam-cáirdeas* or "soul friendship." "A soul without a friend," we say, "is like a body without a head." My friend used to work as a psychotherapist before joining the religious order that he has since abandoned for secular life. He possesses a unique clairvoyant gift, the result of eyes washed clean of self-seeking, which enables him to clearly apprehend the light body or, as I mentioned, "force form" of the person he has before him.

He asked me one day to consider what the purpose of this capacity might be, and whether he should allow it to develop further. My intuitive response to his question was: "Be grateful for this gift. Even if the person is not aware that you are seeing him in the aspect of light and force of will, your very act of perception will affirm his sense of self-worth. This true foundation of being is over-looked or only of passing interest to many today. People need confirmation of the innate purity and goodness of their essential makeup, regardless of any contamination that might have occurred on other levels in the course of their lives."

As I drove away from the monastery that day, I reflected on the hours of expensive therapy it takes to overcome the so-called ego. Yet the surest method and the one most likely to assist in the process of spiritualizing the earth is our attempt to see others as existing out of the same full-ness of importance that we assign to ourselves.

My most enduring friendships are with those rare individuals with whom my mind needs no adjustment. Their understand-ing of my concerns is implicit because of an accord that is natural between us. Anne Stockton is one such cherished friend and mentor. A gifted painter, born in New York in 1910, she founded the Tobias School for art therapy in Forest Row, England, in the early seventies. Anne is a woman of great natural beauty and refined intellect, her soul imbued with the qualities of the living, weaving col-ours that illumine her work. She shines in every company, a charismatic centre of wit and wisdom. To be in her vicin-ity is to experience the warmth of yellow, the dynamism of red, the compassion of blue and the fertile newness of green. Memory lapse is not a feature of Anne's old age. She has an endearing ability in conversation to remain

Anne Stockton receiving the 2000 Sophia award at the Sardello School of Spiritual Psychology in Connecticut. I marvel at her radiant beauty and keen intelligence that seems to grow rather than fade with the years. She was nearing her ninetieth birthday here. PHOTO BY CHERYL SANDERS-SARDELLO focused on a theme until it has been exhausted to our mutual satisfaction. While we give one another licence to wander off at tangents, she invariably holds the thread of our predominant theme. She has honed this facility in her lifelong immersion in the language of colour, on an anthroposophical artistic path that she characterizes as "Beauty reconnecting itself with Truth." She is the most stimulating companion one could hope for, uniquely present to every situation with a delightful childlike curiosity that draws people of all ages to her wherever she is. She is the oldest in years of the people I love most.

I readily responded to her invitation to spend the last days of the century with her in Dornach, Switzerland. We raised our glasses in a toast to the New Year after attending a performance of Beethoven's *Ninth Symphony* at the Goetheanum. She characteristically declared: "My dear, when a thought pops into my head from now on, I shall ask myself if it is an idea that belongs to the new millennium or to the old, because new ideas must always be allowed to come forth and one must guard against resting on one's laurels." In my favourite photograph of Anne she is leaning against the ancient oak tree that shades my writer's cottage, a fitting backdrop for one whose eyes reflect the wisdom of the age.

When I returned from Switzerland to County Clare to put the finishing touches to this book, a pile of Christmas mail awaited me. The first letter I opened bore a British Columbia postmark, turning my thoughts to Canada once again. I recognized the handwriting of a cherished friend, Glada McIntyre. She wrote:

We are wrapped in the cloak of winter today. When snow is falling, the outside world seems far away. How we cherish

these peaceful winter months hidden away on the moun-
taintop. We have all the food and supplies we need until
the Spring, as we have had for the past twenty Winters
here ... It keeps one wonderfully in tune with the natural
earth, going to the spring for water, grinding grain every day
for our bread, fuelling the fire, feeding the animals, milk-
ing the cow and making yoghurt and butter, preparing the
meals from all the delicious living food we are so fortunate
to be able to grow. My days are filled with contemplation
and prayer—the almost involuntary invocation on lighting
the morning candle, or the evening lamps. This was not
common practice in the culture I grew up in, though I think
it was in yours ...

I first met Glada on a warm Sunday morning in August
1995. She happened to enter a hall where I was singing and
recognized my voice as one she had heard on CBC radio
several years before. We established an immediate rap-
port. Two of my sons were with me. Later as we relaxed
outside in the glorious sunshine, a horse-drawn wagon
driven by an imposing bearded man pulled up, and we
were soon lumbering up a forest trail, holding on for dear
life. The location was Argenta, a remote outlying region
beyond the town of Nelson, not identified on the map. I
had driven for fifteen hours up the mountains from Van-
couver at the behest of my son Declan. Along the way
Vince, Glada's Irish-born husband, pointed towards their
grazing Kerry cows.

"Two of the last two hundred remaining of that species
in the world. The calf was produced from semen sent over
from Ireland." There was still a trace of his accent.

I noticed patches of vegetables and colourful clusters
of flowers as we gingerly alighted, to make our way along
a mossy path to the clearing they had appropriated many
years before, and could now claim as their own property.

"We grow organic vegetables in fields spread out across various locations on the mountainside and sell them throughout the region," Vince continued. "At first we dug a hole to preserve root vegetables, and then added a glass dome. Soon we had built ourselves a temporary shelter which, in the course of time, became our home," Glada added.

She pulled open a door to the most unusual house I had ever entered—more like the inside of a tree. It was a dwelling hospitable to elemental beings. No running water or electricity, and yet all their domestic needs were ingeniously met. I looked enviously into their storeroom. There was an abundance of canned peaches, tomatoes, plums, apricots, huckleberry jam, homemade cheese and yoghurt. A hearty meal of delicious pancakes was set before us, dripping with freshly churned butter and syrup. A sturdy gas stove was all Glada had to rely on in producing her nutritious breads and pies, and there was a seemingly endless supply of piping-hot organic tea. I asked Glada why there had been such a stir when she entered the hall.

"I was singing, but all heads turned in your direction!" I joked.

"I think it is because of the Singing Forest," she said "I am well known in the area because of it."

"Do tell me more," I said.

A woman of forty-odd years, she stood before us in luminous beauty, framed by the walls of windowed glass in this special sanctuary among the trees.

"I will tell you about a remarkable experience I had on the 15th of June 1990. Vince and I and our crew of tree planters were at work up Howser Creek, in the Purcell Mountains. We were only making twenty cents a tree. It was tough going, mashed woody debris paved into hardpan down on the flat by the creek, and dense yew brush on a fairly steep slope above; a long run to treeline, but not many opportunities to stick in a tree.

"I stood up to stretch. I saw a beam of light ray out from a mountain named the Virgin, over the nearby forest. As my attention was drawn to the illuminated trees, I was struck by their immense verticality. A profound vertical alignment took place in me in response. Suddenly I felt about twelve feet tall. Then I was struck in my solar plexus by an impact of sound. It grew into a swelling symphony, in range and tone unlike anything I had heard before! Emanating from the forested hillsides across the valley, it was unquestionably a hymn of adoration, of joy in creation and praise to the creator! Words cannot possibly express the magnitude of this joyous sound, nor my absolute bliss in hearing it."

We listened enthralled. Glada's eyes began to glisten as she continued: "Tears were streaming down my face; I know that my whole life had led up to this revelation, this was why I had studied forest ecology, had sought out visionary teachers. This is what I was seeking, the underlying reality. This, I knew, is why I have always chosen to live and work in the forest."

Vince interjected "I remember the day so well and the profound way in which Glada was affected. She kept asking me 'Do you hear it?' asking others, 'Can you hear?' But only she could hear."

A darker note entered Glada's narrative. "I was revelling in the immensity of the experience. I was washed clean, flooded with joy and strength and awe. Then suddenly the song changed. It was an abrupt change from overwhelming joy to abject sorrow. My cognitive mental faculty was being given a new urgent message. If I could put words to it, they would be as follows:" She paused for breath and recited these lines as if they were a poem:

"Oh noble and worthy exploiters and conquerors
Have mercy. Have mercy. Do not end our singing
Which allows the conditions necessary
For all life on the planet as you know it!"

My son Declan leaned closer to me, "The trees in the Singing Forest in Tenise Creek are a thousand years old!"

Glada continued, "I was haunted by that litany for months, awakening to its echo in the night: 'Have mercy, Have mercy on the children'."

Vince interjected, "She was given a great deal of information almost instantaneously, which totally altered the direction of our lives. Since then Glada has been tireless in her efforts to stop the logging. Many people have joined in her campaign, but we are up against the forces of capitalism."

"I received a number of vivid impressions during this clairaudient revelation," Glada continued. "I know now that the biggest, oldest trees receive broadcast of life-force energy from the inner regions in the vicinity of the valley's headwaters, and that these ancient beings transform and transmit that life-renewing energy throughout the entire ecosystem and that when they are removed, the ecosystem is plunged into chaos, within which biotic succession is not predictable."

Her face brightened again to its customary glow. "The Singing Forest is sacred to the divine spirit of grace and mercy represented in the East by Kwan Yin; in the West, she is called Mary, Holy Mother, or Sophia."

Briain was obviously moved. He looked at me and said, "I think I will remain here with Glada and Vince. They may need help with the harvest or with their work in spreading news of the forest." Then, remembering himself, he shyly asked, "That is, if they would like me to stay...?" The look on their faces gave instant affirmation. Thus began an instructive period for him. Living in their adjacent cabin and working with them daily he established a life-long friendship with two remarkable people and learned the skills he would need for his future life in Clare.

Glada shared another insight with us during that first meeting. It concerned the Yggdrasil tree.

"It represents a sacred place created by the Gods, from whence all life is sustained. There is a clear connection for me between this Viking legend and the revelation of the Singing Forest."

Declan, then aged twenty, subsequently also settled near the McIntyre's and often visited them. Glada became a mentor for him when he took up the study of Norse mythology. He found an old map, printed in 1890, that identified neighbouring mountains, all bearing names associated with Nordic lore. In the same spirit with which Yeats restored old stories to popular consciousness, Declan set to writing a play that would give local people new imaginative connection with the majestic ranges that surrounded them. His multimedia production entitled *Shadows of the Yggdrasil Tree* was soon in rehearsal in Nelson. Seventy young people played their part in this brave cooperative endeavour, either on stage or off, with Declan conducting operations while also playing the part of Baldur.

No sooner had I arrived back at the gate lodge of Tinarana House than the summons came from on high: "Mom, please come to Nelson. The play is opening on February 9th. I have written you into a scene. You must come!" How could I refuse? I made the arduous journey across a continent to the furthest northern point I knew, arriving only minutes before the final rehearsal. Declan hailed me from a company of lavishly costumed Gods and Godesses.

"Oh good! You're here, Mom! Can you please come on

stage? Baldur is just about to die and I would like you to sing a keen over my body."

Jet lag notwithstanding, I hastened to obey the Sun God's command! Next evening, I sat with Vince and Glada in the theatre and gave thanks with them for inspiration well received. The night's audience was rising in a standing ovation. Then it was back to Tinarana House to the steadily rising pile of pages. The book was nearing its end and that meant that a new beginning was coming into view.

Shortly after returning I began to help organize a conference the North Carolina-based School of Spiritual Psychology was planning to convene at the already mentioned, nearby Benedictine monastery, Glenstal Abbey. This was the fulfilment of my cherished wish to facilitate a gathering in Ireland of North American friends, which Robert Sardello and his wife, Cheryl Sanders, would lead. "The Healing Field of the Soul" was the theme for the event, which a number of speakers would address, amongst them John O'Donohue, Therese Schroeder-Sheker, Christopher Bamford, Sardello, Sanders and myself. As one participant later remarked, "Here we have a meeting of opportunity and hospitality." Opportunity is the hallmark of North American incentive, while the tradition of hospitality in Irish monasteries is legendary, and entirely upheld on this occasion. A confluence of tributaries representing Spiritual Psychology, Irish monasticism, Anthroposophy,

The lavishly costumed Declan as Baldur in the Nelson, B.C., production I describe. On the strength of writing, directing, and producing this colourful pageant, my son won a scholarship to Concordia University in Montreal where he studied playwriting and was recognized as the "most outstanding student" in his final year, 2004, from amongst a student body that numbered 30,000.

Mark Patrick Hederman and Anne Stockton on Dublin's Parnell Square, meeting outside the hotel where Anne and I were staying. I recommended that Anne wear her blue suit and noted with serendipitous delight that Brother Mark Patrick was wearing a tie of the very same blue! Shades of a looming blue butterfly in the wings perhaps? PHOTO BY TREASA O'DRISCOLL

Jungian psychology and Mysticism, duly converged on Glenstal.

> *Maybe we shall know each other better*
> *When the tunnels meet beneath the mountain…*

Brother Mark Patrick Hederman quoted these lines by Louis MacNiece at the opening of the conference. Remarking that no meeting takes place by chance, he said, "It was meant to be, and has only come to be, because a number of historical—cultural circumstances have cleared its way…" Mark Patrick is a Glenstal monk, an inspired philosopher who carries a clear vision for the social renewal that is possible when Ireland faces its own peculiar darkness. Consciousness soul shines through every gesture and word of this contemporary poet, teacher and best selling author.

Wonder and inquiry stirred our minds and hearts throughout those days and enriched the soul forces of all present. White-robed monks made their procession towards the altar several times a day, forming a reverent circle with outstretched hands when the host was raised above the chalice.

"They remind me of the Grail Brotherhood," remarked Anne Stockton, who knelt beside me.

I gave thanks. The adventure of my year in Ireland was coming to full circle. My new book would speak an echoing voice that reverberated in the meeting of these complementary streams of knowledge and wisdom, the formative substance of my thinking and writing. The thought came to me that it was Irish druids who first began the work of opening human hearts to the mystery of love, often in rural settings like this one. The continuation of this task still remains a living purpose on this small island at the windswept edge of Europe. The continuity of spiritual tradition within Irish monasticism had been enlivened, I

Cheryl and Robert Sardello, dear friends and mentors who invited
me to perform at five of their wonderful Spiritual Psychology Con-
ferences and with whom I collaborated in preparing the 1999 event
at Glenstal Abbey. I met Joy Kwapien, Anne Stockton and Patrick
Boyer, publisher of this book, through the Sardello auspices and
Robert's books occupy pride of place on my shelves.

knew, in this encounter with connected offshoots of a
common Christian root.

I looked around at the faces of my friends: some new,
some of a lifetime. They were assembled in a farewell cir-
cle on the monastery green on the last day. These men and
women devote their lives to the work of awakening con-
sciousness through their writing, teaching, meditation and
clinical practices. It was indeed a motley crew of monks,
minstrels, scholars, poets and jacks-of-all-trades who were
gathered with me from near and far. A red rose passed
around the gathering from hand to hand. When it was
my turn, I gave thanks. Thanks for the encounters and

reflections recorded in my fledgling writing; thanks for the warm convergence of kindred spirits. I am astonished at the glory of the friendship I share with such a diversity of people across continents and years. I am heartened by this love between friends that forms a radiant circle around every heart, rippling out into halos of stars that merge and glow above the roads we travel.

Sources

Adilakshmi. *The Mother*. Germany: Mother Meera Publications, 1995.

AE. *Collected Poems by AE*. London: MacMillan, 1913.

Balough, Teresa. *May Human Beings Hear It*. NP: Circle Publishers, 2000.

Bamford, Christopher. *An Endless Trace*. New York: Codhill Press, 2003.

Bradley, Ian. *The Celtic Way*. London: Darton, Longman and Todd, 1993.

Brown, Paula. "The New Mary." *Ariadne's Awakening*. Ed. Margli Matthews. Stroud, United Kingdom: Hawthorn Press, 1986.

Carmichael, Alexander. *The Sun Dances: Prayers and Blessings from the Gaelic*. Edinburgh: Floris Books, 1997.

De Fréine, Seán. *The Great Silence*. Cork: Mercier Press, 1994.

Eliot, T.S. *Collected Poems, 1909–1962*. New York: Harcourt Brace, 1963.

———. *Four Quartets*. New York: Harcourt Brace & Company, 1973.

Fitzgerald, Astrid. *The Artist's Book of Inspiration*. Hudson, NY: Lindisfarne Press, 1996.

Flower, Robin. *The Irish Tradition*. Oxford: Oxford University Press, 1947.

Heaney, Seamus. *Opened Ground: Selected Poems 1966–1996*. London: Faber and Faber, 1998.

———. *Preoccupations: Selected Prose 1968–1978*. London: Faber and Faber, 1980.

———. *The Redress of Poetry*. London: Faber and Faber, 1995.

Hederman, Mark Patrick. *Kissing the Dark*. Dublin: Veritas Publications, 1999.

Hull, Eleanor. *Cuchulainn*. London: George & Harrap Co., 1913.

Kühlewind, Georg. *Becoming Aware of the Logos*. Hudson, NY: Lindisfarne Press, 1984.

———. *From Normal to Healthy*. Great Barrington, MA: Lindisfarne Press, 1988.

Laing, R.D. *Knots*. London: Random House, 1972.

Lawrence, D.H. *Complete Poems*. London: Penguin Books, 1994.

Lipson, Michael. *Stairway of Surprise: Six Steps to a Creative Life*. Great Barrington, MA: Anthroposophic Press, 2002.

Lusseryan, Jacques. *Conversation Amourese*. Fair Oaks, CA: Rudolf Steiner College Press.

Matthews, Paul. *Sing Me the Creation*. Stroud, UK: Hawthorn Press, 1994.

Moriarty, John. *Invoking Ireland*. Dublin: Lilliput Press, 2005.

O'Connor, Frank. *Kings, Lord and Commons*. London: MacMillan, 1962.

O'Driscoll, Robert. *An Ascendancy of the Heart*. Dublin: The Dolmen Press, 1976.

————. *The Celtic Consciousness*. Toronto: McClelland and Stewart, 1981.

————. *The Irish in Canada: The Untold Story*. Toronto: Celtic Arts of Canada, 1988.

O'Faolain, Nuala. *My Dream of You*. London; New York: Penguin Books, 2001.

O Muirithe, Diarmuid. *A Seat Behind the Coachman*. Dublin: Gill and Macmillan,1972.

Osho, Rajneesh. *Tantric Transformation*. New York: Element, 1994.

Pietzner, Carlo. *Inner Development and the Landscape of the Ego*. Botton, UK: Camphill Publications, 1993.

Raine, Kathleen. *Selected Poems*. Great Barrington, MA: Lindisfarne Press, 1988.

Ramsey, Jay. *Out of Time*. Glastonbury, UK: PS Avalon Publishing, 2008.

Redfield, James. *The Tenth Insight*. New York: Warner Books, 1998.

Reid, Alec. *All I Can Manage, More than I Could*. Dublin: Dolmen Press, 1968.

Rilke, Rainer Maria. *Ahead of All Parting: The Selected Poetry and Prose of Rainer Maria Rilke*. Trans. and ed. Stephen Mitchell. New York: Modern Library, 1995.

————. *Duino Elegies*. Trans. David Young. New York; London: W.W. Norton & Co, 1978.

————. *On Love and Other Difficulties*. New York; London: W.W. Norton & Co., 1993.

————. *Rodin and Other Prose Pieces*. London: Quartet Books, 1986.

Sardello, Robert. *Facing the World with Soul*. Hudson, NY: Lindisfarne Press 1992.

————. *Freeing the Soul from Fear*. New York: Riverhead Books, 1999.

————. *Love and the Soul*. New York: HarperCollins, 1995.

———. *The Power of Soul*. Charlottesville, VA: Hampton Roads, 2002.

Soesman, Albert. *Our Twelve Senses*. Stroud, UK: Hawthorn Press, 1990.

Solovyov, Vladimir. *The Meaning of Love*. Hudson, NY: Lindisfarne Press, 1985.

Steiner, Rudolf. *The Calendar of the Soul*. Illus. Anne Stockton. Forest Row, UK: Temple Lodge, 2004.

———. *Christianity as Mystical Fact*. Great Barrington, MA: Anthroposophic Press, 1972.

———. *Cosmic Memory: Prehistory of Earth and Man*. Great Barrington, MA: Lindisfarne Press 1990.

———. *The Druids*. Ed. Andrew J. Welburn. Forest Row, UK: Rudolf Steiner Press, 2001.

———. *From the History and Contents of the First Esoteric School, 1904–1914*. Great Barrington, MA: Anthroposophic Press, 1998.

———. *The Gospel of John, lectures*. Great Barrington, MA: Anthroposophic Press, 1962.

———. *Intuitive Thinking as a Spiritual Path*. Trans. and ed. Michael Lipson. Great Barrington, MA: Anthroposophic Press, 1995.

———. *Occult Science*. Great Barrington, MA: Anthroposophic Press, 1972.

———. *Self Transformation*. Forest Row, UK: Rudolf Steiner Press, 1995.

———. *Start Now! A Book of Soul and Spiritual Exercises*. Ed. Christopher Bamford. Forest Row, UK: Rudolf Steiner Books, 2004.

Stephens, James. *James, Sēamus and Jacques*. London: Macmillan, 1964.

Sussman, Linda. *The Speech of the Grail*. Hudson, NY: Lindisfarne Press, 1997.

Von Eschenbach, Wilhelm. *Parzival*. New York: Vintage Books, 1961.

Welburn, Andrew J. "Yeats, the Rosicrucians and Rudolf Steiner." *Journal for Anthroposophy* Summer 1988.

Whyte, David. *Fire in the Earth*. Langley, WA: Many Rivers Press, 1997.

Yeats, W.B. *The Collected Poems*. London: Macmillan, 1974.

Zeldin, Theodore. *Conversation*. London: Harvill Press, 1998.

Index

Credits

This book was born out of friendship.

A first draft emerged by grace of the practical support and encouragement of two American friends, Joy and Bob Kwapien. Cherished friends Anne Stockton and her son, the late Rufus Goodwin, subsequently brought the manuscript to the attention of their friend, Kieran O'Mahoney, who helped in the development of a second draft.

Conversations with soul-friend and mentor Claude Bellin were always inspiring and thought provoking. Kate Somerville, another valued friend, graciously applied her literary acumen to the reading of further revisions.

I am deeply grateful to several friends and colleagues in Barrie—Chris and Annemarie Heintz, Werner and Linda Fabian, Chuck and Diane Kyd, and Richard Mulock; all have assisted in keeping me on track and have supported me in far-reaching ways.

I thank my Irish mother and siblings, and my four children, Briain, Robert, Declan, and Emer, for loyalty through thick and thin, on both sides of the Atlantic.

I am most of all indebted to Patrick Boyer, distinguished

and visionary publisher of Blue Butterfly Books, who granted me the honour of inclusion in his inaugural roster of authors. Patrick astutely assigned me Dominic Farrell, an editor whose uncanny ability to read between the lines brought hitherto unfathomed elements of my journey to light. I thank Dominic for the unique combination of tough love and sensitivity that exacted the extensive rewrite and revision required. This collaboration made me aware how greatly the editorial process advanced the ultimate making of this book to which designer Gary Long contributed so much.

Michael Yeats, whom I had known and admired since 1965, graciously gave his permission for the inclusion of extracts from his father's published works. He regrettably passed away before the book was finished and his widow, Gráinne, has generously renewed the permission.

I thank Robert Sardello for allowing me to quote from his several books and for his insightful commentary on my original draft. My initial encounters with Joy Kwapien and Patrick Boyer were fatefully and respectively orchestrated by Robert and his remarkable partner in life and work, Cheryl.

Editor-in-chief Christopher Bamford, another admired friend and mentor, has encouraged my endeavours over many years and I thank him for permission to quote from a number of Lindisfarne Books/Steiner Books and Anthroposophic Press publications.

I thank poet Seamus Heaney for personally granting me permission to quote from cherished works of his.

I acknowledge Pollinger Limited and the Estate of Frieda Lawrence Ravagli for permission to quote passages from the works of D.H. Lawrence.

I am grateful to Hawthorn Press (www.hawthornpress.com) for permission to quote lines from *The New Mary* and references reproduced from "Ariadne's Awakening", by Margli Matthews, Signe Schaefer and Betty Staley, and from "Sing Me The Creation" by Paul Matthews.

Interview with the Author

You've given scores of public performances across Europe and North America. How does engaging a live audience compare with writing a book for unseen readers?

TREASA O'DRISCOLL: A live presentation exists only in the moment of performance whereas the written word remains and can be revisited. Also, as my editor and I discovered, you can constantly revise a manuscript but you cannot recast a performance once it has been given. So you just rehearse more before going on stage, instead!

However, the engagement of either a visible audience or unseen readers requires striking a fine balance between the universal and the personal. Mood, venue and audience participation are variables, of course, in the performing experience. I found that my stage experience helped shape an art of communication that in fact prepared me for the more solitary and exacting enterprise that writing entails.

What motivated you to write Celtic Woman?

O'DRISCOLL: My husband, a professor of English, a scholar, and champion of Celtic Studies, was always encouraging me to write. Then books and writers were a central feature of our life together, as well. I came into contact with several accomplished artists about whom I aspired to write, so that, too, was part of the motivation.

My study of Rudolf Steiner's writings was itself an inspiring and significant spur in getting me going, I realize, as was my ever-keen reading of poetry.

I had already decided to write a book when unexpectedly a friend, Joy Redfield-Kwapien, commissioned this memoir after I accompanied her and her husband on a tour of Ireland. Our conversations on the road touched on such mutual interest as poetry, memory, spirituality, destiny, friendship and the Irish/Celtic tradition in which I had been reared. She urged me to put in writing what flowed so naturally from my experiences and learning as we spoke, so those touring talks actually provided content around which parts of this book was formed.

Do you have a succinct definition for what love is, since you mention it so often in the book?

O'DRISCOLL: I approach love from the point of view of force rather than sentiment. This force expresses itself in and through us in a threefold way—as idea at the level of mind, as meaning or beauty at the level of feeling, and as action at the physical level of the body.

The human soul, regardless of one's cultural background, circumstance or belief, is eternally nourished and expanded by love. This is one of the great wonders of life, the stuff of relationship, and the true source of happiness. That kind of love, as force, is accessible to all.

Your book will surely appeal to men and women of all ages, but among your early readers, women in particular have expressed appreciation for your chapter on sexual love. Can you explain why?

O'DRISCOLL: There is a psychological component to a woman's sexual nature, which leads in turn to fascination with any methodology or philosophy that can advance her more conscious, and thus healthier, engagement with this aspect of the game of life.

For most women, sex is primarily a function of relationship and not something to be cultivated for its own sake. A woman's need for relationship is as compelling in her as the physical desire of the body is urgent in the man. Enduring attraction between the sexes depends on the perpetuation and recognition of these differences.

That particular chapter is my attempt to bridge the gap between the mystification that surrounded sex in the Ireland of my youth and the gathered wisdom of my own experience. I am, needless to say, still learning!

Is there a central message you would like the book to convey?

O'DRISCOLL: My fundamental approach to life coincides with that of poet John Keats who characterized our world as a "vale of soul making" rather than the "vale of tears" it is often made out to be.

Significantly, the original word for poetry in Greek is making, and what poetry makes is meaning. Every human life is a work of art in the making, like poetry, and that is my "message." Also, there is satisfaction, as I discovered, in tracing the patterns of serendipity that weave through one's life and story. So the message in that is for each person to see such patterns in his or her own life because they help keep us on the track of meaning and destiny.

Robert Sardello, the internationally renowned author of Freeing the Soul from Fear *and founder of the School of Spiritual Psychology in North Carolina, praises your book as the forerunner of a new genre he calls a "soul memoir." What do you think he means by that term?*

O'DRISCOLL: It's a lovely expression, isn't it? Dr. Sardello, like any other reader, finds that this memoir recalls events, ideas, and encounters that have variously tried, tempered, and enriched my soul. Of course the soul is where impressions of the senses and intuitions of the spirit are distilled into meaning. When feelings of sympathy and antipathy are brought into balance, soul qualities such as equanimity, courage, patience, and truthfulness arise of their own accord. The self-development of each individual in turn has its bearing on the whole, since the world soul reflects the evolutionary patterns of all human souls. Because I approach the journey of life from this point of view, Robert Sardello observed that reading my story "heightened the possibility of others consciously discovering their own soul life."

If *Celtic Woman* provides this key to unlock meaning in someone else's life, I'll be delighted—whatever genre the work itself gets classified under!

About this Book

Celtic Woman explores with open honesty and engaging irony how cycles of personal discovery have connected international performing artist Treasa O'Driscoll to heaven and earth—but not the way you'd expect.

This surprising memoir of an Irish woman attuned to poetic updrafts and spiritual downloads in the lives of real people, many of them celebrities in Ireland and North America she counts as personal friends, exudes her Celtic heritage on every page.

Her encounters in life have been testing, tragic, romantic, and highly comic. The stars drew O'Driscoll to musicians, poets, teachers, artists, actors, farmers, unexpected strangers and familiar drunkards. Their lives all became a single interwoven tapestry of common meaning connected at the level of the soul.